T H E
YIN-YANG
BUTTERFLY

OTHER BOOKS BY VALENTIN CHU

*Ta Ta Tan Tan (Fight Fight, Talk Talk):
The Inside Story of Communist China*

Thailand Today: A Visit to Modern Siam

THE
YIN-YANG
BUTTERFLY

Ancient Chinese
Sexual Secrets
for Western Lovers

VALENTIN CHU

A Jeremy P. Tarcher/Putnam Book
published by
G. P. Putnam's Sons
New York

A Jeremy P. Tarcher/Putnam Book
Published by G. P. Putnam's Sons
Publishers Since 1838
200 Madison Avenue
New York, NY 10016

Library of Congress Cataloging-in-Publication Data

Chu, Valentin
    The yin-yang butterfly : Ancient Chinese sexual secrets for western lovers / Valentin Chu.
        p.   cm.
    "A Jeremy P. Tarcher/Putnam Book."
    Includes bibliographical references and index.
    ISBN 0-87477-747-X
    1. Sex customs—China—History.   2. Sex instruction—China—History.
3. Hygiene, Sexual—China—History.   I. Title.
HQ18.C6C53   1993   92-39628 CIP
306.7'0951—dc20

Designed by Lee Fukui
Printed in the United States of America
1   2   3   4   5   6   7   8   9   10

To Vickie

The Wisdom of the East is based on practical knowledge coming from the flower of Chinese intelligence, which we have not the slightest justification for undervaluing.

CARL JUNG, commentary to
The Secret of the Golden Flower

Acknowledgments

My deep gratitude goes to Sigrid MacRae, whose gift to the Prime Unicorn started it all; to Larissa Lawrynenko, who gave me constant encouragement and many insightful suggestions; to Carl Solberg, who read the manuscript and rendered valuable comments; to Richard and Polly Fisher, whose timely help was a magical blend of aesthetics and logic; and to Roy Rowan, whose tips helped me get away from a sticky spot.

I thank my publisher, Jeremy Tarcher, for his intuitive feeling, critical appraisal, and artistic taste, which largely were responsible for molding my manuscript into this finished book; my editor, Connie Zweig, for her contribution to the beauty of the book; and Lee Fukui and Lisa Amoroso, for the elegant design, cover, and illustrations. Thanks are due also to Coral Tysliava, Diane Lomonaco, and Allen Mikaelian for their coordinating work.

My heartfelt thanks to Julian Bach, literary agent extraordinaire, who not only found a good birthplace for this book but took the trouble to guide me through the publishing jungle.

To many friends—author friends, friends in the media, artist friends, and just good friends—I express my appreciation for their eagerness and good wishes, which inspired me to keep on with this esoteric project all these years.

Contents

Preface

THIS IS A BOOK on sex and eroticism, themes intimately linked to health and longevity. It is intended for weekend readers who enjoy stories and anecdotes about a titillating subject, avid aficionados of sexuality who are not averse to a bit of ancient bedroom wisdom, and modern lovers who seek a new dimension in their sex lives.

Although the book's area of interest and practical applications are universal and contemporary, its background is more circumscribed and remote—namely, ancient China. We will look at China in centuries, indeed millennia, past, and more specifically, into its bedrooms. Most Westerners are not aware that the world's earliest known sexology classics came from China, and that the Chinese used them for more than a millennium before they began to disappear about a thousand years ago.

More recently some of these "lost" classics have been discovered or reconstructed, both inside and outside China. A careful study of them shows that within the antiquated and esoteric writing are hidden remarkable theories and observations about human sexuality that happen to agree with the latest theories of modern sexologists.

WHY I WROTE THIS BOOK

In the 1970s, I came upon several of these Chinese sexology texts, dating from about two thousand years ago. They were interesting enough, but the ancient classical writing was so abstruse that I felt they would mean little to people today. Even in contemporary China, where vernacular Chinese is flourishing, classical writing is a dying language to most of the younger generation.

These ancient texts advocate many theories and practices, and make the claims that good health leads to good sex, and good sex leads to good health—and even rejuvenation and long life. Are such claims grounded in mysticism, or do they have a scientific basis? No contemporary scientist or sexologist has made a serious study of these claims, and because most people are not aware of the existence of ancient Chinese sexology, there is no real "expert" on the subject. I recognized this back in the seventies, and it is still true today.

While there is no expert, there *are* students. And it was as a student that, a decade ago, I began my arduous, but by no means unpleasant, research into these ancient classics, as well as contemporary Western sexology and health sciences. What started as a hobby soon became an intense pursuit.

My research revealed some extraordinary facts. First, in spite of its Confucian mask, China has seen interest in erotic techniques and sexual potency for thousands of years. Second, the Chinese were using mind-body practices centuries ago, not only in advanced martial arts, but also in advanced marital arts. And third, an increasing number of ancient Chinese concepts relating to health and sexology appear to be endorsed, albeit unwittingly, by contemporary Western health scientists and sexologists.

Here was something intellectually fascinating, and perhaps useful. I decided I might try to introduce and interpret relevant parts of the ancient sexology, within a modern frame of reference, for the benefit of today's readers. To my surprise, I discovered that Chinese scholars who understood the ancient classics knew little about modern health science and sexology. Western writers who had that modern knowledge, predictably enough, could not read ancient Chinese classical writing without Chinese help.

I wondered whether I was qualified to write such a book. I was born and educated in China, and I know Chinese classical language and literature well. My academic training in the sciences and my professional experience with popular books on health, medicine, psychology, nature, and other subjects, would help. In addition, I had worked as an editor and writer for major American publishers. This experience equipped me to evaluate the ancient theories and practices in the obscure classics with the yardsticks of contemporary science and sexology, and then share what I had found with Western readers.

My findings do not represent a definitive scientific study. Rather, I present them as intellectual teasers; health scientists and sexologists may want to examine them further. Although individuals who have practiced aspects of this ancient art of lovemaking have sworn to its efficacy, I leave the laboratory proof to health scientists and sexologists. My intent here is to introduce and analyze selected ancient theories and practices for contemporary readers. I believe the knowledge gained from the ancients may enrich people's sex lives today and, as the ancients maintained, also benefit health, youthfulness, and even longevity.

SOURCES AND ORGANIZATION

I must admit I was somewhat intimidated by the vast amount of material available on the subject. Not only were there the ancient Chinese sexology texts themselves, but I also had dynastic histories, official records, scholarly chronicles, literary treatises, fiction, folklore, and art to choose from. Of these, most of the original-language sources had never appeared in English. Equally important were the latest writings on sexology and health. I have used material freely from all these sources: the subject merits a multidimensional treatment, and a touch of color.

The information collected here demands an appropriate structure, of course, and an appropriate title. As to the latter: Yin and Yang are, respectively, female and male sexual energy. The butterfly is a Chinese symbol of conjugal happiness as well as sensual desire. A favorite of poets and painters, it signifies both flirtatious coquetry and tender intimacy.

The Yin–Yang Butterfly, then, is divided into three parts. The first, "The Sensual Landscape," is a voyeur's view of sexual customs and practices in ancient China. The second part, titled "The Art of the Bedchamber," highlights what the remarkable bedchamber sages taught many centuries ago about joyous lovemaking and all its ramifications. The third section, "Ancient Secrets for Modern Lovers," brings the past into the present and directly addresses contemporary readers. It is in a sense a recipe book for sexuality, based on or inspired by ancient erotic techniques and mind-body therapy to enhance sexual vitality.

BENEFITS—AND A CAUTION

You do not have to be Chinese, or ancient, to understand or benefit from this book. You can use selected features of the Art of the Bedchamber, especially as adapted in the third section, and fit them into your own lifestyle.

If you are in your twenties, you may not need this book—yet. Youthful virility neither requires nor appreciates sexual savoir faire. If you are thirty-something, the book will spice up your sex life now and strengthen your sexual well-being in ensuing decades. If you are in your forties, fifties, or sixties, and are enjoying or would like to enjoy sex, this book should open new vistas for you. If you are seventy or beyond and are still sexually active, you already may be familiar with a few things discussed here. On the other hand, if you have not had a sex life for many years, you can read the book as a fantasy, or keep it for your next incarnation.

A word of caution: The ancients enjoyed sex in those halcyon days when sexually transmitted diseases were unknown, and many of their techniques of lovemaking involved an exchange of sexual secretions. In this age of sexual perils, readers are warned that some practices mentioned in this book are for confirmed "safe partners" only—those who have been in long-term monogamous relationships with each other, and who have tested negative for HIV. Otherwise, stringent safe-sex measures, such as the use of condoms, are imperative. And until cures and vaccinations for such diseases as herpes genitalis and AIDS are found, even these protective measures are not absolutely safe.

The sexual nutrients, sexual exercises, and erotic techniques described in this book were popular with, and used in moderation by, the ancients. They come with no warranty attached. Readers should check with their own physicians before trying them.

A NOTE ON TRANSLATION

Written Chinese is an ideographic language: its characters derive from images. It is also extremely condensed and cryptic. It has no prepositions, no verb tense, no number differentiations, and until this century, it had no punctuation. The part of speech of a word is conveyed by its context. Yet this ancient tongue, or rather the modern, vernacular variation of its ancient, classical form, today is used by the largest number of people in the world.

The ancient Chinese sources for this book are all in classical Chinese. There is really no such thing as a literal translation from classical Chinese, into English or any other language; this is especially true in the case of ancient Chinese poetry. In this book, I have rendered all the quotations from original Chinese texts—whether shorter terms or longer passages—directly into English myself. I found some already existing translations of the same texts to be inaccurate, or simply inadequate. In some instances, I have styled the English translation very much like the original, deliberately using faulty grammar, fragments, and so on, to give the flavor of the Chinese version.

Chinese terms rendered phonetically in English always have been a source of confusion to many Westerners. In the past, phoneticization was based mainly on the Wade-Giles and Mathews systems. The newer pinyin system, sponsored by the Beijing government, is more accurate for most pronunciation, but some letters it uses are pronounced differently from how they normally are in English (or Romance languages). Chinese spellings here follow mainly a mixture of Wade-Giles and Mathews systems; where the pinyin system obviously excels, in geographic names, for example, it is used.

The long history of China, like that of ancient Egypt, is customarily designated by dynasties. Each dynasty, referred to by name rather than number, is divided into the reigns of kings or emperors. Each reign is in turn divided into individual years designated by special names, some computed from the sixty-year Cycle of Heavenly Stems and Earthly Branches. In citing historic events, I use the customary monarchical designations, as well as dates of the Christian era.

What I have plucked from ancient Chinese sexology is, obviously, from another land, another era, another culture. *The Yin–Yang Butterfly* touches on both the mystical and the scientific, and should be read with this inclusiveness in mind.

The book is intended to help readers dispel their bedroom blahs and add spice to their sex lives. The more adventurous may want to experiment, judiciously, with some of the ancient practices, aiming at enhanced sexuality, health, and youthfulness. Whatever the results of such experimentaion, one thing is sure: It is fun to try.

Part One

THE SENSUAL
LANDSCAPE

EUROPEAN ALCHEMY, Japanese geishas, Indian Tantric cults, venetian blinds, fireworks, wedding rings—these and many other disparate technological and cultural features from around the world originated in ancient Chinese sexual practices.

For more than a millennium, sexuality was enjoyed by the people of China, sometimes openly but more often discreetly, as a healthy part of life. Then came a century of political turmoil, followed by waves of prudish neo-Confucianism that swept across China during the past nine centuries or so. The great variety of Chinese sexual practices has been erased from the memory of contemporary China, and is virtually unknown to the West.

If we look deeper, however, we find many surprises. What allows us to look deeper is the penchant of the Chinese for recording anything and everything they believed worthwhile during the past five thousand years, from philosophical speculation to poetic eroticism, from events in the heavens to the coital thrusts of emperors in bed. They studied, wrote, and published so many books, essays, and chronicles that, by the estimate of European scholars in the eighteenth century, Chinese written records exceeded in volume the written records of all other languages put together.

Perhaps that is not so surprising: after all, the Chinese invented paper and printing. For thousands of years, among the educated elite and illiterate peasants alike, the respect for scholarship has bordered on mania. And one of the subjects of that scholarship was sexuality. From all that has been written about it by the Chinese, we have unexpected vistas of a sensual landscape.

1

The Culture That Nurtures

The Quest for Sexuality

ONE HALLMARK OF CIVILIZATION, it is said, is cuisine. Indeed, the human race has come a long way from wolfing down bloody raw meat to savoring the subtle taste, aroma, and texture of a variety of foods. Another hallmark of civilization is sexuality. Humans have progressed from merely satisfying their carnal animal instincts to sharing loving intimacy, with all its passion and tenderness, its sensuality and playfulness. A healthy refinement of cuisine and sexuality is often the natural consequence of a stable, mature, sophisticated civilization. The way in which a people refine their skills in fulfilling their basic needs of food and sex, and distill them into art forms may be measurements as significant as all the conquests made, monuments erected, and wealth amassed.

In this respect let us note a contrast. French cuisine, to name one, is a favorite for many around the world, and the reputation of French lovers legendary. While Chinese cuisine has become popular among Westerners—but this only after World War II—Chinese sexology and sexuality are still virtually unheard of in the West. This gap has its reasons; it is easier to monitor the kitchen than the bedroom. And in the eyes of the world, China is a puritanical culture.

Symptomatic of this idea is the prevailing myth among Westerners that the Chinese do not kiss mouth to mouth. This myth was perpetuated by Western missionaries in China who knew

3

nothing of the sex lives of their flocks, and by such respected Western sexologists as Theodore Van de Velde. In his 1928 best-seller *Ideal Marriage*, the otherwise very perceptive gynecologist writes: "Japanese, Chinese, Annamese [Indochinese] do not *kiss* as we understand the term." In fact, lip kissing is described and praised in Chinese sexology classics and in Chinese fiction and poetry. Deep kissing has delighted lovers all these centuries in China and elsewhere in the Orient. The only sources of research used by Van de Velde and the missionaries appear to have been Confucian classics.

But if we look behind this formidable Confucian façade, we find something quite different. The Chinese culture is the only major one that for thousands of years has been seriously, relentlessly—but discreetly—pursuing erotic techniques and sexual potency as a means to health, youthfulness, and longer life. India's Tantrism, which advocates ritualistic sexual union, has some superficial similarities with the Chinese approach. But it aims at religious salvation, while the Chinese pursuit is pragmatic and earth-bound, aiming at health and longevity. And, yet, as will be discussed later, some historians believe that Indian Tantrism was inspired by Chinese sexual practices.

The Art of the Bedchamber

For thousands of years, the ancient Chinese were intensely interested in the links among sex, health, and longevity. Their spirited research into sexuality is embodied in what loosely has been called the Art of the Bedchamber. This body of knowledge was developed by the ancient Chinese Taoist philosophers and proto-scientists who seriously pursued bodily immortality, first through magic, then through alchemy, and finally through sexual practices. They experimented with means for greater sexual energy, which they believed was inseparable from better health and longer life. The techniques they developed, incidentally, enabled a polygamous husband to satisfy as many as ten spouses in a single night and still not self-destruct.

The mystical, at times sophisticated experimentation in all aspects of sexuality was practiced eagerly by people in China for more than a thousand years. But it was shielded very well from the outside world. About ten centuries ago, much of the ancient Chinese core sexual knowledge began to disappear. As a result, during the ensuing centuries, when prudery ruled supreme, the Chinese forgot, or never learned, quite a few ancient sexual practices taught by their ancestors. They thus became known as a prudish people who lusted only after Confucianism or communism. But their interest in sexual nutrients and sexual exercises continued in subdued or disguised forms, and fortunately for posterity, the Art of the Bedchamber was not lost completely. Evidence of it was discovered early in this century, and we can now reconstruct it in more detail.

For centuries, many Chinese have practiced the Art of the Bedchamber more or less openly or secretly, consciously or unconsciously. They have eaten specific foods and herbs, and exercised their sexual muscles and sexual nerves to enhance bedroom prowess and nurture sexual vigor. They have invented ingenious toys to intensify coital pleasure or console lonely women, and devised a sexual physiognomy to predict an individual's sexual proclivities by simply looking at facial (and other bodily) features. They have made insightful use of love-play to forestall problems of potency and build stamina in sexual union. They have discovered erotic acupressure points and refined erotic massage to liven up love-play.

The Chinese were the first to develop systematically a spectrum of therapeutic sexual positions, aimed at health, conception, and pleasure—though not necessarily in that order. They contrived various secret techniques for both men and women in the bedchamber: orgasm control to prolong sexual union, titillating patterns of coital thrusts, other tactics to heighten ecstasy. They spent countless hours in meditative breathing to enhance their life-force and enrich their sexual energy.

The Chinese art of lovemaking was developed by the intellectual elite: Taoist immortality-seekers, physicians, scholars, mandarins (high government officials chosen from among top scholars), poets, painters, and master chefs who felt that lasting longer in bed was as desirable as living longer in life. Not surprisingly, the Art of the Bedchamber, with its theory of Yin and Yang, erotic techniques, and promise of long life, perhaps even immortality, was extremely popular with the royalty. The aristocrats were therefore the most enthusiastic patrons of this Art.

For five thousand years China had an absolute monarchy. Its rulers by tradition maintained forbidden palaces, essentially harems, with thousands of palace ladies guarded by eunuchs. When a man was surrounded by countless beautiful and available women, his most ardent scientific research would involve coping with one bedmate after another, delighting and vanquishing, doing it again and again. To many sexually exhausted male aristocrats, happiness was the delicious bedroom art that could repeatedly bring a woman to ecstasy, or an elixir that could raise a "dead" phallus.

A HISTORICAL QUEST

Sex was an important feature in the dynastic history of ancient China, as was the search for immortality. In the earliest time and for many centuries thereafter, Chinese monarchs firmly believed in the Taoist pursuit of immortality. In the third century B.C., the First Emperor of Chin sent three thousand young men and women, all virgins, to search for the legendary herb of immortality in the eastern seas, where the sun rises. The young people and their leader, the Taoist Hsu Fu, were never heard from again. They may have been shipwrecked or, as is generally believed, may have landed and settled in Japan. During the Han dynasty (c. 206 B.C.–A.D. 220), when the Art of the Bedchamber began to be practiced widely, one emperor had a giant dish built atop a 270-foot tower to collect dew, which, he believed, would increase his sexual stamina. Many emperors were known to seek the so-called elixir of immortality. They eagerly consumed this sexually oriented concoction prepared by experimental alchemists—and sometimes met with disastrous results.

In the thirteenth and fourteenth centuries, during the Yuan dynasty, the Mongolians who conquered and ruled China made Lamaism the state religion and spent two-thirds of their imperial budget on it. Lamaism was inspired in part by Indian Tantrism, which in turn may have been inspired by China's Art of the Bedchamber.

The Chinese drove out the Mongolians and established the Ming dynasty in the second half of the fourteenth century. The new emperors returned to the Taoist Art of the Bedchamber, although some vestiges of the Lamaist sex practices remained. By then much of Taoist sexology had degenerated into a mumbo-jumbo mixture of mysticism and alchemy. Charlatan Taoists formed sex cults among the common people, and made spurious elixirs which were taken thirstily by several Ming emperors hoping for increased sexual potency and long life. Emperors Shih Tsung (ruled 1522–1567) and Kuan Tsung (ruled 1620–1621) both died from consuming such elixirs. The death of Kuan Tsung was one of the great Ming scandals, involving accusations, counteraccusations, investigations, and impeachments of high court officials. A less tragic and more amusing case involved Emperor Mu Tsung (ruled 1567–1573). After taking an aphrodisiac, he got an erection that refused to go away. He was forced to cancel his regular audiences for a few days until his priapism subsided.

From the seventeenth through the early twentieth centuries, the Manchurian emperors of the Ching dynasty reverted to some Lamaist practices but avoided excess. In their palace was a Lamaist temple filled with "joyous Buddhas," Tantric idols in sexual embrace, some with movable genitalia. These were used as three-dimensional sex manuals by the Lamaist priests who customarily coached royal princes who had reached a marriageable age.

APHRODISIAC HEALTH TONICS

These later rulers of China were much more cautious in their quest for sexual vitality. They turned to safer aphrodisiac health tonics, which to this day are still taken earnestly by the Chinese. The Empress Dowager, for instance, meticulously ingested pulverized pearls and many other deluxe substances such as ginseng, bird's nest, and silvery tree ears (a tree fungus) to enhance her looks and health. Her skin was said to resemble a baby's. Her husband, Emperor Yen Feng (ruled 1851–1862), kept two hundred plum blossom deer in a royal garden so that every day he could drink deer blood, a health and sexual tonic. In the summer of 1860, during one of the several invasions of foreign troops after the Second Opium War, British and French troops occupied the imperial capital of Beijing and burned several palaces. The emperor fled to Jehol, a province north of the Great Wall, and as a result of his hasty flight he had to do without his daily tonic. Eventually, after moaning in vain on his deathbed for the precious deer blood, he died from debility.

During that same invasion in 1860, European troops burned Yuan Ming Yuan, a palace northwest of the Forbidden City. Some years earlier, a high government official named Ting Wen-cheng had gone for a private audience with the emperor in the palace. Early for his appointment, Ting was told to wait for the monarch in a small reception room. There he saw a bowl containing a dozen innocent-looking purple grapes. He sampled one and soon felt a growing heat below his navel, followed by a monster erection. Since his thin muslin summer gown could hardly hide his condition, Ting had to pretend to be violently ill; he doubled over and put his hand on his abdomen, and cried out in pain. He was led from the palace through a side door by courtiers who later told the emperor of Ting's "sudden sickness." Clearly, someone in the palace, perhaps the emperor, was using potent aphrodisiacs. However, most royal tonics were of the aphrodisiac health type.

A Long-Lasting Pursuit

The Chinese desire for heightened sexuality was, and is, due partly to the Confucian obsession for siring heirs, partly to a Taoist concern for health and longevity, but mostly to the delightful nature of their pursuit. This pursuit went on openly at first, and sometimes unwisely. Then it became more cautious, modest, almost covert. But even when it was carried on secretly, this quest went on, as it had before, for centuries.

Whatever our level of sophistication and depth of knowledge today, we can learn from the ancient Chinese in matters sexual: how they used food and herbs to benefit their sexual vitality, how they exercised to train their sexual muscles and nerves, what erotic techniques they devised to enhance sexual union. They fervently believed in and enthusiastically practiced activities they felt would nurture their health in general and their sexual vitality in particular. Chinese culture has been called many things by many people: as far as sexuality is concerned, it may be called a culture that nurtures.

2

The Mating of Yin and Yang

Sexual Cosmology, Taoism, and Confucianism

YIN AND YANG, AND BEYOND

Ancient China had a distinctive, deceptively simple cosmology—a sexual cosmology. In the primeval void was Tai Chi, the Grand Ultimate, immaterial, formless, and impalpable. It moved and produced Yang, or male energy. Having moved to the utmost, it rested, and then produced Yin, female energy. The dual elements of Yin and Yang, opposite but complementary, mated and produced Tao, the Way that cannot be charted, the Name that cannot be described, the Truth that is unknowable. Tao encompasses heaven, earth, and humankind, all things material and spiritual.

When Yin and Yang are in harmony, whether in nature, the world, or the human body, crops thrive, nations are at peace, individuals enjoy health. When that harmony is upset, natural calamities, wars, diseases emerge. The basic dualism of Yin and Yang is conveyed in the symbol of Tai Chi. This common motif in Chinese art consists of a circle divided into two equal curvy halves, each resembling a plump tadpole with a single eye. These two halves represent Yin and Yang mating into a harmonious whole, and thus the essence of Chinese cosmology. Although the theory was later reconstructed and elaborated by various metaphysicians and philosophers, this cosmology goes back to the distant beginnings of Chinese culture, more than five thousand years ago.

The idea of cosmic sexuality, the mating of Yin and Yang, would color the attitude toward sex in ancient China. It was considered a natural and guiltless human activity, and enhancing sexual vigor and sexual pleasure was a legitimate pursuit in a healthy life. The sexual cosmology is also the foundation of Taoism, China's oldest indigenous philosophy, which later branched out into religion and proto-science.

Many basic concepts in this cosmic outlook are found in *I Ching,* or *The Book of Changes,* one of the oldest, most revered, and least understood Chinese classics. This unique book was compiled by various authors between the sixth and the fourth centuries B.C. It centers around sixty-four hexagrams, each consisting of two trigrams, or a total of six whole (Yang) or broken (Yin) sticks arranged in various combinations, to denote various modes of coupling between Yin and Yang. Attached to each hexagram are two brief texts, "Judgment" and "Image," which have been used as oracles for divination since antiquity. Subsequent commentaries by anonymous cosmologists and metaphysicians expanded these commentaries and made this abstruse text the basis of philosophical speculation for many Chinese thinkers.

I Ching is thus a book of both divination and, more important, philosophy. Poetic in language, cryptic in meaning, profound in philosophical implications, it is the seedbed of Chinese thought and culture. It is also the cradle of cosmic sexuality in China. The sixty-third hexagram, for instance, is a symbol for sexual intercourse, with the female trigram atop the male one, or Yin above Yang. In other words, Yin (woman) takes precedence. The sixty-third hexagram is emblematic of Taoism, whose notion of female superiority distinguishes it markedly from Confucianism with its ideas of female inferiority.

(Incidentally, the binary system, the counting system used in computers, was inspired by the Yin and Yang sticks of the *I Ching* hexagrams. The inventor of the binary system reportedly got the idea from a Frenchman who lived in China and was intrigued by the ancient text.)

Chinese cosmologists amplified the sexual dualism of Yin

Tai Chi symbol

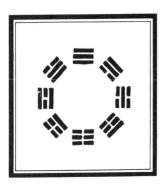

The eight trigrams of
I Ching

and Yang metaphysically and philosophically. Innumerable pairs of opposites—among them earth and heaven, shadow and light, softness and hardness, quiescence and activity, absorption and penetration—came to symbolize these two forces. These sexual ramifications are so pervasive in China, so accepted as natural, in fact, that they seem to affect every facet of Chinese culture.

The concept of Yin and Yang must have been partly responsible for the secret, luxurious sex lives of this supposedly inscrutable people. To understand their sexuality, however, and to make use of some of their bedroom secrets, it is essential first to take a brief look at what the Chinese have been thinking and doing.

ANCIENT ACHIEVEMENTS

China as a nation has the oldest living and longest-lasting civilization. Until only a few centuries ago the Chinese had been developing their own distinctive culture with recurrent flowerings in science and technology as well as philosophy. The English philosopher Francis Bacon once named three inventions—printing, gunpowder, and the magnet—as having done more than any others to speed humankind's progress into the modern world. He termed the origins of these inventions "obscure and inglorious," and never learned that all of them were Chinese. And those were by no means the only Chinese contributions toward human progress. The compass, block and movable-type printing, paper, porcelain, and lacquerware are among the many well-documented Chinese inventions.

Since World War II, a new breed of Western Sinologists has been claiming that for some twenty centuries Chinese culture was in many respects far more advanced than that of Europe. Joseph Needham of Cambridge University, author of the monumental *Science and Civilisation in China,* has commented: "During the first fourteen centuries of the Christian era . . . China transmitted to Europe a veritable abundance of discoveries and inventions which were often received by the West with no clear idea of where they had originated." Between the fifth century B.C. and the fifteenth century A.D., according to Needham, the standard of living in China was higher than that in Europe.

In the preface to *The Genius of China,* Robert Temple writes:

"One of the greatest untold secrets of history is that the 'modern world' in which we live is a unique synthesis of Chinese and Western ingredients. Possibly more than half of the basic inventions and discoveries upon which the 'modern world' rests come from China. And yet few people know this."

Orthodox Sinologists of the old school, it should be emphasized, were obsessed with China's Confucianism but oblivious to what Temple calls "untold secrets." And the Chinese themselves today have forgotten much of what their ancestors discovered and developed.

Many centuries ago the Chinese built the 1,700-mile Great Wall, the only manmade structure visible from the moon, and the 1,300-mile Grand Canal, with its innovative system of locks. According to Needham, Temple, and other Westerners, they were also the first to make cast iron and steel, and the first to deep-drill for oil and natural gas. They invented the seismograph, the rocket, the umbrella, and the parachute (and this fifteen centuries before Leonardo da Vinci's parachute sketches).

It may be hard to believe all this if one looks at China today, however. Why did China, so advanced in science and technology during ancient and medieval times, suddenly lose its advantage when modern science began to flourish in the West in the seventeenth century? Why has it lagged so far behind that today it is in some senses underdeveloped? There are various answers, but the main ones involve overpopulation, overemphasis on literary and artistic pursuits, and a disastrous encounter with opium.

The ancient Chinese had a keen understanding of biology, and devised quite a few lasting tricks with living beings. Bonsai, the art of dwarfing old trees and "aging" young ones, was invented in China. The Chinese developed tiny, brilliant-hued goldfish from large, dark-colored carp, and bred and rebred a ferocious four-hundred-pound war dog into the small Pekingese, a lapdog known around the world. Moreover, the Chinese applied their knowledge of biology to human medicine and physiology. Because their ancient practice was based on theories that were alien to the West, it was largely and consistently ignored.

Taoist and Zen meditation, which originated in China, have been considered as pure mysticism by many Westerners. But Western science is beginning to find that such meditation generates brain waves that enable the mind to benefit the body. The Chinese have been using acupuncture as a medical treatment for more than three thousand years; only relatively recently has it been discovered by Westerners. The martial arts practiced in various Asian countries today all can be traced to ancient Chinese monasteries where Buddhist and Taoist priests devised unarmed but deadly methods of self-defense. In these and other ways, the ancient Chinese—and their descendants—cultivated knowledge of the living organism, of life, and of sexuality.

PHILOSOPHY AND RELIGION

More significant than science and technology in shaping ancient Chinese culture were philosophy and religion. Here we may enumerate three great molding forces: Confucianism, Taoism, and Buddhism. The first two were already in full bloom in the sixth century B.C., before the time of Socrates, before the spread of Christianity. Notable among the sages were the humanist Confucius, with his doctrine of ethics; the pacifist Mo Tzu, who taught universal love; the legalist Hanfei Tzu, who inspired the earliest known form of totalitarianism; and the Taoists Lao Tzu and Chuang Tzu, who advocated individualism and naturalism. Of these, Confucius and Lao Tzu have left the most lasting imprints on Chinese civilization.

Confucianism is a philosophy of morals and a code of ethics; it is centered around the complex Chinese family system and extends to the entire nation. According to this doctrine, every individual in a hierarchy, from the family to the nation, has a specific authority and duty, and is guided by innate morals in dealing with others. The highest moral value lies in filial piety. The Confucian utopia is a world not only at peace but in total harmony (which, incidentally, may preclude democracy).

The self-contained, rigidly structured Confucian universe thrived on meticulously prescribed etiquette, forms of dress and address, rites and rituals; it even spelled out comportment as specific as a gentleman's walking gait. In essence, Confucianism advocated innate, personal morals in a humanist society steeped in social consciousness. Confucianism limits itself to pragmatic human relations. In its original form, it did not bother with cosmology or acknowledge the supernatural or metaphysical.

Counterpoint to worldly Confucianism is otherworldly Taoism, a curious trinity of philosophy, religion, and proto-science inspired by the pursuit of immortality. Taoism speculates boldly on such profound ideas as creation, nature and human nature, matter and spirit, time and change, being and nonbeing. As a proto-philosophy it grew from the earliest indigenous ideas of the Chinese race and had an amorphous existence long before Confucianism was born. Lao Tzu, an older contemporary of Confucius, shaped it into a philosophy, which was amplified and elaborated by Chuang Tzu more than a century later. Chuang Tzu is celebrated for his dream in which he was a butterfly flitting among the flowers; when he awoke, he was not sure whether he was Chuang Tzu who had dreamed of being a butterfly, or a butterfly dreaming of being Chuang Tzu.

In its cosmic sense, Tao is the ultimate, unknowable reality, which governs everything in the universe. It has been described as resembling an infinite web of perpetual movement and change. All physical objects, living beings, events in nature and human nature are mere changing shapes and phases in the contractions and expansions, ripples and undulations of this infinite web. Everything changes ceaselessly. Nothing that exists, nothing that happens, ever repeats itself exactly. Taoists believe that mortals may glean an instant of this constant change and delude themselves with the evanescent image as reality. Ancient as it may be, this concept of reality applies to our modern science of quantum physics, which in effect looks at what we call reality as an illusion.

Taoists scorn the Confucianist doctrines of propriety and social status as overdecorous and pompous. Taoists, who in contrast value spontaneity and intuitiveness, believe that resilience triumphs over rigidity, and quiescence over activity. Their outlook on life leans to nature and the natural. Happiness comes from merging into and harmonizing with nature, not in conquering it, and certainly not in the foolhardy pursuit of things worldly—such as power, fame, and wealth. To people enjoying success, Taoism mentions failure, and to those suffering failure, it calls to mind success. Taoism depends on many paradoxical aphorisms, such as, "Great wisdom resembles stupidity." In the past, some Taoists, rebelling against the rigid Confucian establishment and the ancient Chinese version of the rat race, went about with disheveled hair and unkempt clothing, sometimes reeling from too much wine. One might consider them the original hippies.

Taoism dismisses as futile such intellectual exercises as hair-splitting examination and debate. It values instead the intuitive leap and is responsible for the characteristic Chinese thought process, namely, synthesis rather than analysis. Imaginative and romantic, Taoism has affected the life philosophy of all Chinese, even the most rabid Confucianists. For many Chinese the choice between Confucianism and Taoism has been delightfully convenient: one can be a Confucianist in success and a Taoist in failure, a Confucianist in public and a Taoist in private, a Confucianist by day and a Taoist by night.

Even in early times, Taoism, while it intrigued intellectuals with its pondering on esoteric subjects, began to interest other, less cerebral people. During the second century A.D., under the influence of a Taoist philosopher and metaphysicist, a religious offshoot began to grow from the main philosophical trunk. This Taoist religion was based strongly on the popular Yin–Yang cosmology and was enriched with elements of folk legend. Eventually it became an organized religion, complete with a pantheon of gods, goddesses, and immortals.

THE IMMORTALS

The immortals, or *hsien,* represent a uniquely Taoist concept. They are humans who have discovered the secrets of everlasting life and acquired an astral body resembling their physical one. These men and women stopped aging once they achieved immortality. The early Taoists not only believed in this bodily immortality but seriously pursued it, with centuries of research and experiment. Their spirited quest was to leave fascinating imprints on science in the West and bedroom art in the East. With its unlikely mixture of proto-science and mysticism, Taoism lured devotees to try to perfect an elixir of immortality (*hsien tan*), first in the alchemist's crucible, then in the human body itself.

Some Western scholars believe that alchemy originated in China under this impulse several centuries before the Christian era; it later spread westward to Arabia and Europe. But while medieval European alchemists engaged almost exclusively in trying to transmute base metals into gold, their Chinese counterparts focused on concocting the elixir of immortality. This elixir,

it was believed, would not only confer immortality and stop aging but also boost sexual vitality.

In Europe, alchemy directly or indirectly inspired chemistry. Although the alchemists failed to turn base metals into gold, they have in a way been vindicated. Metals *can* be transmuted, not in the alchemist's crucible but in the nuclear physicist's cyclotron.

In China, Taoists believed that the secret of the elixir of immortality was locked in several ingredients, including cinnabar, naturally occurring mercury sulfide. They used this potent mineral in a number of ancient recipes, and many Taoists and a couple of emperors died of mercury poisoning after ingesting the elixir. Taoist alchemists eventually abandoned their crucibles, but not before they had—accidentally—invented gunpowder.

SEXUAL ALCHEMY

In their research the Taoists turned their attention to "inner alchemy," or sexual alchemy. This was nothing less than an effort to perfect an elixir of immortality inside the human body. A key Taoist concept is *chi,* primeval life-energy or life-force. The ancient Chinese believed that all living organisms possessed this force, the essence of life. This vital, ceaseless energy not only permeated all living beings but also emanated from inanimate objects. It ebbed and flowed in heaven and on earth. *Chi* was thus the supreme universal energy. The mystical Taoist search for immortality eventually developed into a more pragmatic quest for longevity and health—through sexual energy.

When Buddhism was introduced into China from India in the first century A.D., it encountered a sophisticated, deeply entrenched civilization already several thousand years old. Through the centuries the three formidable systems of philosophy and religion—Confucianism, Taoism, and Buddhism—were to compete against, copy from, and influence each other in myriad ways. The result was the crystallization of Chinese culture and, in addition, the enrichment of sex life on the Asian continent.

The school of Buddhism that reached China was Mahayana (Great Vehicle). By the seventh century, Mahayana Buddhism in China had absorbed elements of Taoist metaphysics and mind-body practices. Chinese Buddhists revised the concept of nirvana, the ultimate blissful state of salvation, which Indian Buddhists believed could be attained only through multiple incarnations; Chinese Buddhists held that it could be achieved by intuitive, antirational transcendental meditation until enlightenment suddenly came. Historians call this radically altered form of Buddhism, known as Zen or Chan Buddhism, a purely Chinese phenomenon; it is actually modified with a generous dose of Taoism. In the twelfth century Zen was exported to Japan, where it still thrives today. In China, Zen Buddhism has been practiced mainly by the educated elite. For many among the illiterate, Mahayana Buddhism degenerated into mere superstitious idol worship.

Zen Buddhism has left lasting marks on China, especially in the notions of compassion and reincarnation. The religiously eclectic Chinese tend to mix and match selected beliefs, whether they call themselves Buddhists, Taoists, Muslims, Christians, or even agnostics. Most acknowledge a supreme intelligence-morality they term "heaven," which is a concept of God. Individuals are guided not so much by the fear of fire and brimstone as by their own conscience. The Chinese do not conceive of original sin and venerate no implacable gods.

During the Tang dynasty (618–907), often recognized as the golden age of China, Taoism was made a state religion. The two-pronged pursuit of immortality through alchemy and sexual union was at a zenith. This was the heyday of ancient Chinese sexology.

TANTRISM

Probably around the end of the seventh century, according to Joseph Needham, R. H. Van Gulik, and other Western Sinologists, Taoist sexual theory was introduced to India. Within a single century Tantrism emerged there. Indian Buddhism, which previously had espoused the elimination of all human desires, had a new school, Vajrayana, which preached that salvation could be attained through ritual sexual intercourse. The Vajrayana scriptures indicate that an Indian holy man was taught this when he visited China.

Soon a Hindu sect, Saiva Sakta, appeared, with a nearly identical sexual doctrine for salvation. The beliefs and practices of both sects are called loosely Tantrism. Today, the writhing couples carved on the temples of Khajuraho and Konarak are a solid testimony to Indian Tantrism. Vajrayana Buddhism, which com-

bined with folk religion to form Lamaism in Tibet, Nepal, and Mongolia, died out in India. Saiva Sakta Tantrism still exists there.

In the first half of the eighth century, Tantric missionaries from India journeyed to China, where the Tang Chinese, who had been cheerfully practicing their own Taoist sexual exercises, incorporated mystical Tantric features into their sex classics. A principal belief the Chinese adopted was that semen undischarged in the practice of nonejaculation could "return" to the body's reservoir of life and sexual energy, via a point in the brain. Whether as a result of Tantric feedback or not, Taoist sexual classics became increasingly mystical and obsessed with the idea of nonejaculation, especially in the fifteenth and sixteenth centuries.

CONFUCIANISM ADAPTS

Drastic changes in religion and philosophy came during the Sung and Southern Sung dynasty (960–1280). To compete with Taoism and Buddhism, Confucianists adopted many elements of these other two systems. The revised ideology, known as neo-Confucianism, incorporated the Taoist theory of Yin and Yang and some Buddhist cosmology. It touched on metaphysics and the supernatural, subjects not found in the original teachings of Confucius. *I Ching,* considered a Confucian classic but neither written nor edited by Confucius, became the bible of neo-Confucianists, even though it was based on Taoist thinking.

While strategically incorporating Taoist and Buddhist features, the neo-Confucianists went further than Confucius himself in exaggerating loyalty to the emperor and sexual propriety. They insisted on separation of sexes, even within the family. Chinese emperors gladly seized neo-Confucianism as an ideological justification for their authoritarian rule. They were likely to frown on pure Taoism: the freedom-loving, iconoclastic Taoists, unlike the Confucian conformists, had been the fountainhead of many a bloody rebellion.

A UNIQUE SOCIETY

The civilization of this ancient empire, having developed in virtual isolation for centuries, was in many aspects antithetical to that of the West. Of course, it is impossible to generalize on the complexities and paradoxes of China, which every once in a while would spring a surprise to the rest of the world. China enjoyed long centuries of peace and prosperity, and despite intermittent periods of turmoil and violence it remained fairly stable. This stability was due to the powerful influence of its three main schools of thought, as well as to its solidly entrenched social and political structures.

For several thousand years the country was fed by a vast population of farmers, and ruled by an emperor through the mandarins, high-ranking officials chosen at competitive imperial examinations. The scholars who wrote the most erudite essays, composed the most sensitive poetry, and rendered the most aesthetic calligraphy or painting became mandarins. While dynasties rose and fell, and emperors came and went, the mandarin bureaucracy endured. In effect, China was ruled for many centuries by "egghead" governments.

At the top of Chinese society were mandarins, scholars, poets, calligraphers, painters, and master chefs. All Chinese, including illiterate peasants, revered them. Farmers who tilled the land were respected, at least in an abstract sense. No Chinese, whether prince or peasant, would leave even a single grain of rice in his bowl uneaten: rice symbolized the back-breaking labor of the peasants, and wasting it was a moral sin.

Next down the social ladder were traders, merchants, and craftsmen. The business of making money, though respectable, was not considered a noble pursuit. If a businessman was lucky enough to make a fortune, he was never accepted into the elite. Only his offspring could rise socially—and then only if they became scholars. When a man became suddenly wealthy, his priority was to engage tutors to teach his children poetry, calligraphy, and painting.

Because of the strong Confucian influence, the Chinese always have valued harmony and disdained contention. Even an aggressive person in an adversarial situation would disguise himself in a cloak of harmony. Disputes were settled usually through mediation rather than lawsuits. In some eras, in fact, lawyers were grouped socially just above prostitutes.

The monolithic Confucian family system made filial piety the highest moral; the mistreatment of parents was the greatest sin.

Young children were pampered, but as soon as they reached the age of reasoning, they were taught self-discipline. The family institution was formidable; divorce was rare, and even a man's mistress was integrated into his family as a concubine. Significant milestones—births and major birthdays, weddings, deaths—were celebrated with colorful, elaborate ceremonies.

Confucianism, with its strong family values, did not exist alone, as we have seen. Buddhism contributed the concept of reincarnation and the practice of anonymous charity to accumulate merits in heaven. Taoism made the Chinese tolerant of others and eclectic in their philosophy of life.

THE FALL OF AN EMPIRE

The reverence for scholarship became so strong in China that eventually it backfired. By the middle of the eighteenth century, the long, relentless emphasis on belles lettres had left a mark of effeteness on the culture. The brightest minds scorned science and technology as inelegant "petty skills." Scholars looked down on physical activity and labor, comfortable in their silk robes with long, loose sleeves, and at times growing their fingernails several inches, to show that their activities were exclusively inside the head.

Corruption in government was facilitated under inept monarchs and the powerful, scheming eunuchs in their courts. Between 1741 and 1851 the population of China more than tripled from 140 million to 430 million. The cause of this explosion has puzzled historians, yet its effects on a nation with limited arable land are undeniable: seemingly insoluble economic problems, and food shortages, have plagued China to this day.

The shaky Dragon Throne might have survived its problems, as it had before, if there had been no outside forces to tip the balance. But at this time, driven by the trading imperatives of the Industrial Revolution, European powers were casting their eyes on the promise of rich profits in the East. Despite repeated protests by the Chinese government, British traders flooded China with increasing amounts of Indian-grown opium. When a Chinese imperial commissioner seized a British shipment of opium in Canton and burned it, the British sent their gunboats to China, thus launching the First Opium War (1839–1842).

The Chinese had invented various weapons, but their descendants by then had forgotten about them. The "barbarians" from the West had improved and modernized these guns and cannons, which, when carried on fighting ships, rendered their bearers virtually invincible. The once proud Celestial Empire was brought to its knees. China was, in the end, a paper tiger. The pigtails sported by Chinese men, as specified by imperial decree, and the bound feet of Chinese women became symbols of a backward, degraded people. The elite of the nation increasingly sought solace and escape in opium, which was everywhere.

Thus was triggered the disintegration of an ancient empire, a resplendent civilization. For more than half a century Britain, Japan, and other colonial powers repeatedly encroached on Chinese sovereign rights. Whenever the Chinese balked, European gunboats and troops invaded China. Only the Open Door policy (equal opportunity for all powers), advocated by the United States, saved China from being partitioned into colonies the way the African continent was.

Outrage at the indignities inflicted on them by the "foreign devils" touched off decades of violent uprisings among the Chinese. The Boxer Rebellion, which culminated in 1900, was one such rabidly antiforeign uprising. Early in this century, a boy monarch ascended to the throne, and the millennia-old monarchy soon was toppled by republican revolutionaries. During the next half-century China was devastated by battles among warlords and repeated Japanese invasions. The internal convulsions became more and more violent and senseless, and the Maoist Red Guards fought this violence with more violence. In this turbulent period, the so-called Cultural Revolution, many people were tortured or killed, and countless invaluable cultural artifacts destroyed. It will take years, perhaps generations, for China to recover from this cultural catastrophe.

The traumatic loss of national prestige over the past two centuries has brought the once proud Chinese to lose faith in their own cultural heritage. Many, especially the educated, have begun to scorn things Chinese and worship the West. Today the Chinese know only vaguely of their past cultural brilliance; many are unaware of their ancestors' sophistication in many areas, sex included.

3

When Confucius Wasn't Looking

Customs, Courtesies, and Courtesans

Sexuality has been all-pervasive in the Chinese psyche, whether in the primeval sexual cosmology or everyday customs and traditions. Through the centuries, however, this cosmic sexuality has been subtly symbolized and stylized, so that the sexual origin has been often obscured, and sometimes even forgotten.

China has had no overt phallic worship. Nevertheless, the symbolic phallus, as well as the symbolic vulva, recur frequently. Chinese written characters, many of which are composed of two or more elements, or radicals, developed from pictures, representational images. Although most characters have evolved into stylized forms, some can be traced easily to their pictorial origin. The character for "sun," for instance, is a square (originally a circle) with a dot (sun spot) inside. The character for "prisoner" recalls a human figure held in a stockade. The character for "ancestor" is formed by two radicals, but its older form consisted of only one, resembling an erect phallus with two ridges around it. The character for "mother," made with several curves and two dots, came from the image of the breasts and nipples of a nursing woman. The character for "woman" is a spread-eagle human form with a

22

hole in the appropriate place. The character for "debauchery" consists of three of these spread-eagle forms.

Sexual symbolism has entered into ritual and common customs as well. Until a century ago, at a festival held at the first full moon of the Lunar New Year, Chinese women customarily would visit the Cheng Yang Gate of the old city wall of Beijing. The massive doors of the gate were studded with thick, blunt stylized nails which protruded several inches from the doors. The women would fondle these undeniably phallic-shaped nails with their hands to ensure good health and fertility.

Chinese art and crafts, with the exception of Buddhist sculpture and murals, are full of sexual symbolism. Landscape painting often features lofty, craggy mountains in the background, dotted with knarled trees and shrouded in clouds; in the foreground is a lake, a bubbling stream, or a waterfall tumbling through wispy mists. Such elegant, poetic scenes are also sexual, for the Yin–Yang polarity runs throughout them. Mountain peaks and craggy rocks are Yang; valleys and bodies of water are Yin. Swirling clouds and mists symbolize female sexual secretions; rain, male semen. The Yin and Yang in works of art symbolize arousal; each energizes its opposite with a vital sexual energy. Harmonizing between Yin and Yang is the genesis of everything in the Chinese universe. Paintings other than landscapes may be equally laden with sexuality. One famous work shows two women in a misty garden, surrounded by peonies and *ling-chih* (divine mushrooms); a male phoenix hovers above them. Here the Yin of women, peonies, mushrooms, and mist is being energized by, and is harmonizing with, the Yang of the male phoenix.

The subtle vocabulary of sexual symbolism is endless. A perfect harmony between Yin and Yang is the union of the Yin earth and the Yang heaven. Emanations from earth—water, clouds, mists—are Yin, while things from heaven—rain, dragons, jade (thought to be congealed dragon semen)—are Yang. Yang symbols in art include stallions, rams, cocks, and unicorns. Yin symbols include the peach, peony, lotus, and chrysanthemum, all of which suggest the vulva. The cloud-shaped *ling-chih* mushroom, valued by Taoists as the plant of immortality, symbolizes female effluvia.

Vases and other containers are Yin symbols. Medicine cups were often made of rhinoceros horn, which symbolizes the vulva with its dripping Yin essence. Incense burners consist of a bowl (female organ) on a tripod (male organ). The good-luck emblem *ju-i* ("as you wish"), a favorite in reception halls and at wedding ceremonies, is a stylized scepter, often carved in jade. Its graceful shape belies its origin: the *ju-i* is a discreet phallic symbol.

In the past in China, personal seals were used instead of signatures; they functioned as a symbol of authority. An emperor's edicts, for instance, had to carry his royal seal. Paintings too have always borne the artist's personal seal. Besides the carved scripts on the bottom, necessary for imprinting, seals are often decorated on the sides with representations of mountains, dragons, and other subjects. Many seals have a rounded top, a subtle phallic shape. Until recently, gold and silver in China were cast in the form of *yuan-pao* (prime treasure) instead of ingots and bars; the boat-shaped *yuan-pao* is a vulva symbol.

Many Chinese paintings depict an old man sitting serenely near winter-flowering plum blossoms, which signify sexual pleasure in old age. As long as he did not behave like a lecher, a sexually active old man in traditional China was not considered a dirty old man. Instead he was regarded as a fortunate, healthy male who enjoyed sex and longevity. Countless paintings, designs on porcelain, jade and wood carvings, and embroidered robes show cloud-shrouded dragons pursuing and toying with a giant pearl, which sometimes has flames shooting out of it. This pearl represents the condensed essence of mingled male and female sexual energy.

PRUDISHNESS AND LASCIVIOUSNESS

Despite the pervasive, even formalized sexual symbolism in art and elsewhere, the pendulum of sexuality has swung widely—and wildly—in China. Among the cultures of the world, China has known some of the most restrictive, as well as some of the most licentious, practices.

During the most prudish times, respectable Chinese women could talk to men who were not blood relatives only from behind a screen. A maiden whose bare arm was accidentally touched, or whose partial nudity was accidentally seen, by a male stranger had to marry him to preserve her virtue. A married sister could not sit at the same family dining table with her own brother. Husbands and wives were not to touch each other outside their bedroom, and their clothes were not to be hung next to each other on the same rack. Widows who refused to remarry were honored by their communities with stone monuments.

Incest taboos were severe, and included a "name incest," which forbade a man to marry a woman with the same last name, even if they were not at all related. The obsession with virginity was rampant; in some regions a piece of bloodstained cloth had to be exhibited by the proud husband the morning after the wedding night. In southern China the groom's family would send a whole roast suckling pig ceremoniously through the streets when the bride visited her family three days after the wedding—but only if she had been found to be a virgin. Through this ritual the whole community would know her condition. Suicides, murders, and bloody clan feuds sometimes resulted if a young woman was found not to be a virgin.

On the other hand, an emperor of China might have anywhere from 3,000 to 40,000 women in his inner sanctum, where, guarded by eunuchs, he could have sex with any of them. The feats of some of the most lecherous emperors, empresses, and aristocrats were faithfully recorded for posterity in official histories and scholarly chronicles.

From time to time, sex cults engaged in mass orgies. In the fourteenth century aristocrats and commoners alike, coached by cult priests, indulged in such practices. For privacy in warm weather, participants shielded their windows with *tiao-hsien*, ingenious blinds made of bamboo slats. They were used so widely on brothel windows that they eventually came to symbolize these establishments. (Earlier, *tiao-hsien* had inspired a foreign visitor named Marco Polo; the result was the so-called venetian blind.)

A top attraction at Chinese festivals in the eleventh century consisted of wrestling matches between naked women. In some areas people practiced a custom we might think of as "rent-a-wife," whereby a man could rent a wife from her husband for a contracted period, whether as a baby-maker or sexual partner. A famous prime minister of the Sung dynasty was born of such a contract. In spite of the seclusion of young women, men were able to seduce them in clandestine liaisons; these have inspired some of the finest classical poetry and drama. Affairs between fathers-in-law and daughters-in-law, known as "raking ashes" in Chinese, were prevalent among the royalty during certain eras. In recent centuries, a standard punishment for sexual misconduct was public spanking; a big paddle would be used on naked buttocks, of men as well as women, right inside the courtroom.

Neo-Confucianism Takes Over

Up to a thousand years ago, then, sexual life in China was colorful. The Art of the Bedchamber flourished and was practiced openly. During the three centuries of the Tang dynasty (618–907), sex and sexuality were robust and freewheeling, not only in the imperial courts but also among the commoners. And women were as forward as men in their sexual pursuits, seductions, and clandestine trysts.

During the Sung and Southern Sung dynasty, however, neo-Confucianists began to advocate segregation of the sexes even within the family, and sex for procreation only; underlying this was their belief in the inferiority of women. Their puritanical public stance has dominated China for almost the past thousand years. The neo-Confucianists were not against sex; they were just overdecorous prudes, who restricted sex to the sanctuary of the bedchamber, outside which they pretended to see no sex, hear no sex, and speak no sex.

They did, though, maintain the old Confucian obsession with begetting heirs. Even the most diehard neo-Confucianists copulated, often spiritedly, to sire sons. In fact, they had utter contempt for voluntary celibacy and saw the celibacy of Buddhist monks and nuns as unnatural. To the neo-Confucianists, family was the bedrock of social and political systems, so they practiced polygamy with a straight face.

Until the recent past, polygamy had been customary in China. The upper and middle classes practiced it if they wanted, when they could afford it. They could justify it morally on the grounds that it was a way to guarantee male heirs to carry on the family line. The Chinese had a curious form of polygamy, distinct from that of other cultures. If a man had several wives, the first remained the female head of the household; she could not be divorced unless she was caught in serious misconduct. The concubines, or subsequent and minor wives, had to defer to her. No one could usurp the first wife's status in the family hierarchy, whatever the husband's emotional or sexual preferences. Under such an all-encompassing family structure, there could be virtually no "scarlet women" or illegitimate children.

The Chinese system of polygamy obligated the husband to satisfy his wife and all his concubines sexually. This seemingly superhuman feat was not impossible if the husband was an adept in the Art of the Bedchamber. Husbands who were exhausted or bored by conjugal duty at home sometimes would take a night off and visit high-class courtesans, in whose company they would indulge in wine, poetry, and music.

Judging whether a Chinese concubine was happier or unhappier than an American divorcée or a French mistress is outside the scope of this book. Yet it is relevant to look, if only briefly, at the position of women in ancient China. As in many if not most ancient and medieval cultures, women in ancient China were deemed inferior to men, especially when neo-Confucianism prevailed. While neo-Confucianists did not say explicitly, they created moral codes that belittled or restricted women. A typical neo-Confucian "rule" held that a woman without talent was virtuous.

Although the neo-Confucianists considered women inferior, they did not despise them in the way medieval European churchmen, for instance, did; and even when Chinese women had little standing in society at large, they wielded considerable power within the family. This was partly due to the emphasis in Confucianism on filial piety toward both parents. Even a grown-up son with his own family had to defer to his mother as long as she lived. And when it was necessary, it seems, Chinese women knew how to fight back. Chronicles abound with cases of politically or socially prominent men, their faces scratched or battered, appearing in court with their wives for mediation of marital fights. Some of the most feared Chinese men met their match in their wives; some were even henpecked. Chinese women may have mastered the Taoist secret of conquering hardness with softness.

HOMOSEXUALITY

As in most civilizations, homosexuality is found in much of China's history. Quite a few emperors, members of royalty, liter-

ary figures, and especially actors are known to have been homosexuals. Most homosexual relations were between grown men and prepubescent boys, who traditionally were kept as pages by the royalty and the wealthy. When these boys reached puberty and their voices began to change, they would be released. As a reward for their prepubescent functions, they often were helped to find spouses.

When, in the middle of the fifteenth century, a Ming emperor banned legalized, high-class prostitution for court and government mandarins, these bored men directed their libido elsewhere. In the traditional Chinese theater, both male and female roles were played by men; many actors who played female roles onstage played similar roles in bed. These actors, as well as specially trained young singers, became the objects of affection for upper-class men seeking a homosexual relationship. It was fashionable for the rich and famous (and lecherous) to keep in their households not only wives, concubines, and dancing girls but also pretty page boys and homosexual actors. During the nineteenth century, noted literary figures wrote books, essays, and poems describing and praising homosexual love. Most of the men engaging in homosexual activities, it should be noted, were bisexuals, who carried on heterosexual relationships as well.

Lesbianism was tolerated, sometimes even encouraged. Ingenious erotic devices for women were invented in China. When the last emperor of China was toppled from his throne early in this century, revolutionaries found more than a thousand such sexual aids in the women's palaces of the Forbidden City.

A CURIOUS SEXUAL VOGUE

Sex life in ancient China, richly varied as it was, was remarkably healthy. It had little of what some today would call "pathological" or "perverse" behavior—except for one solidly entrenched sexual fetish. The binding of women's feet was in essence an erotic practice. One might say that it got out of hand for almost a thousand years; the modern Chinese, and many Westerners, condemn it as a painful symbol of the social bondage of women.

It was during the centuries of neo-Confucian sexual puritanism that the curious custom of foot-binding began. Yao Niang, a willowy, featherlike dancer, was the favorite consort of the tenth-century Southern Tang dynasty king Li Yu. Yao Niang bound her feet with cloth ribbons to strengthen them but keep them looking dainty when she danced. She made such a hit in the imperial court that high-born ladies began to bind their feet in imitation of her. The fashion became a fad, and the fad became a mania; women of all classes—except peasant women—bound their feet. A woman would not be considered beautiful, in men's eyes or her own, unless she had tiny bound feet. Parents subjected their daughters to this grueling beauty treatment when the girls were no more than six years old. The aim was to produce dainty little "golden lotuses"—the ideal shape for the bound feet—five, four, even three inches long.

During the nineteenth century, Europeans brought back from China the horror story of foot-binding, which they condemned as a barbaric custom. These Westerners, however, overlooked their own Victorian female fashion for tight-laced wasp waists—a practice that caused cardiac and pulmonary damage. And flagellation, avidly enjoyed by some Victorian gentlemen and ladies to satisfy their lust, might seem as strange as foot-binding.

Thus foot-binding, which began as a feminine beauty treatment with its accompanying daily routine and suffering, eventually became an entrenched custom affecting Chinese social and sexual life. Generations of Chinese men developed a passionate fetish for small feet; they went into ecstasy merely upon touching a woman's foot. A woman's bound foot might be an even more potent aphrodisiacal symbol to men than the vulva. When a woman had had her feet touched and fondled by a man, she would be completely powerless to resist his seduction.

A Ming dynasty politician once proposed, with perfect seriousness, to stop the incursions on China's northern borders by introducing foot-binding to the northern barbarians. He reasoned that the invaders, seduced and enchanted by the golden lotuses of their own women, would lose interest in China. The government never adopted this proposed strategy, and the northern barbarians—the Manchus—ended up conquering China. During the three centuries of their rule, they forbade their own women to follow the practice of foot-binding.

Although foot-binding forced a woman to walk with a wobble, it was believed to strengthen the muscles of her buttocks and

vagina. Combined with certain forms of exercise and deep breathing, foot-binding was said to have prodigious effects on women's copulative prowess. At one time the women of Tatung in northwest China were regarded highly by Chinese bedroom sportsmen. Women from this city were not known for their beauty, but they were celebrated for three superlatives: they had the tiniest feet, their vaginas had the tightest "double doors," and they were most generous with "bed calls" during lovemaking.

Connoisseurs of eroticism during the Ming dynasty perfected a set of forty-eight techniques of sexual dalliance, all involving those dainty golden lotuses. They ranged from a man's using his tongue to pick out seeds and raisins placed in the hollow of a woman's foot, to his tying her feet high from the latticework of the traditional curtained bedstead with her foot-binding ribbons. The techniques included also various ways of holding, massaging, and moving a woman's feet during foreplay and coitus.

Small feminine feet, then, became an aesthetic and erotic symbol. And so did the shoes that went on them. It was a daring accomplishment for a man to drink wine from a woman's tiny silk shoe. The scholar Yang Tieh-yai loved partying, which in his time involved entertainment by professional female singers and dancers. Whenever he saw one with especially tiny feet, he would remove one of her soft silk shoes and drink wine from it. His friend Ni Yin-lin, a renowned landscape and erotic painter, and a compulsively neat individual, was repulsed by Yang's habit. Every time Yang toasted with a woman's shoe, Ni would angrily stalk out of the party, amid roars of laughter from the other celebrants. A Ming scholar who obtained the shoe of a famous courtesan, used it as a wine cup to treat his friends, who invariably got drunk. The shoe became a coveted conversation piece.

THE SEX LIFE OF MEN AND WOMEN OF CULTURE

Literary and artistic figures in ancient China were no prudes in their private lives. The Ming scholar Tang Po-hu, famous as a writer, poet, calligrapher, and painter, was known also for his womanizing. Chu Cho-to, a seventeenth-century poet, is remembered for his two hundred love poems describing in detail his stolen moments with his sister-in-law, with whom he had a torrid affair. The famous Tang Taoist priestess Yu Hsien-chi was celebrated for the impromptu poems she composed while carousing with male literati. The Tang poet Tu Mu had affairs with countless women. Another Tang poet, Sung Chih-weng, tried to ingratiate himself to the lascivious empress Wu Tse-tien by humbling himself and holding the urinal for the empress's male concubine while the latter performed his toilet. But when Sung finally met the empress, she rejected him because of his halitosis. The brokenhearted Sung was left to write many poems about his "love lost." This was poetic license gone berserk.

The renowned Sung dynasty poet Soo Tung-po, a mandarin and magistrate, once sat in judgment over a Buddhist monk who had been accused of killing a courtesan during a jealous dispute. Soo sentenced the monk to death, delivering his verdict in verse. His official duties did not reflect his own personal life. He would often call on a friend, Ta Tung, a pious Buddhist abbot, to sip wine and converse in impromptu verse. Sometimes Soo would bring along a courtesan, thus embarrassing the abbot; but Soo himself thought nothing of it. He once tried, as a lark, to have the courtesan seduce the great monk. Ta Tung, however, resisted the temptation and sent Soo a poem that reiterated his own moral philosophy; he thereby gained Soo's great respect.

Another of Soo's friends, the abbot Fu Yin, once teasingly asked Soo's younger sister, who had just become a bride, to describe her wedding night. She replied bashfully that it would be difficult for her to do so outright; she would put it into a poem. The next day she told the abbot to look for her poem inside the huge temple bell of his monastery. When Fu Yin poked his shaven head into the bell, he saw a note saying simply: "It was exactly like this!" The visual joke sent the normally sedate abbot into hysterical laughter.

CULTURED COURTESANS

The fact that the great poet Soo brought along a courtesan when he called on his abbot friend may have embarrassed the devout Buddhist monk, but it is not shocking when viewed against the contemporary mores. Ancient China, after all, was familiar with the world's oldest profession. During the Tang dynasty, courtesans were visited by upper-class men only, among them scholars, poets, painters, and high mandarins. (Merchants, no matter how wealthy, were never considered upper-class.) Though technically prostitutes, these courtesans were professional hostesses trained in performing music and singing, dancing, painting, composing poetry, and discussing literature with their clients. They granted sexual favors only when the clients wooed them for a certain period and only if the wooing was accepted. With their own code of ethics and professional pride, these courtesans would spurn any vulgar man, no matter how rich. Some were even celebrated for their "chastity." (Incidentally, the geishas of Japan are a relic of this Chinese system.)

Probably because of increasingly strict moral standards advocated by neo-Confucianists, and the related curtailment of women's freedom, prostitution in China grew rapidly from the tenth century on, and its standards steadily deteriorated. It flourished in the fourteenth century, during the Ming dynasty. Courtesans regularly entered the imperial palaces in Nanking to entertain at banquets; later, however, they were banned by one of the emperors. The capital had no fewer than sixteen officially registered "houses of joy." The government levied a "rouge-and-powder tax" on a vast army of courtesans, "singsong girls," and proliferating common prostitutes.

The Sung emperor Hui Tsung (ruled 1101–1126) carried on a five-year affair with the courtesan Li Sze-sze, the only one mentioned in the official history of the Sung dynasty. One day he visited her incognito, accompanied by his trusted eunuchs. Like all her clients, the emperor had to take a bath, as insisted by Li's madam, who did not know his true identity. While Li was playing music for him, the impatient emperor tried to get to the basics. She brushed him off so angrily that he fell on the floor, then left in a huff. Soon rumors circulated about the emperor's visit. The madam almost died of fright; but as Li had predicted, within a month the emperor returned, having sent her a gift of a treasured musical instrument and a quantity of silver.

Because of her fame, Li Sze-sze invited the poet Chou Pang-ni to write lyrics for her songs. One day when Chou was at Li's, comfortably settled in her boudoir, the emperor arrived unannounced. Chou had to hide under Li's bed while the emperor shared it with her. Then and there Chou was inspired to write some lyrics, which he later gave to Li. On the emperor's next visit when he heard Li singing this new song, he realized that it contained intimate details that should be known only to himself and her. He asked who had written it, and, enraged, ordered Chou into exile.

On his next visit to her house, the emperor found that Li was out. She was saying farewell to Chou. Upon her tearful return she brought back Chou's latest poem, describing the sweet sorrows of parting. The emperor was so moved by its beauty that he decreed Chou be brought back to the capital and given a high position in government.

The emperor Hui Tsung could have moved the courtesan Li Sze-sze into his palace and made her an imperial consort, but for some reason he never did. Perhaps the neo-Confucianists objected, or perhaps it was more stimulating for him to go to a courtesan's house, but the emperor continued to visit her as a client. So he would not have to travel in disguise, he ordered the construction of a tunnel more than a mile long between his suburban palace and Li's house; it took two and a half years to build. During their relationship he gave Li gifts galore, including generous amounts of gold and silver, a collection of jeweled lamps, and a master painting that today is in the British Museum.

Demon Lovers and Real Animals

One fascinating theme in ancient Chinese folklore and literature was sexual union between human beings and supposed demon lovers. Tales of such liaisons usually involve lonely young male scholars who are seduced by exquisitely beautiful women, who, it turns out, are fox spirits. A ghostly temptress would visit a solitary young man night after night and have intercourse with him, and he would be powerless to resist. Some demon lovers would drain their victims to death sexually, while others would fall genuinely in love and eventually depart in a sentimental farewell. Whether they represent purely literary fantasy or sexual delusion in lonely young men, tales of fox spirits copulating with men were believed widely.

Sexual beliefs concerned not only demons but also animals. In southeast China, male mountain beavers were said to be so lewd that exhausted female beavers had to evacuate an area soon after the mating season began. A mateless male beaver, denied of his natural outlet, would embed its penis in a tree. If hunters came upon such a mating scene, they would kill the beaver and cut off the penis, which would then be dried in the sun and sold at a high price as an aphrodisiac. In spring, when women went to collect herbs in the mountains, male beavers would go after them in droves. The women would kill these lustful animals, cut off their penises, and sell them to herbalists. Fraud was common for such an expensive item, and to test one a woman would rub together her palms until they were warm, then place the dehydrated penis in her palm. If it stood erect, it was genuine beaver; if it remained lifeless, it was a fake.

The southern Chinese treasured snake bile as a medicinal tonic for sexual potency. On the island of Hainan, one variety of python was said to be irresistibly attracted to the sexual odor of women. A hunter who came upon a python would cover the snake's head with a woman's underpants. It would then become so intoxicated that the hunter could bind it with rattan, slice it with a sharp knife, and take out its bile. The python then would be released and would live on.

Turtles too figured among the Chinese sex menagerie. The turtle was a symbol of venerable longevity, especially during the Tang dynasty, when the image of the animal, or even the written character for the word, appeared as a common good-luck charm on gifts, paintings, scrolls, and other festive items. Folklore told of female turtles' mating with male snakes, and eventually the turtle became a symbol of cuckoldry. Today, as in past centuries, calling a man in China a turtle is a vile insult. Because some turtles have green moss on their shells, even the term "green hat" is offensive; no Chinese male would ever put a green hat on his head. (In Japan, which derived much of its culture from China during the Tang dynasty, the turtle is still a symbol of long life; the world for "turtle" occurs in many Japanese names.)

SPICING UP SEXUAL UNION

With their spices and seasonings, the Chinese can turn the most mundane ingredients into gourmet dishes. They have tried the same with conjugal unions, which otherwise might turn stale.

34

After all, in the words of Confucius, "Food and sex are human instincts." He was discerning enough to admit: "I have never seen people love morals more than they love sex."

The great sage Confucius, for twenty-five centuries the ultimate arbiter of Chinese morals, was not the fanatical ascetic some might think. After being criticized for calling on Nan-tzu, the notoriously lascivious wife of the Prince of Wei, Confucius defended himself by claiming that during their meeting Nan-tzu spoke to him from behind a screen, as was the custom. But he never told his disciples the details of that rather lengthy interview. Confucius reportedly divorced his wife because she was a poor cook. Sex was not unimportant to him, and indeed, it was considered necessary by all schools of Confucians. In the puritanical centuries of Chinese history, Confucius's image was transformed so that he became the stern overseer of Chinese morals. But despite this looming presence, the Chinese have enjoyed food and sex in their own natural ways, especially when they thought Confucius wasn't looking.

4

In the Forbidden Palace

Amorous Emperors and
Lascivious Ladies

IT IS EARLY in the seventh century, at the Grand Canal of China. Thousands of cavalrymen ride on horseback along the banks. A flotilla of a thousand boats, extending for seventy miles, sails slowly southward in the canal. Near the middle of the flotilla glides a giant barge with a hundred halls and cabins on its four decks. On this breezeless summer day, the boat's colorful sails are folded at the base of its bright red masts. On the towpaths, five hundred chanting, giggling young palace maids in pastel silk dresses are pulling the barge with multihued silk ropes. On a spacious stage at the stern of the boat, twenty lithe female dancers move sinuously with their gossamer silk scarves to music played by an all-female string and wind orchestra. Noblewomen, high imperial officials, and a sprinkling of Buddhist monks and Taoist priests stroll on the open decks, sip wine, and sniff the exotic flowers set in wooden planters. In the throne room on the top deck sits the emperor, surrounded by his royal consorts and gazing imperiously at his subjects kowtowing on the banks.

Such was the royal voyage of the Sui dynasty emperor Yang (ruled 605–617), builder of the Grand Canal, royal highways, and grandiose palaces, renovator of the Great Wall, epicurean, tyrant—and lecher. Once on the throne, he forcibly moved thousands of affluent merchants and their familes from other cities to the capital of Loyang. As part of his giant construction project in the western suburb of the capital, lakes were dug, all linked by canals. The soil that was dug up was used to make a number of hills, each a few hundred feet high. A master architect built sixteen luxurious palaces on the hills and by the lakes. Rare plants and animals and odd-shaped boulders from all over China dotted the artificial landscape.

For the construction of the Grand Canal, Yang conscripted more than 3 million men as forced laborers, and assigned 50,000 soldiers as task masters. Hundreds of thousands died in the building of the canal. The emperor conscripted more than a million slave laborers to repair the Great Wall, which was started by another tyrant nine centuries earlier to keep the northern barbarians out. In addition, the restless Yang had palaces built in far-flung provinces, for his many travels.

On this voyage the emperor was sailing to Yangchow, a great city of pleasure he had visited before. When his barge ran aground at a shallow spot, he ordered a complete survey of the canal. The canal bottom was found shallower than the specified depth in 129 spots, and Yang promptly commanded that the engineers and laborers responsible, some 50,000 men in all, be executed.

Even though he was surrounded by thousands of beautiful women on his palatial playgrounds, Emperor Yang was constantly looking for new thrills, and he cultivated a number of hobbies accordingly. His Maze Palace was decorated with erotic murals. The walls of his bedchamber had nine large bronze mirrors so he could watch himself indulge with his women. A talented imperial aide invented two of his most treasured toys. One was a couch with straps and cuffs, designed especially to restrain unwilling virgins so he could deflower them more easily. The other, known as the "carriage of the heart's desire," featured a bed that would rock and vibrate when the vehicle moved. If the passengers became too passionately noisy, the carriage's many tinkling jade bells would drown out the noise. The emperor brought these and other devices along when he traveled.

Emperor Yang's lavish spending, and his tyranny and debauchery, soon caught up with him. As his flotilla reached Yangchow, he received reports of unrest and rebellion from all over China. He made his way back to the capital, but insurgents eventually killed him. A rebel general succeeded in ending the brief glory of the Sui dynasty and founded the great dynasty, the Tang, that brought three centuries of peace, prosperity, and cultural refinement to China.

Emperor Yang's outrageous conduct made him one of the more notorious examples of disastrous tyranny in Chinese history. His splendid lifestyle and love of erotic pleasure were, however, the norm rather than the exception in the long line of emperors of China.

According to a solidly entrenched Confucian dictum, the emperor had a mandate from heaven to rule his people like an authoritative but benevolent father. The people had to obey and be loyal under this paternalism. If the emperor misruled, the mandate would be withdrawn. In reality, of course, he might be benevolent or tyrannical, able or incompetent, virtuous or licentious. His mandate from heaven could be withdrawn only by a palace coup or a popular revolution. Whatever the case, the emperor had the prerogative of life and death over his subjects, and the privilege of choosing whom he went to bed with. Even virtuous emperors exercised this privilege.

THE POWER OF EUNUCHS

Libidinous emperors were able to keep thousands of women in their courts safe from amorous complication through an ingenious and diabolical system. Since the first or second century B.C., besides the emperor, the only males allowed in the royal sanctum were eunuchs. The emperor's women were tucked away safely, protected outside by imperial guards and inside by sexually neutral eunuchs. The system of forbidden palaces went on for two thousand years.

Where were recruits for this special corps found? Initially they came from punished families: as everything else in China, the penal system was family-oriented, and when a high imperial official was executed by the emperor, his daughters were put in the palace as maids and his sons were castrated and became court eunuchs. Eventually, being a eunuch ceased to be a punishment. Sons of poor families or young men who wanted to work as eunuchs had themselves castrated.

In many cases, especially in earlier centuries, castration involved the removal of only the testicles. The penis was left intact but rendered sexually useless. During the later dynasties, surgeons sometimes removed the entire genitalia. If a boy was castrated before puberty, he grew up with a squeaky voice, enlarged hips, and hair on his scalp but little elsewhere. If an adult were castrated, he retained his male voice and body hair. Even though a eunuch's sexual capability had been taken away, his sexual desire might remain, especially if he was castrated after puberty or in his adult years. During the last two dynasties, some high eunuchs were known to frequent brothels. One Ming dynasty eunuch even had a wife and several concubines—although this probably was more for show than for substance. During some dynasties, eunuchs were allowed to sleep with palace ladies to give them "a touch of Yang essence." They would engage in various forms of sex play but no actual intercourse.

If the operation was not done properly, the supposedly castrated man still could have erections. Such was suspected in the case of An Teh-hai, chief eunuch under Tzu Hsi, the celebrated Empress Dowager who virtually ruled—or misruled—China from 1862 to 1908. Informally called the Western Empress because her quarters were in the western part of the palace, the Empress Dowager and the Eastern Empress were co-regents for Tzu Hsi's son, the boy emperor Tung Chih (ruled 1862–1875). Young, handsome, and smart, An was not only Tzu Hsi's majordomo and factotum but also her unofficial political advisor. An controlled the access of all imperial officials to the empress, notwithstanding dynastic laws that forbade political roles for eunuchs. As her ultimate confidant, he spent an inordinate amount of time with her in private; rumors, naturally, soon were being whispered in the palace. Once the young emperor saw An leaving his mother's chamber after a lengthy visit. He ordered his retainers to seize and strip the chief eunuch on the spot, and a young eunuch to masturbate him. Either An's castration was complete or he was too frightened; his penis remained limp, and the emperor had to let him go.

An became increasingly arrogant. Even though by law eunuchs were not allowed to leave the capital, he went on an imperial mission to another city to order ceremonial robes for the Empress Dowager, who gave him permission. Her palace enemies persuaded her co-regent to apprehend An and have him executed in public for violating the imperial law. The Empress Dowager was devastated but could do nothing.

Empress Tzu Hsi then cultivated another favorite eunuch, Li Lien-ying, who became even more powerful than An, although he managed to be more discreet. As regent for her five-year-old nephew, the emperor Kuang Hsu (ruled 1875–1908), the Empress Dowager had free rein, with Li as her confidant. Li was later instrumental in the imprisonment of the young emperor, who advocated reform and modernization of the country. China, by then rapidly deteriorating, was on the verge of being dismembered by greedy European powers, and the erratic policy of the Empress Dowager and her favorite eunuchs propelled the empire down a disastrous path of disintegration.

Because of their proximity to the seat of power, the men who had been mutilated deliberately to safeguard the sexual sovereignty of polygamous monarchs ended up not only engaging in palace intrigues but also meddling in state politics. Eunuchs and the system supporting them were an indirect cause of the decline and fall of four of China's greatest dynasties, the Han, Tang, Ming, and Ching.

THE FORBIDDEN PARADISE

If the forbidden palaces of ancient China gave these half-men unsuspected opportunities for self-aggrandizement, they were a paradise for the emperors with their absolute sexual prerogative. The number of women in the palace varied according to the reigning monarch's treasury and libido. There were usually between 3,000 and 8,000 women at court; among them, a smaller number constituted the emperor's consorts and potential consorts, while the majority held various roles, from high-ranking officials to scullery maids.

The method of recruiting palace women differed from dynasty to dynasty. A victorious war usually brought in a rich feminine booty. Some tyrannical emperors would send out search parties to conscript young and attractive girls, often setting off nationwide panic. Weddings were hastily arranged, and attractive girls disguised themselves with rags and dirt to dodge the royal draft.

In later dynasties the recruitment of women was more civilized. During the Ming dynasty, palace ladies, the empress included, were chosen from the people, somewhat as in a beauty contest. Emissaries combed the empire for candidates, and the best were selected as potential consorts of the emperor. Especially educated and talented women were appointed high palace officials, while the rest served as palace maids. Women who were eliminated from the running received gold, jewelry, brocade, and imperial certificates. These young women were eagerly sought after by eligible bachelors of the upper class.

Whatever the emperor's sexual fancy, he traditionally accepted a spousal hierarchy. Huang Ti, the legendary Yellow Emperor (ruled c. 2697 B.C.) had four consorts who gave him twenty-five sons. This is the earliest known instance of Chinese royal polygamy. During the Hsia dynasty (2205–1766 B.C.) each monarch had twelve consorts. The quota was increased to thirty-nine in the next dynasty. During the Chou dynasty (1122–255 B.C.), rulers by tradition each had 121 spouses, ranked in five grades. In later dynasties, the system of ranking became less rigid.

The method of selecting the empress and other high-ranking consorts varied greatly. Some were picked from the inner palaces; others, as in the Han dynasty, were chosen from prominent families. One Han emperor drew lots for his empress, from among four finalists. Ming crown princes usually chose three finalists, then let their mothers pick the lucky one from the trio. One fourth-century emperor is known to have made a humble, homely weaving girl his empress, upon the advice of a physiognomist. Physiognomists, who could supposedly tell a person's temperament, character, health outlook, sexual proclivities, and fortune in life from facial and other bodily features, were as respected in ancient China as many psychoanalysts are in modern America.

Becoming empress or consort meant great honor and fortune, but it did not necessarily lead to a happy ending. During certain dynasties, when an empress or imperial consort gave birth to a son who could someday become the crown prince, by law she had to die. The mother of a crown prince might meddle in palace and state politics, so for the alleged sake of the nation she had to die. The infant then was reared by a wet nurse. Consequently, a crown prince often grew up emotionally attached to his wet nurse. When

he inherited the throne, he might make her a high-ranking aristocrat. During later centuries, even the husband of a wet nurse might receive an aristocratic title.

A Bedmate for the Night

While choosing the emperor's consorts was more or less dictated by custom and tradition, choosing his bedmate for the night was another matter. In antiquity, royal astrologers usually planned the king's copulatory schedule, and a female official of the royal chamber handled the arrangements. The sovereigns of the Chou dynasty, each with his 121 spouses, followed a preordained schedule each lunar month: From day 1 through day 9, the king slept each night with nine of the eighty-one lowest-ranking concubines. From day 10 through day 12, he slept each night with nine of his twenty-seven honorable dames. On day 13 he spent a single night with his nine royal consorts, and the next night was given to his three royal concubines. Day 15, the time of the full moon, was devoted to the queen. During the second half of the month, the monarch's sexual obligations were reversed, and he worked his way down from the queen to the lowest rank.

The Art of the Bedchamber thus was already in its embryonic stage some three thousand years ago. A schedule like that of the Chou dynasty was based on the theory that if the king absorbed sufficient Yin essence from his various partners, when it came time for a close encounter with the queen, his Yang essence would peak, and give him the best chance to sire a healthy, bright son and heir.

This rigid schedule was discarded in the Han dynasty. Emperors began to choose their bedmates with capriciousness and diabolical ingenuity. One emperor would roam his palace grounds daily, in a cart pulled by three or four goats. When the goats stopped, the nearest woman would be his sexual partner for the night. To push their luck a bit, palace ladies would put bamboo leaves and salt outside their quarters, knowing how eagerly the goats ate them. The Han emperor Cheng, who had a fetish for the color black, used that very fixation to choose his bedmates. His night palace had black walls, black drapery, and black furniture, and all his women wore black dresses and black veils. At night he often extinguished all the candles, which were black too, and groped around in the dark. Whoever he caught would be his bedmate—in pitch-darkness.

The Tang emperor Hsuan Tsung would make his selection by giving each of his three thousand consorts a flower for her hair, then releasing a giant butterfly. His bedmate for the night would be the consort on whose hair the butterfly landed. Another Tang emperor, Ching Tsung, would shoot sachets of musk or other perfumed powder at his women with a bow. Whoever got hit, and covered with the scented powder, was his lady for the night. Even more elaborate and poetic was the technique of the Ming emperor Cheng Tsung, who at dusk in springtime would sail on the palace lake with a group of women. He would release hundreds of fireflies, and the women on whose hair the fireflies settled became finalists. The woman who attracted the most fireflies was queen for the night. Many women smeared crushed rose petals in their hair to lure the fireflies. Another of Cheng Tsung's methods was literally poetic: He would inscribe the first two lines of several well-known four-line Tang poems on a tree leaf, and his ladies would write on their own leaves the last two lines. The leaves then were set adrift in a palace canal. When one of the emperor's leaves drifted alongside one of the ladies', the leaves were fished out and read. If the lines were from the same poem, the woman who had inscribed the lines was the emperor's for the night.

During the Ching dynasty (1644–1911), emperors' methods for choosing a nocturnal companion were less whimsical, though often equally bizarre. This dynasty was founded by a northern tribe, the Manchus, who in conquering China adopted so much of its native culture that they were eventually assimilated. Fearing assassination by their Chinese subjects, Manchu emperors took strict security measures. On the morning that he chose a woman as bedmate, the monarch had her name displayed prominently on a special green plaque in the palace. She would spend the day preparing herself by washing and burning incense, and in the evening a eunuch would come to check her identity. She was stripped completely and searched closely, wrapped in a big silk bag, and then carried on the eunuch's back to the emperor's bedchamber. After the union she was repackaged and carried back to her quarters.

MONITORING IMPERIAL SEX

One of the most fascinating aspects of an emperor's sex life was the official monitoring of his intercourse. In order to verify the time and circumstances of conception and authenticate the emperor's paternity when a consort gave birth to a son, complete records were kept of the emperor's sexual activities: date, hour, name of consort, duration of intercourse, even the number of imperial thrusts. These records were classified as top secret, but they became known when dynasties fell. As early as the twelfth century B.C., a female official in the royal palace had as her sole duty the programming and monitoring of the king's sexual unions. She arranged particular bedmates for him, and when the hour approached, she put a silver ring on the chosen consort's right hand and escorted her to the emperor's bedchamber. She observed the encounter and recorded the details with a vermilion brush-pen. After the union she shifted the ring to the woman's left hand and escorted her away. If the woman became pregnant later, she would be given a gold ring to wear. (This rite, by the way is believed to be the origin of the modern custom of wedding rings.)

In later centuries, during the Ching dynasty for instance, a eunuch did the monitoring, and the ritual became more elaborate. Right after the emperor's ejaculation, the eunuch would crawl on all fours by his bed, kowtow, and ask: "Your Majesty, retain or not?" If the emperor said no, another eunuch, a grand master of acupressure massage, would immediately take the woman to an adjoining chamber and work vigorously on her pubic region to expel the royal sperm. Records do not indicate conclusively whether this method of birth control was effective.

The typical Manchu emperor led a very frustrating sex life. Not only was he monitored, but he could be stopped in the middle of intercourse by a eunuch, should the latter deem that the intercourse had been too lengthy for the emperor's health. If an emperor in the throes of passion ignored such a request, the eunuch had a foolproof way of cutting short the imperial motions: he would kneel down and start reading a hortatory memorandum from the emperor's father or grandfather, or another ancestor. It was a strict tradition among many Chinese to hold sacred such family memorandums urging the descendants to morality, diligence, and other virtues; indeed, these documents were read reverently from time to time, like the Bible. If a eunuch started reading one of these family admonitions, the emperor would feel obliged to suspend his activity and kneel down at once. The occasion was something like hearing a national anthem.

Understandably, monitoring and related killjoy rituals shattered the romantic prospects and the pleasure element in an emperor's sex life. Some monarchs managed to abolish the monitoring during their reigns, while others circumvented the practice—sowing their wild oats or even visiting prostitutes, away from the imperial voyeurs.

DEVOTION AND DECADENCE

In spite of their absolute sexual privileges, many monarchs led reasonable conjugal lives. Some were known for their loyalty to a single mate. One Ming emperor was so enamored of his mother's chambermaid, who was seventeen years his senior, that he made her his imperial concubine as soon as he got on the throne. His devotion to her lasted twenty-three years, until she died; he was unshakably despondent after her death, and died a year later.

Such examples of marital constancy, however, were not as well-known as those of licentious lavishness. In the eighteenth century B.C., the last monarch of the Hsia dynasty had an artificial lake filled with wine, and trees in a forest hung with barbecued meat. He set loose three thousand naked noblemen and noblewomen to engage in drunken orgies and posted lifeguards to fish out drunks who fell into the wine lake. The tenth-century ruler Wei Chung frolicked with palace ladies on an enormous bed behind crystal folding screens. Other monarchs would have naked women row on palace lakes in summer and play in hot tubs in winter.

These practices often turned utterly decadent. A Ming nobleman used the mouths of maidservants as spittoons. In his mansion were numerous female statues, dressed in finery and decorated with powder and rouge. These figures, which either kneeled or lay on their back, with their open mouths, were used as urinals by his male guests.

One of the lewdest monarchs was the Yuan emperor Shun (ruled 1333–1368), who twice a year collected virgins from all over

China for his pleasure, and who is said to have raped at least forty noblewomen. He installed two charlatan lamas as palace priests to coach him in sexual techniques. One of them was awarded the majestic title of "Grand Master of the Great Yuan Empire." Under Shun's reign civil strife and rebellion spread through that great empire, and eventually Shun was pursued by rebel troops. To slow down the pursuing army, he left clusters of beautiful palace women here and there along his escape route as bait. The strategy worked, and he managed to flee to his ancestral home in Mongolia. With his flight ended eighty-eight years of Mongolian rule of China.

The rebel leader who then seized the throne was a Buddhist monk. He founded the illustrious Ming dynasty, under which Chinese culture enjoyed a great renaissance, with the arts—and the cult of elegant living—reaching their zenith. This dynasty had its own lecherous black sheep, Emperor Wu Tsung (ruled 1506–1522). He was notorious for dropping in on his wealthier subjects and sampling not only the delicacies on their table but also their wives and daughters. If he liked what he tasted, he would carry it—or her—off to his palace. His subjects so dreaded his visits that at word of his coming, streets emptied and most houses were locked. Wealthy families even built secret rooms and cellars for their women to hide in when the emperor was on the prowl.

A number of monarchs are known for their romantic eroticism. The Tang emperor Mu Tsung (ruled 821–825) wrote love poems on silk blouses, which his consorts then donned when they were summoned to his chambers. He would read the poems aloud while copulating. Meng Chang of the Later Shu dynasty (925–960), tall and handsome, was an eminent poet. One day, while walking in the street incognito, he saw an attractive woman beating up several men who had been making passes at her on the street. He became enamored of the woman and took her to his palace. Not only was she a martial arts expert, a poet, and a musician, but she was also good in bed. She was so good in fact that he bestowed on her the poetic title of "Madame Flower Pistil." In Chinese literature, "flower pistil," like "flower heart," refers to the innermost part of the vagina, the cervix.

Li Yu (ruled 962–978) was a romantic, and tragic, monarch of the Southern Tang kingdom. He was an excellent painter, poet, calligrapher, chess player, and zither player. His queen was talented in music and poetry, and a composer of songs. The two spent most of their time writing poems and playing music. Their cultural pursuits, unfortunately, were no match for a hungry neighboring power, and Li Yu died a captive in prison.

Perhaps the most renowned amorous monarch of China was the Tang emperor Hsuan Tsung (ruled 713–756), whose poignant life is immortalized in Chinese poetry and drama. He had 40,000 palace women, the highest number on record, of whom 3,000 were his consorts, served and guarded by 3,000 eunuchs in his three palaces in the capital of Changan (now Xian). Hsuan Tsung was the emperor who chose his bedmates with butterflies—until he fell in love with a nun, who had been his late father's consort. He made her Imperial Concubine Yang and canceled his daily morning audience so he could spend time with her.

Hsuan Tsung's devotion was more one-sided than he realized, however. He had a trusted aide named An Loh-shan, a Tartar, from the north. Bright and wily, An was fat but an agile dancer. With the emperor's consent, Yang playfully called An her godson. An paid more than normal respect to his "godmother," and showed her more than normal affection.

Yang had exquisite porcelain skin and was on the plump side, as was the fashion for women of the Tang era. She enjoyed bathing in the famous hot springs of the emperor's Hua Ching palace near Changan. Whenever she was intoxicated, she loved to expose her breasts, described by the emperor as "newly skinned foxnuts" and by her loving godson as "congealed yogurt." The godson was once so hungry for this yogurt that he left fingernail marks on her breasts. To cover up the telltale sign, Yang devised a bosom covering of red silk, and the fashion immediately caught on among palace ladies.

Yang's status in the bedchamber brought instant aristocracy and wealth to her three sisters and a foster brother. They vied with each other and with the emperor's brothers in their sumptuous, erotic lifestyles.

In part because of this concentration on eroticism, Emperor Hsuan Tsung neglected his governmental duties. Eventually An Loh-shan started a revolt, and the emperor fled the capital with Yang's family. At one point the emperor's restive troops refused to go farther unless he executed her and all her family members. The grief-stricken monarch was forced to give the order. After his beloved consort was strangled with a silk scarf, Hsuan Tsung continued his flight. At the site where the famous beauty had died, a poor old crone displayed a stocking she claimed was Yang's. She charged a fee for a sniff and made a fortune.

Seven years later, the emperor—by then retired—returned from his exile to Changan; he was heartbroken as he walked by his old palace, now overgrown with weeds, murmuring Yang's name. This story inspired the great Tang poet Po Chu-i to write one of the most touching narrative poems of classical Chinese literature, *The Song of Long Sorrows.*

LASCIVIOUS LADIES

The behavior of some monarchs in treating women like property or toys, while characteristic of many ancient cultures, might seem even more pronounced in ancient China, because of its socially entrenched customs regarding women. But whenever the tables were turned, women acted exactly like men. Once in control, they too played the game of power intrigues. Given the opportunity, women could lead lascivious lives and treat men like sexual toys.

An early example is the mother of the First Emperor of Chin, in the third century B.C. She had a lover who, sexually exhausted by her, tried to detach himself from her. He found a replacement candidate, an unusually well-endowed man named Lao Ai, and chose a method of introduction at once subtle and blatant. At his suggestion, Lao marched at a carnival with a wagon wheel on his erect penis, spinning it while parading. Naturally this feat became the talk of the capital, and Lao soon was summoned into the bedchamber of the emperor's mother.

Sometimes, male partners were supplied to women by their sons, as in the case of King Yueh Ling in the sixth century. One day the monarch asked his mother why she looked unhappy. She replied that while he was enjoying life, she wondered if he ever thought of her. The king got the hint and gave his mother a present of forty male concubines.

San Yin, sister of Emperor Fei of the Sung dynasty (of the House of Liu), complained to her brother that while he kept several thousand women in the palace, she had only one mate. Her loving brother assigned thirty male consorts for her pleasure.

The two sisters who became the favorites of the Han emperor Cheng (ruled 32–36 B.C.) were known for their dancing talents, body fragrance, and erotic skill. The older sister, Chao Fei-yi, pretended to be a virgin in front of the emperor. For three nights, her histrionics of shame and pain kept the emperor from consummating their union. She later confided to a close friend that knowing the Art of the Bedchamber had enabled her to fake virginity. She became empress, but had sexual liaisons with so many palace men (the eunuch system had not yet been introduced) that the emperor shifted his affections to her sister Heh-teh, a co-consort. Heh-teh was a tease who, unlike her blatantly sexual older sister, titillated the emperor with her feminine wiles. One day she accidentally killed him with an overdose of aphrodisiac.

Hsia Chi, a noblewoman in the Kingdom of Chen at the time of Confucius, was renowned for her erotic lifestyle. Kings and noblemen vied for her sexual favor, even showing her underwear at court to flaunt their intimacy with her. All those who entered into serious relationships with her died prematurely—whether by murder, in duels, or as a result of illness or debility. This femme fatale—three times a queen, seven times a wife, nine times a widow—was a true connoisseur of the Art of the Bedchamber.

Among the most lascivious women in Chinese history was Empress Chia, whose husband, Emperor Wei (ruled 290–307), was not too bright. When his aides told him that there was a famine, that the people had no grain, he asked: "Why don't they eat mincemeat?" (This was fifteen centuries before Marie Antoinette's supposed "Let them eat cake.") Wanting to produce an heir and thereby consolidate her power, Empress Chia slept with numerous palace officials and servants. This jealous and vicious woman had several of the emperor's pregnant consorts and influential aides killed. Two years older than her husband, she worked hard to preserve her youth and looks. She even kept a stable of young men for weekly extractions of semen, which she drank, mixed with honey, as a health tonic.

Chia kept herself as busy sexually as many an emperor. After she asked the imperial doctor to teach her the Art of the Bedchamber, the two became lovers; their noisy sexual encounters were often heard from outside her bedchamber. She secretly sent emissaries to round up handsome young men for her sexual amusement. The young men knew only that they were taken in a

windowless carriage to a great mansion where they had sex with a highborn lady. If anyone betrayed even a suspicion of the woman's real identity, he paid with his life.

Even more lascivious, and better known, was Empress Wu Tsetien (ruled 684–705), a brilliant monarch and ruthless schemer. At fourteen, the attractive, ambitious girl was the maid of the chamber pot to the Tang emperor Tai Tsung (ruled 627–650). She was made his concubine but became a nun after his death.

When fate stepped in a few years later, Wu's ambition was realized beyond her wildest dreams. Her husband's son, the reigning emperor Kao Tsung (ruled 650–684), favored his imperial concubine Hsiao over his official spouse, Empress Wang. The unhappy empress came up with a plan to sink her rival. First she ordered Wu to grow back the hair she had had to cut off as a nun. Then one evening she gave a banquet for the emperor at her quarters, where she presented the stunning Wu, dressed seductively and now with long flowing hair. That very night the emperor was enthralled by the former nun in his bedchamber. Empress Wang was glad: she had replaced her rival with an ally. Or so she thought.

Installed as the emperor's favorite, Wu gave birth to an infant girl. She devised a diabolical plot. One day, right after the friendly empress visited Wu's quarters, Wu strangled her own baby and covered the body with a blanket. Then she invited the emperor to visit her and in his presence "discovered" that her baby had been murdered. The only person known to have come by earlier that day, Empress Wang, became the prime suspect. The angry emperor deposed her and made Wu empress. Once firmly in power, Wu ordered the murder of Wang and hundreds of nobles and palace officials whom she considered potential rivals.

In 690, at the age of sixty-seven, Wu usurped the Tang throne, proclaimed herself reigning empress, and started her own dynasty, the Chou. She ruled brilliantly for more than a decade, with the help of many capable imperial administrators, until a palace revolution ended her reign.

Empress Wu was something of a feminist in her day. She issued a decree permitting all nuns, whose ordination and retirement had been controlled by the government, to cancel their vows, leave their nunneries, and marry, if they so desired. She rejected a petition by top imperial officials to honor widows who

refused to remarry, and in fact offically persuaded widows to remarry.

Empress Wu's colorful sex life might seem to overshadow
those pioneering political achievements. Although in her late sixties when she took over the throne, she looked more like a voluptuous woman in her thirties. Understandably, Wu had numerous
lovers. One, a Buddhist monk, built a huge image of the Buddha
and a lavish temple on her palace grounds. At the same time she
was carrying on with him, she had a torrid affair with the imperial doctor, who coached her in the Art of the Bedchamber and
concocted sexual recipes for her. The doctor had the monk's temple burned to the ground.

When the empress tired of the two lovers, her secretary discreetly supplied her with new recruits. Wu's daughter Tai Ping offered her own love interest, Chang Chang-tsung, to her mother.
Wu, quite taken with him, made him her main consort.

Empress Wu was noted for her voracious sexual appetite.
When she had intercourse with her lovers, palace gossips said,
they sounded like "eight horses rolling in wet mud." To camou-
flage the embarrassing sounds, she kept a band of musicians outside her bedchamber to play while she indulged in her favorite
sport. A specific type of music, *tai ko,* is believed to have evolved
from these unique bedchamber concerts.

When the empress became old and sick, her daughter and others engineered a coup that restored the Tang dynasty, with Wu's
son, whom she earlier had deposed, as emperor. During the coup
Chang Chang-tsung was killed and his body cut up by a mob.
Wu's secretary retrieved Chang's penis and brought it to her. Wu
took one look and burst out tearfully: "This is Loh Long!" (This
was the pet name she used for Chang.) She placed the severed
organ lovingly in a jade box and ordered that it be buried with her
when she died.

Wu's sexual behavior set a pattern for many around her. Her
daughter Tai Ping married twice, then had affairs with dozens of
noblemen, palace officials, and prime ministers. Many erotic aids
were found in her palace after her death.

Upon Wu's death her secretary, Shangkuan Wan-erh, became
very influential at court. Among her numerous lovers was the
minister of the army, Tsui Shih, a former bedmate of the empress. Tsui later had an affair with Tai Ping, who jilted her own

lover, a duke. The outraged duke threatened to expose Tsui's affair with the princess to the powerful Shangkuan—unless Tsui let him spend a night with his beauteous wife. To pacify the duke and protect his own career, Tsui offered his wife to the duke, who turned out to be a tattletale: soon other noblemen were demanding that Tsui pacify them too. Tsui ended up offering not only his wife but his two stepdaughters as well.

THE POWER OF WOMEN

The course of ancient Chinese history was altered sometimes by women, but even more often because of women. Hsi Shih, an exquisite woman in the fifth century B.C., was given as tribute by the king of the conquered state of Yu to the king of the state of Wu. The latter, softened by his romantic life with the storied beauty, neglected affairs of state. Meanwhile, the monarch he bested, living a spartan life of vigilance, strengthened his own position. Eventually Wu was vanquished by Yu.

In 33 B.C., a Han emperor gave a palace beauty, Wang Chao-cheun, to a Hun chieftain. The chieftain was so happy with her that the Huns did not attack China's border for decades.

In the eighteenth century, the Ching emperor Chien Lung sent a military expedition to Sinkiang for the specific purpose of capturing a Muslim princess celebrated for the fragrance of her body. Brought back to the capital, the princess became Fragrant Imperial Concubine. Although the emperor tried everything to please her and alleviate her homesickness—even building a palace with a mosque—she remained unhappy and eventually committed suicide.

The rebel general who unseated the Sui emperor Yang, the canal builder, raised his banner of revolution because of a woman. He was having an affair with the emperor's favorite concubine when the illicit liaison became known. To save his own neck the desperate general had to stage a revolt. He was successful against the unpopular tyrant and founded the Tang dynasty. This resplendent dynasty later was weakened and brought to its end because of another woman, the imperial concubine Yang, as recounted above.

The immediate cause of the fall of the great Ming dynasty

was a beautiful woman. In the seventeenth century the Ming line was enfeebled by meddling eunuchs and plagued by revolts. A powerful rebel, Li Tzu-cheng, captured the capital of Beijing, where the last Ming emperor hanged himself. There Li captured the famous beauty Chen Yuen-yuen, the beloved concubine of the Ming general Wu San-kuei, who was guarding the Great Wall along China's northern border with Manchuria. When he learned of the capture of his woman by Li's rebels and realized that the Ming troops were powerless to oust them, Wu asked the Manchus for help. He opened the fortress gates of the Great Wall and let Manchu troops into China. Once inside, the Manchus did not wish to leave. Thus began three centuries of Manchu rule under the Ching dynasty.

This chapter may have given the impression that imperial China was ruled by monarchs who did little but seek out members of the opposite sex. Certainly, the privileges accorded an absolute monarch were a strong temptation for sexual excess. But most of the nearly thousand rulers of ancient China were not sexual activists like those described above—even when they did engage in polygamy. Some monarchs were valiant warriors and great conquerors. Others were wise rulers who made the empire prosper. Many were highly cultured and enthusiastic patrons of art and literature. Still others tried, within the framework of the monarchy, to establish contacts with their humble subjects by incognito direct inspections. Quite a few erected what may be called a drum of injustice at the palace gate. Any lowly person wronged by a high bureaucrat or nobleman could beat the sonorous drum, and his grievances would be heard by the emperor.

But those monarchs who were especially active sexually made their own type of contribution to Chinese culture. Besides adding spice to history, they were responsible for nurturing and promoting the Art of the Bedchamber.

5

Five Thousand Years of Erotica

Voluptuous Poems, Bawdy Novels, and Spicy Woodcuts

THE EROTIC LITERATURE and art of the Chinese reflect their particular style of treating sex as a natural human phenomenon, without sensationalism. One detects little if any guilt associated with sex, and finds few if any references to pathological traits or practices—child molestation, incest, rape, sadomasochism.

However difficult it may be to spell out, there is a distinction between pornography and erotica. The smut peddler, often abetted by the dialectician, claims that even what might be judged as obscene is an exercise in free speech and therefore sacrosanct. The stern moralist insists that anything depicting sex is dirty, sinful, and depraved. Both are extremists. Neither knows the difference between pornography and erotica. The public is pulled back and forth in the middle of a tug-of-war, as opinions fly from pulpit and witness stand.

This book uses the following working definitions: Pornography is that which presents sex in a crude and vulgar manner, and the sexual act as an animalistic encounter of raw sexual organs. Some pornography might seem simply coarse, and harmless to the mature mind, but it may be detrimental to adolescents, whose sexuality is still amorphous. Pornography that involves degradation, pathological perversity, and violence is destructive to immature youths and, when it has an adverse influence on the psychologically unbalanced, especially the criminally insane, disastrous to society in general. Much of pornography is actually anti-erotic in effect.

Erotica, on the other hand, depicts sex as part of life, in modes ranging from the delicately subtle to the brazenly explicit. It usually portrays the sexual act within a framework of emotions or a social milieu, and the emphasis is more on sensuality than sensations, more on sexuality than sex. It is sometimes impossible to draw a clear line between the erotic and the pornographic, as they may merge into each other.

On the basis of this rough distinction, much of the sexual literature and art of China can be categorized as erotica. This is especially true of poetry, which always has played a significant role in Chinese literary life. Partly because of the nature of the classical language, perhaps, descriptions of the most passionate love scenes are couched in cryptic, elegant imagery that subtly suggests, rather than explicitly narrates.

As has been mentioned before, the Chinese language is extremely condensed, and the context in which words are placed decides their function. Its richness of imagery enables Chinese to offer a thousand shades of emotion. When translated into English, it may appear even more florid than in the original Chinese. The purity of diction and vividness of images characterizing Chinese classical poetry were well suited to erotic suggestiveness.

EARLY EROTIC POEMS

Much of the oldest classical Chinese poetry is found in *The Book of Odes* (*Shih Ching*), a collection of 305 poems, ceremonial chants, religious hymns, and folk songs dating from the twelfth to the sixth centuries B.C. When neo-Confucian puritanism ruled supreme, scholars arbitrarily interpreted the odes to be about propriety, morals, and chastity. Modern Chinese scholars, however, rebelled against this literary dogmatism and read many of the odes as love songs. Such a reading is understandable: they may be laden with arcane symbolism, but these songs explicitly concern love and sexual seduction.

The oldest and best-known sexual ode tells of a young hunter encountering a maiden in the woods and seducing her:

In the wilderness lies a dead roebuck;
It is wrapped with white ramie.
In the woods walks a desirous maiden;
She is lured by a lucky young man.

The fallen dwarf oaks in the woods,
The dead roebuck in the wilderness
Are wrapped and bound with white ramie.
The maiden is like fine jade.

"Oh, be slow! Oh, be gentle!
Pull not at my loincloth!
Make not the sleeping dogs bark!"

Although quite a few odes in this classic depict sex between lovers—sometimes between strangers, as in this poem—they are too esoteric to qualify as genuine erotic literature.

Since antiquity, the Yin-Yang cosmology of the Chinese has brought them to interpret natural phenomena in terms of sex, and sexual phenomena in terms of nature. Among the most frequently used literary allusions, as we have seen, are clouds, which symbolize female sexual secretions, and rain, symbolizing male semen. These allusions were set forth in the poetic essay "Kao-tang Fu," attributed to Sung Yu, a well-known poet of the third century B.C. Highly esteemed, for its literary value as well as its lyrical portrayal of feminine charms and amorous dalliance, the essay is an early example of erotic literature. Its preface tells of a feudal king who dreams that he meets a beautiful woman; she identifies herself as the goddess from the Sorcerer's Mountain and offers to "share pillow and mat" with him. They make love, and the goddess teaches him much about the art of love. When they part she says: "I am the morning clouds at dawn, and the pouring rain at dusk." Ever since, "clouds and rain" (*yun-yu*) has been an elegant and picturesque literary term for sexual intercourse.

Traditional classical poetry reached its zenith during the Tang dynasty, when sex was footloose and sexology classics flourished. Paradoxically, most of the renowned Tang poems were about nature, bureaucratic corruption, or the ravages of war. Chinese poetry, which had been written in rigid four- and five-character lines, extended to seven-character lines during the Tang dynasty. Later it evolved into a new form, *tzu*. In this form, the number of characters in each line differs in a variety of patterns. All Chinese characters are monosyllabic, so *tzu* meant a change from the old metronomic meter to a syncopation of musical phrases. The new poetic form ushered in other changes: vivid classical word imagery was combined with zippy vernacular expression. Chinese poetry thus was liberated, and moved from the exclusive preserve of esoteric scholars to the popular playground of the literati.

VOLUPTUOUS POETRY

The liberated poetry was better equipped to portray the luxuriant nature of sexual love. There was a virtual explosion of "voluptuous poetry" (*yen-shih*), which thrived from the tenth century on. Most of this poetry consisted of lively gems about sexual love and passion. As Chinese women became increasingly secluded in public and most marriages came to be arranged by parents, poetry provided an outlet; it sang of clandestine trysts involving lovestruck maidens who in spite of convention and their own bashfulness give themselves to their paramours. The portrayals were quite delicately drawn; it was up to the reader to sense their eroticism. The following excerpts from more noted voluptuous poems date from the tenth through the seventeenth centuries.

The wedding night was a popular topic. The bride's loss of her virginity was often described with natural metaphors:

> *The peach blossom is overwhelmed*
> *By persistent raindrops.*
> *The secret heart glows*
> *With stolen glances.*

> *Too shy*
> *To ask for gentleness,*
> *She only grits her teeth.*
> *Suddenly, a thrush trill.*

57

The thrush trill alludes to the sexual gasp made by a woman in pleasure or pain. Other birds, as well as bees, flowers, and fruits were favorite symbols in erotic poetry, as in this Tang poem:

> *The bee steals wild nectar*
> *And savors its first taste;*
> *The golden oriole pecks at the peach,*
> *Melting the soft pulp in its mouth.*
>
> *Rippling ardor*
> *Makes her slightly pant;*
> *Tender passion*
> *Brings gentle delight.*

The peach is a Chinese symbol for the vulva, as well as for longevity.

The freer forms of *tzu* poems enabled poets to employ florid classical imagery and enliven it with a vernacular twist. In this poem two lovers are making hasty love outdoors:

> *I find her in a noisy crowd.*
> *We look for a secluded spot.*
> *Fallen blossoms are our mattress.*
>
> *Her phoenix toes are raised high*
> *Like a clashing of silver hooks.*
>
> *Teased, her face blushes deeply;*
> *Nowhere to hide,*
> *She closes her starry eyes*
> *And speaks in a low, low voice;*
> *Words inaudible, words lost.*
> *Shame, shame!*
>
> *With an agitated heart*
> *She cries repeatedly:*
> *"Watch out! Does anybody see us?"*

This Sung poem portrays a woman's exquisite postcoital listlessness:

Extreme pleasure
Brings bashfulness and languor.
Jade softens,
Blossoms droop.
My hairpin hangs on my sleeve.
My hair flows down my arms.

Mercilessly the slanting lamp stares at me.
I am damp with perspiration,
And my eyes are dim with intoxication.

I am sleepy,
I am sleepy,
Oh, my love, I am sleepy.

The renowned Ming scholar, painter, and poet Tang Po-hu is known for his voluptuous poems and erotic paintings. He uses metaphors of nature to suggest intercourse:

She sheds her clothes coyly,
A peony cringing in the autumnal wind.
Crimson dampness seeps through and through,
Peach blossoms scattered on the stream,
Red leaves floating in the jeweled gulch.

Who could endure this moment of wild passion!

Peach blossoms and fallen petals suggest the stains left by clouds and rain.

Another poem of his, about remembrance of delights past, is much more explicit:

I have not seen her after our parting.
When can her slippers cross with mine again,
Her feet hugging my waist,
Raising to my shoulders,
Her hands gripping my back?

A RISQUÉ NOVELETTE

Chinese erotic poetry gradually evolved into erotic prose. Several short novels combining prose and poetry appeared during the

Tang dynasty. A delightful erotic novelette of the seventh century, *A Visit to an Immortal Grotto* (*Yu Hsien Ku*), combines witty prose and ribald poetry. This work, long lost in China and later discovered in Japan, was written by Chang Wen-cheng, whose literary works were highly valued in both China and Japan. *A Visit* is a fantasy about the author as a young scholar traveling in the foothills of mountains in northwest China. He comes upon a great mansion, actually the cave of a female immortal, Shih Niang, and her female aide, Wu Sao. Chang enjoys an evening with the two women, sipping wine and composing elegant but racy poems in a mirthful exchange with the immortal. Finally, he spends the night in Shih Niang's bed.

The dialogue is full of double entendre and sexual innuendo. At dinner Shih Niang wants to play a wine game. Chang says: "I'm not good at drinking, so I can't play the wine game. I prefer to play the sleeping game." Asked how, he explains: "We play *shuang-lo* [a card game]. If I lose, I must sleep with you for the night. If you lose, you must sleep with me for the night." Wu Sao adds drily: "You don't have to play the game. Even if Shih Niang doesn't play, tonight she won't be able to get out of this."

Much of the story is told in poetry, at times ribald. When Chang is pouring wine into Shih Niang's goblet, he composes this ditty:

> *Its tail must not wobble,*
> *Its head must not dip low.*
> *Hold your goblet firmly,*
> *Shallow or deep as you desire.*

The female immortal's skills are equal to her guest's. When they are playing a game of tossing arrows into a vase, Shih Niang versifies:

> *Draw back the shaft,*
> *And you miss it.*
> *Raise the arrow head,*
> *And you overshoot it.*
> *Aim below the navel,*
> *And you enter it.*

Later, Chang and Shih Niang sit facing each other. In an increasingly romantic exchange of impromptu verses, he propositions her and she replies coquettishly. Their flirtations progress from the poetic to the physical, and from kissing to fondling and beyond. When he touches her at a certain spot, she rhapsodizes:

In days past I played it myself.
Tonight another plays it for me.

While the two have flirted throughout the story, using titillating dialogue and suggestive verse, their lovemaking is described only cursorily. The eroticism of this novelette, the romantic mood that may be inspired in the reader, lies in verbal foreplay rather than physical union.

The Supreme Joy of Sexual Union

Not all Chinese erotic writing, it should be noted, is as sensually elegant as the voluptuous poetry or as humorously risqué as the novelette described above. One formerly unknown piece of Tang erotica was discovered by French Sinologist Paul Pelliot in 1907 in the Tun Huang grottoes, in an oasis at the edge of the Gobi Desert. This fascinating item, dating from the ninth century, is *The Poetical Essay on the Supreme Joy of the Pleasurable Union of Heaven and Earth, and Yin and Yang,* by Po Hsing-chien, younger brother of the famous poet Po Chu-i. The manuscript has numerous copying errors and the last section is missing. An unabashed rhapsody of sexual union and eroticism, it is written in elegant but explicit classical language.

Its preface underlines the Yin-Yang cosmological outlook for sexual union, which it considers natural and fundamental to human beings. Nothing brings greater joy to men and women than sexual union—hence the title. This passage describes a wedding night:

The groom takes out his crimson bird. He pulls down the bride's red trousers, raises her naked feet, and fondles her fleshy portal. She grasps his stalk, her heart palpitating. He sucks at her tongue with his mouth, his mind in a whirl. When the fluids are plentiful, they rub against each other and receive their pleasure with

affection. Her cleft is slightly open, but at first he refrains from dashing forward. Only when his stalk is greatly swollen does he pierce her. He looks down at her virgin gate and sees her crimson drops mixed with his rivulets of semen. Then they wipe themselves with a piece of cloth and put it in a basket. From now on they are husband and wife, according to the principles of Yin and Yang.

This is followed by a more detailed description of the joy of subsequent marital unions:

After this union, they will always open to each other. Sometimes high in a moonlit pavilion, sometimes behind closed windows in early spring, together they read *The Classic of the Elemental Maid.* The beauteous woman lies on a reclining cushion behind a circular screen. She takes off her gauze skirt and loosens her embroidered trousers. Her eyebrows are like a bouquet of flowers; her waist is like a roll of silk. With tender passion she stretches out furtively, and she gazes coyly at her own body. They first pat and knead their flexed bodies, and caress each other from head to toe. Sometimes her legs are raised above his shoulders. Sometimes her blouse is pushed above her navel. The sobbing mouth seeks the tongue; snowy haunches are raised up high. The jade stalk rears its head in violent anger; the golden gulch opens its lips in tremulous fear. The lone peak rises by the chasm; the hidden valley quivers by the chicken terrace. Secretions flow; lascivious juices surge.

The woman pushes her face into the pillow, bending her waist. The man leans against the bed with sloping knees. His jade stalk moves to and fro, up and down, left and right. The Yang stem thrusts straight ahead or stabs obliquely. It loiters by the lute string or grinds erratically against the grain seed, scraping upward or piercing downward. They pull at the shoulders and rub buttocks. They rock and shake. It is warm, slippery, wet, and dewy. Sometimes the jade stalk advances leisurely and dips shallowly, like a nipple in an infant's mouth. Sometimes it thrusts deeply, like a chilled snake entering its nest. Toying and winnowing, she half swallows the fruit pit; rushing and striking, he buries himself to the root. Suddenly shallow, suddenly deep. Floating again, sinking again. Her tongue thrusts into his mouth as his stalk stabs at her flower heart. Sometimes seizing, sometimes pressing down. Sometimes staying immersed, sometimes rapidly slipping away.

He wipes their parts with a towel and again puts the stalk

into her. The orchid bags, now dried, sway confusedly. The stalk, now inside the ramparts, assaults deeply. He is eliciting from her the seven sounds of the infant, mixed with gasps. He raises her trembling feet, pausing to regain energy while letting her lasciviousness overflow. Then, using the Art of the Bedchamber, he moves in the style of nine-shallow, one-deep. He pauses and alternates sudden rapidity with sudden leisureliness, while looking down at the exiting and entering.

Now the woman's countenance is transfigured and her voice trembles. Her hairpins have fallen and her hair is in disarray. Her eyes are covered by loose hair and her comb has slipped like a half-moon on her shoulder. His eyes are misty and his five limbs are drooping. His semen has seeped into her womb; their secretions have soaked the cinnabar grotto.

Quite an encounter! Next the essay tells how a woman and her husband disrobe in the moonlight and carry on playful sexual games, and describes the joys of sexual union in each of the four seasons, in boudoir and secluded garden. It details sexual seductions, with sportive characterizations of stolen love: how a man and a woman meet unexpectedly and make impromptu love by a wall, on a meadow, or deep in some flowering bushes, spreading their clothes on the grass or crouching against a pillar. Such a hurried, clandestine tryst, the author says, is a hundred times more exciting than one in a safe bed.

AMOROUS BALLADS

Around the middle of the thirteenth century, the Mongols invaded China; in 1280, Kublai Khan was on the Chinese throne, beginning the Mongolian Yuan dynasty. (It was at this time that Marco Polo visited the Celestial Empire.) Under the oppressive Mongolian rule, and encouraged by neo-Confucianist prudery, the Chinese began to seclude their women and send their sex life underground. Afraid to spark the ire of their Mongolian conquerors, Chinese scholars turned from serious classical essays and poetry to more frivolous forms of literature. *Tzu* poetry, for one, was transformed, into *chu*, chanted verse or ballads. This sung poetry retained some classical terms but used mostly colloquial expressions. Its popularity zoomed, and its description of sexual love became more realistic and revealing than in classical poetry. The following conjures a nighttime encounter between two lovers:

Light, light sighs,
Low, low murmurs.

Playing pull and tug, pinch and press.
Unused to such games,
The maiden is confused and uncertain.

Through the sheer gauze
Her breasts loom like white ivory;
My hand in her bosom,
Holding tight.

Smooth, resilient, and protruding,
Arching, quivering in my grasp.

My hand still tingles.

The most remarkable literary development during the Yuan dynasty was the rise of Chinese drama, in the form of dialogue and *chu*. Ballads were sung by a single actor with musical accompaniment, while the dialogue was spoken by various actors. Most of the dramas were about romantic love, often of the stolen variety. In a sense they were like Western operas, but with few episodic and melodramatic qualities. The singing parts might be likened to a hybrid of today's light opera and American country music.

The growth of Chinese drama in the Yuan and Ming dynasties was remarkable. All other varieties of drama and folk opera in China grew from the Yuan drama. The chanted verse in most of these dramas was of the voluptuous variety and expressed passionate love among youths who defied the conventions of neo-Confucian society. The playwrights were usually producers as well, who organized their own traveling troupes.

A Lovers' Tryst in a Monastery Chamber

The best-known of the early dramas is *The Story of the Western Chamber* (*Hsi Hsiang Chi*), by Wang Shih-fu. Its plot involves a young scholar, Chang Chun-shui, who rents a cell in a monastery after he sees a lovely damsel staying in the same monastery. She, her mother, and a maid are accompanying the coffin of her father, a former prime minister, to its burial place. Because of unrest in the countryside, they have sought temporary safety in the monastery.

One day several thousand bandits surround the monastery, threatening to kill everyone inside unless the maiden, a famous beauty, consents to marry the bandit leader. Her frantic mother promises her daughter's hand to anyone who can end the siege. As it happens, the garrison commander in the area is a former classmate and good friend of the scholar, and he responds to the scholar's plea for help with his troops. After the siege has been lifted, however, the mother goes back on her word. With the help of the sympathetic maidservant, the lovesick scholar has a passionate tryst with the young woman. The complicated plot eventually has the two marrying each other. The following describes, in ballad form, a rendezvous of the two lovers:

> *Her embroidered slippers are lusciously tiny,*
> *Her willow waist fits a delicious handful.*
> *Bashful, she will not raise her head,*
> *But leans it against the pillow.*
> *Her hairpins are fallen,*
> *Her hair is awry.*
>
> *He undoes her buttons,*
> *Unties her silken waistband.*
> *Orchid scent wafts through the secluded chamber.*
>
> *"Dear rascal, would you hurt me?"*
> *"Hey! Why won't you turn your face to me?" . . .*
>
> *Slowly, slowly, she sways her willow waist.*
> *Tenderly, tenderly, he splits the flower heart.*
> *Dew drips into the opening peony.*
>
> *Dipping for a touch of rapture! . . .*
> *The tender pistil shivers with delicate scent,*
> *The butterfly sips without restraint.*

Half resisting, half yielding,
As if in fright, as if in love,
The red mouth brushes the scented cheek.

These dramas, once published and staged, became the rage of old China. One work, *The Peony Pavilion* (*Mou Tan Ting*), by the sixteenth-century Ming scholar Tang Hsien-tsu, tells of a romance between a young man and a young woman. They are strangers but have met already in a dream, making love in a peony garden pavilion. The woman, who actually lives in such a garden, dies and is buried near a plum tree in the garden. On a journey the young man comes upon the site of his dream and a portrait of the dead woman. Her ghost appears and makes love with him for many nights. Eventually, she is resurrected and marries the young man.

When this drama was published, sentimental youths avidly read and reread it. A woman who saw her own life reflected in the drama was said to have died of a broken heart after reading it. An actress who had had an unhappy love affair killed herself after playing the young woman. The most famous incident involved Chin Feng-tien, an accomplished calligrapher and poet. She vowed never to marry any other man except the author of *The Peony Pavilion*. She wrote him a fan letter, which was ignored. Her second letter moved him so much that he traveled by canal boat to her distant city. Upon his arrival he learned she had died a month earlier. Buried with her, he was told, was a copy of his drama.

EROTIC NOVELS

The Yuan dramas of the fourteenth century, with their romantic plots and melodious ballads, developed into novels. In their earliest form these novels were meant to be recited by storytellers rather than read silently. They were written in vernacular language, usually with classical poetry interspersed. Most of the major novels have a hundred chapters or more, and their long, involved plots and subplots match those of Tolstoy and Dostoevsky.

Of the five most famous Chinese novels, two are erotic: *Gold Vase Plum* (*Chin Ping Mei*) and *The Dream of the Red Chamber* (*Hung Lou Meng*). Each is a novel of manners involving a big household, and each appears to be a roman à clef; both are considered great literary works, and are the subject of numerous scholarly books and critical essays. But here their similarities end. *Gold Vase Plum* is a blatantly realistic story about a carnal nouveau riche and his many women. *The Dream of the Red Chamber* is a phantasmagoric romance about a sentimental youth and his many female relatives and maidservants sharing an enormous genteel estate with picturesque pavilions and gardens. The former novel's sexual explicitness borders on pornography, while the latter's eroticism is delicate and hauntingly suggestive.

WILD LOVE UNDER THE GRAPE ARBOR

Written by an anonymous author during the second half of the sixteenth century, *Gold Vase Plum* tells of the lecherous playboy Hsi-men Chin, who is affluent but uncultured, and Pan Chin-lien (Golden Lotus), his nymphomaniacal concubine. The novel depicts Hsi-men as a gauche, malevolent man without love, affection, or even passion. He vents his carnal lust not only on his spouses but indiscriminately on maidservants, wet nurses, shopkeepers' wives, and prostitutes. He has sex with forty-six women and two page boys, and dies from an overdose of aphrodisiac. The hundred chapters of the novel employ vernacular prose and elegant classical poetry to describe Hsi-men's sexual exploits. The sketches of the physical environment and the rendering of social mores are superb, and the dialogue brings out the individuality of each major character.

Because of its graphic passages, the novel was banned during the reign of the eighteenth-century Ching emperor Chien Lung. Later editions were published with the juicy parts expurgated, but each deletion was accompanied by a note saying exactly how many characters were deleted. Enterprising students have counted a total of 13,123 such characters. The longest censored passage numbers 633 characters, and the shortest, four.

Below I have translated two expurgated passages, about a wanton romp of Hsi-men and Golden Lotus under the grape arbor in their secluded garden. On a sultry midsummer afternoon Golden Lotus strips herself naked, leaving only foot ribbons and slippers on her feet. She reclines languidly on a mat, fanning herself with a white muslin fan. The sight arouses Hsi-men, who disrobes and sits on a porcelain garden stool.

> He wriggles his big toe into her flower heart, making lubricious juices ooze out of her like the mucus of a snail. He takes off her embroidered slippers, toys with them, unwinds her foot ribbons, and then uses them to tie her feet so they hang from the grape arbor. Now her legs are like the outstretched claws of a golden dragon. Her widely opened vulva shows a pair of full red lips with a chicken tongue in between.
>
> He crouches down above her, holding his duster handle with one hand to aim at the Yin gate. Then, using the other hand to steady himself on a pillow, he penetrates her with his inverted tasseled spear. He strokes energetically into her abundant fluids, an eel moving in slippery mud. The woman underneath him keeps on exclaiming, "Da da!"

Their activity is interrupted by the arrival of the maid Spring Plum. When she sees the two, she puts down the wine flask she has brought and runs toward a pavilion, ignoring Hsi-men's call for her to return. He disengages himself and chases after her. Once he has caught her, he carries her giggling back to the arbor. He seats himself on the porcelain stool, places Spring Plum on his lap, and refreshes himself and her from a wine cup.

Golden Lotus pleads for him to untie her, but he doesn't listen. Instead, he plays a dart game with plums, her gaping grotto as the target. He hits the bull's-eye three times, and each time rewards himself with a cup of wine. When he tires of this, he inserts a plum into the grotto of the protesting woman and returns to his wine cup, as the maid fans him. Finally he falls asleep, and Spring Plum skitters away. The tale unfolds:

> When Hsi-men wakes up an hour later, he sees Spring Plum has disappeared. But Golden Lotus's two white legs still hang from the arbor. His lust is rekindled. "Little Wanton," he says, "I'm going to spend myself inside you." He plucks the plum from her vagina and puts it in her mouth. . . .
>
> Now he begins to work on her. At first he moves his jade stalk only at the entrance of her grotto, refusing to go deeper. The woman raises her hips, exclaiming "Da da, get in quick! You are making the Little Wanton frantic! . . ."
>
> Laughingly, he says, "Little Wanton! Now that you realize this, we can set things right."

He smears boudoir mewl powder on the frog mouth of his stem and inserts its tip into her Yin gate. He moves slightly a few times while looking down at the stalk. Soon it raises itself angrily and expands with bulging veins. As he thrusts in and pulls out, the woman rubs her misty, half-closed eyes on the pillow and moans. "You big-tooled Da da!" she babbles. "What tricks are you playing on me? Why don't you go deeper? This Little Wanton's flower heart is itching, down to the marrow of her bones. Have pity on me! Kill me!"

While lewd words continue to bubble out of the woman, Hsi-men thrusts into her relentlessly, some four hundred times. With his hands on the mat, he raises and lowers his loins, withdrawing his stalk to its tip, then penetrating to its root. He does this vigorously for another hundred thrusts. The woman wipes her juices with a handkerchief, but once they are wiped away, more seep out again. Soon the mat is drenched.

For all its lurid passages, *Gold Vase Plum* is, as has been mentioned, considered a major literary work. Its coarse sexual narratives are jocular, almost Rabelaisian. Its characters engage in a wide variety of sexual activities, including frequent "playing the flute" by women, "drinking at the jade fountain" by men, anal intercourse, and some homosexual and lesbian practices. The popularity of this novel resulted in at least three sequels, also by anonymous authors.

There was a brief but spirited appearance of pornographic novels in the early seventeenth century, the later years of the Ming dynasty. A cult of elegant living had flourished in China throughout the period. The exquisite, translucent delicacy of Ming porcelain and simple, elegant lines of Ming furniture became world-famous. Architecture reached its zenith, as the magnificent palaces still standing in Beijing today attest. The art of landscaping transformed Chinese gardens into secluded havens edged with bamboo groves and dotted with jasmine and peony bushes and bizarre-shaped rocks. Freeform lotus ponds arched over by narrow vermilion bridges, and pavilions and swings were mainstays of these gardens.

By the late Ming period, however, the saturation point had been reached. The prevailing mood was typically fin-de-siècle. World-weary scholars and artists were disenchanted with politics and tired of the pursuit of elegance. Out of fashionable despair, some took themselves to Buddhist and Taoist monasteries in remote mountains. Others turned to writing outrageously obscene novels, characterized by coarse slang and sometimes scatological details. Many of China's pornographic novels were written at this time, but most disappeared under the puritanical censorship of an emperor of the next dynasty. A few were preserved in Japan or by private Chinese collectors. These are of scant literary value, although the voluptuous poems interspersed in them are as good as any.

The best-known of this genre with some literary value is *The Prayer Cushion of Flesh* (*Jou Pu Tuan*). The Sinologist Franz Kuhn, who translated *Jou Pu Tuan* and several other Chinese works into German, called it an "erotic moral novel" and praised it as superior in literary value to *Gold Vase Plum.* Chinese scholars strongly dispute such an evaluation.

Reading the original Chinese texts of both novels gives the unmistakable impression that whatever literary value *Prayer Cushion* has cannot be compared with that of *Gold Vase Plum.* The plot of the former revolves around a scholar who, tired of his wedded life, leaves his wife in search of greener pastures. To improve his sexual prowess, he has an itinerant surgeon transplant slices of a dog's penis onto his own. Armed with this unique weapon, the scholar begins a carnal spree, seducing several women. The husband of one of them exacts his vengeance by seducing the scholar's wife and eventually selling her to a brothel, where she becomes famous for her erotic skill. The scholar, seeking ever new thrills, visits the renowned prostitute without realizing she is his wife. At the sight of her prodigal husband, she hangs herself. Humiliated and remorseful, the scholar castrates himself and becomes a Buddhist monk. The purported theme of the novel is that a man attains ultimate Enlightenment through carnal indulgence.

While the sex scenes of *Prayer Cushion* are as explicit as those of *Gold Vase Plum,* they constitute almost all the story; one has the sense that the author's only purpose was to portray sexual encounters. Unlike *Gold Vase Plum,* the novel has no character development and no description of social or physical background. Seduction scenes are unrealistic, with every seduced woman acting from the beginning like a brazen whore. *Prayer Cushion* does show some insight into sexual psychology, but it is evident that the author knew nothing of the Art of the Bedchamber. In spite of the raw and at times obscene narrative, the book has no sadistic or degrading elements.

A Dream of Eroticism

The Dream of the Red Chamber, which together with *Gold Vase Plum* is one of the two most celebrated erotic novels in Chinese literature, was published in the mid-1700s. Its author, Tsao Hsueh-chin was the scion of a prominent family that had gone bankrupt. As has been mentioned, *Gold Vase Plum* and *Dream* differ completely in their approach and presentation. *Dream* describes life in an enormous, affluent household of more than three hundred who live in a rambling complex of mansions and elegant gardens. The protagonist, Chia Pao-yu, is a brooding, sentimental youngster pampered by a large flock of female relatives—aunts, nieces, cousins—and numerous maidservants. The author alludes and allegorizes, without explicating things. There is not a single lewd word in the book, and it is pervaded with a delicate, elusive, eroticism. Although the book touches on such subjects as homosexuality, lesbianism, and incest, these are only discreetly hinted at.

Dream has been rendered into English and German in condensed form. But even the best translation cannot do justice to such a dreamlike work. I have translated some excerpts here, to give a taste of the work. Chia Pao-yu, visiting a part of the family complex not his usual haunts, feels drowsy and wants to take a nap. The wife of a nephew of his, Chin Ko-ching, by clan hierarchy his niece but by age a mature woman, suggests that he nap in her room.

> As they enter Madame Chin's bedroom, they are greeted by a delicate, sweet fragrance. Pao-yu's eyes grow dim and his bones turn soft. He says with a smile: "So fragrant! . . . This place is good! This place is good!" Madame Chin says: "This room of mine is good enough for an immortal." . . . As soon as Pao-yu closes his eyes, he falls willy-nilly into sleep. In his dream he walks behind Madame Chin.

In this shimmering, ethereal dream world, he is greeted by a beautiful female immortal who lets him glance—but only fleet-

ingly—into celestial books with enigmatic poetry and paintings. The immortal gives him food and wine, and tells him she wants to make her younger sister Ko-ching (namesake of Madame Chin) his spouse. And this very night is to be the wedding night.

> Having instructed him in the secrets of clouds and rain, she pushes him into the bridal chamber, closes the door, and leaves. Pao-yu dreamily follows the immortal's instructions and makes love to Ko-ching. The next day the two become hopelessly entangled with each other with tender words and loving caresses. . . .
>
> Pao-yu wakes from his dream and sits up in bewilderment, as if he has just lost something. When the chambermaid Hsi-jen helps him to adjust his trousers, her hand accidentally touches his crotch, and she feels something cold, wet, and sticky. She hastily withdraws her hand, saying: "What happened?" Pao-yu blushes profusely and lightly pinches her hand. Hsi-jen is a bright girl and two years older than Pao-yu. She is beginning to understand some of the things between the sexes. When Pao-yu behaves like this, she half understands what has happened. Her powdered face suddenly flushes a bright crimson. . . .
>
> Bashfully Pao-yu begs her: "My good girl, don't you tell anyone!" Hsi-jen smiles shyly and asks in a low voice: "How did you—" She stops, looks around, then asks: "Where did the liquid come from?" Pao-yu, red-faced, refuses to answer. Hsi-jen stares at him and keeps smiling. Pao-yu then tells her all the details of his dream. When he recounts the passionate episode of clouds and rain, Hsi-jen covers her face with her hands and crouches down, giggling. Pao-yu has always liked Hsi-jen's coy and bewitching charms, and he tugs and pulls her so that they will enjoy themselves according to the immortal's instructions. . . . After token resistance from her, they make tender love.

The author is masterly in evoking a subtle eroticism. To convey the effect a young woman has on some elderly male relatives, for example, he describes simply her "sudden joys, sudden frowns, her pendant earrings swaying like garden swings." One of his favorite sensual motifs is fragrance. In one passage he describes a languid moment between Pao-yu and his cousin Lin Tai-yu, a fragile girl about his age. The two are lying face to face on a couch, and she sees a crimson spot on his left cheek. She asks whose fingernail was responsible for it. He denies it is a scratch, but says that he may have smudged his cheek when he was helping some other household girls mix their rouge. His cousin wipes the stain off his cheek, pouting. Then:

> Pao-yu does not hear what she is saying. He is aware only of a hidden fragrance issuing from Tai-yu's sleeves, intoxicating his soul and melting his bones. He grabs her sleeve with his hand, trying to see what is inside that is responsible for this. Tai-yu says smilingly: "These days, who would carry any aromatics?" Pao-yu replies, also smilingly: "It is so fragrant! Where does it come from, anyway?" Tai-yu answers: "I don't know this myself."

PEASANT LOVE SONGS

In glaring contrast to the delicately voluptuous style of *The Dream of the Red Chamber* are brazen, earthy peasant love songs, which have been around for centuries. Educated people have scorned them, but during the past century scholars have studied them as a living cultural asset. These love songs, some quite openly sexual, trace their origins to ancient songs such as those collected in *The Book of Odes* and dating back as many as three thousand years ago, when young peasants sang and danced at harvest festivals, and then paired off for more interesting diversions.

Some of these songs are transparently figurative. An example is this ditty from eastern China:

> *Young lass has a little implement,*
> *It can squeeze sugar cane, thick or thin.*
> *If you don't believe this, lad, try it,*
> *The juice squeezed out is sweet and sticky.*

Most are explicit, like this song from the same region entitled "Harvesting Mulberry Leaves":

> *Eight gauze skirts are our bed curtains,*
> *The field is our bed.*
> *The shade of mulberry leaves is our house.*
> *Oh, the sight is delicious in the mulberry orchard!*
>
> *Boy faces girl, girl faces boy.*
> *Our joy is greater than the wedding night.*
> *Boy holds girl, girl holds boy.*

My golden lotuses hook my young lover.
He raises my little feet high,
As if carrying lotus roots by the yellow pond.

My clovelike tongue goes inside his mouth.
Oh, it is better than licking honey.

Our essences are lost, dripping down our thighs.
My newly opened peony bud is plucked by my lover.
You are tasting it ahead of my future husband.

Here is a song of lament:

When you and I first made love,
My white damask trousers were dyed red.
My godbrother,
Oh, it hurt!

Ah ya, ah ya,
My godbrother,
Oh, it hurt!

You have plucked the fresh flower of your little godsister.
Now you love someone else,
You don't come to me anymore.

Ah ya, ah ya, you don't come to me anymore.

Some of the songs praise the male's bedroom prowess:

I give you, my love, my ninth thanks, for your great skill.
You made me die, and you made me live again.
We did all thirty-six positions of the spring palace,
And made one night two nights long.

Other songs are more playful:

The lass sits on the inlaid bed,
The lad climbs in to pluck the flower.
Our skins melt, our flesh tingles.

First we play the goldfish frolicking in the water,
Then we play the bee plucking at the flower heart.

A song from northern China enumerates certain peasant ideals:

The best love songs sing about stolen love;
The best meat to buy is the rump cut;
The best breasts to feel are the lotus bosoms of eighteen-year-olds;
The best mouth to kiss comes with curvy eyebrows, delicate eyes,
*   and bright red lips.*

THE HEYDAY OF EROTIC ART

The erotic art of China has a more limited scope than Chinese erotic literature. Dubbed "spring palace" art, it flourished briefly in the late Ming dynasty, the first half of the seventeenth century. This art was executed mainly in the form of monochrome and color prints, characterized by delicacy of line, hue, and composition. These prints reveal a facet of Chinese eroticism that may intrigue sexologists and cultural anthropologists.

The earliest known erotic art of China, found on tiles and shells in Han dynasty tombs, dates back two thousand years. Later, when sexology classics became popular during the Tang dynasty, artists embellished them with how-to illustrations. Erotic picture scrolls also began to appear during this time. In the next dynasty, the Sung, erotic art was produced even in the imperial art academy.

The heyday of erotic art, however, did not come until the second half of the Ming dynasty, when woodcut prints proliferated. The best erotic prints, in five colors, were produced between 1606 and 1624. After 1644, when the Ming dynasty gave way to the Ching, this art degenerated and soon died out altogether.

Between the ninth and the sixteenth centuries, four famous painters were known principally for their erotic paintings. Most of their creations are lost today. Even though several renowned painters dabbled in erotic art, it was never valued highly by Chinese aesthetic standards. The Chinese always have considered calligraphy, done with the brush-pen, as the highest form of art. Good brush calligraphy has dynamics of movement, freedom of contour, and an eloquent balance of space and brushstrokes. Chinese landscape ("mountain and water") watercolor painting, which presents the artist's subjective impression rather than an exact, "realistic" view, rates almost as high. Less valued than landscapes are paintings of flowers and birds and of people. Lower yet in esteem is illustrative art, which is considered almost artisan's work.

As early as the eighth century, Chinese painters eliminated the rigid outlines of objects in paintings and substituted them with dynamic brushstrokes. Probably more by design than by accident, Chinese painters have never used three-dimensional techniques such as perspective and chiaroscuro, which Renaissance artists of Europe developed so brilliantly. Photographic likeness and pure abstraction have been equally scorned by Chinese artists.

The Chinese have produced some magnificent sculpture, for instance the thousands of life-size terra-cotta soldiers and horses guarding the tomb of the First Emperor, discovered in Xian in the 1970s. Later, however, Chinese sculpture was almost exclusively in the form of Buddhist statues, showing a marked Indian influence. Sculpture of the human figure as seen in classical Greek and Roman works is unknown in China. With its different philosophy and tradition, and view of humankind, Chinese art of the human figure—including the erotic variety—differs, understandably, from that of the West.

Most of Ming erotic art exists as woodcut prints. Often these prints were found in fan-fold albums, usually with a page of art facing a page of poetry. The albums contained twenty-four or thirty-six pictures. Sometimes the albums were horizontal, panoramic scrolls, which could be displayed inside the massive Chinese lattice bed as a connubial inspiration. Erotic pictures also adorned vases, wine cups, and snuff bottles. An amusing type of folding fan displayed innocuous landscapes or flowers and birds on both sides when opened in the normal way, but showed a graphic sexual tableau when opened in reverse. Tiny ivory or porcelain figures of copulating couples discreetly hidden in boxes with sliding lids were favorite conversation pieces.

Chinese erotic art is unique in several respects. As it is of illustrative origin, it is mainly instructional. It is unlike evocative landscape painting, which is filtered through the artist's perception. Human figures are not well proportioned; the torso and upper limbs are often disproportionately large. There is no deliberate exaggeration of genitals as in Japanese erotic art. Facial expressions show little passion. The erotic scenes depicted are almost all static tableaux, but they show faithfully the postures of the participants, including the position of torsos and limbs, and even the orientation of the jade stalk. While the scenes depicted may be neither passionate nor dynamic, they suggest serenity and harmony, often laced with whimsy and playfulness. Many of the sexual encounters are presented as outdoor scenes, and even most indoor scenes have a backdrop of foliage and rocks through a window or pavilion door. This is perhaps due partly to the Taoist fondness for nature, and partly to the fact that Chinese gardens are always secluded from prying eyes. Freedom from prying eyes does not mean absence of the voyeur. Indeed, many amusing scenes show a couple copulating and a young woman peeping, sometimes while playing with herself. Not a single piece of Chinese erotic art shows sexual violence or what modern psychologists would consider pathological behavior.

The great variety of coital positions and situations in Chinese pictorial erotica indicates an intent to dispel boredom in the marital act. Most of the positions prescribed by sexology classics can be found depicted in Chinese erotic paintings and prints. Both erotic literature and art tend to encourage positions in which the female legs are raised or flexed, so that the woman can enjoy keener sensations. A number of positions tend to stimulate various out-of-the-way spots, including the flower heart, sometimes neglected in orthodox positions. This emphasis on female satisfaction is the cornerstone of the ancient Chinese Art of the Bedchamber.

Part Two

THE ART
OF THE
BEDCHAMBER

THE ART OF THE BEDCHAMBER—the sexology of ancient China—
is more than two thousand years old. In recent centuries it was
little-known, shrouded in mists after the core of sexology classics
had disappeared. Several rediscovered sexology classics, however,
tell us that this ancient art of lovemaking is a fascinating mixture
of mysticism and scientific prescience.

A study of the once lost classics, as has been noted, reveals this
theme of ancient Chinese sexology: Sexuality is a natural human
urge which, if satisfied regularly in moderation, and enjoyed with
pleasure, not only will give people greater sexual potency but will
make them live healthier and longer. To enhance a happy sex life,

the classics offer various means of boosting sexual energy, refining love-play, and mastering erotic techniques.

While the male essence is limited, according to these classics, the female essence is inexhaustible. Around this premise, the classics devised elaborate means to boost the male's sexual stamina and thereby to prolong the sexual union.

One happy consequence of the Art of the Bedchamber is assured female satisfaction in bed. It is uncertain whether this approach had anything to do with the fact that the three earliest, most renowned, and most quoted sexologists of ancient China were female.

6

Lady Doctors of Love

Sex Therapists in the First Century

The Yellow Emperor asks the Elemental Maid: "My spirit is weak and disharmonious. My heart is without joy, and my body is filled with apprehensions. What should I do?"

The Elemental Maid replies: "The debility of men is caused by faulty ways in the mating of Yin and Yang. Women prevail over men, just as water prevails over fire. They that know the way are like a good cook, who can blend the five flavors into a tasty soup; they that know the Tao of Yin and Yang can blend the five pleasures. But they that know not may die an untimely death. How could they ever enjoy sexual pleasures?"

THE OPENING PASSAGE from *The Classic of the Elemental Maid* (*Su Nu Ching*) epitomizes the ancient Chinese art of lovemaking by suggesting that good health comes from good sex, and good sex comes from good health. Written in the first century A.D., the *Elemental Maid* predates all known sexology classics of other cultures: India's *Kama Sutra* (third–fourth century A.D.) and *Rati Rahasya* (eleventh century); the Arabian *The Perfumed Garden* (fourteenth–fifteenth centuries); and the Muslim *Ananga Ranga* (fifteenth century). Although written probably around the same time, Ovid's *Art of Love* is about courtship and seduction, not sex.

Actually, the *Elemental Maid* is predated by at least a dozen other Chinese sexology classics. In Hunan province, in 1973, four manuscripts from the second century B.C. were unearthed in a

81

royal tomb of the Han dynasty. These are the oldest extant sexology classics, although their contents are not as well-known and significant as those of the *Elemental Maid.* Additionally, the bibliography of the dynastic history of the Han dynasty lists books from the entire spectrum of Chinese learning at the time. In the section on medicine, under the heading "Inside the Bedchamber," are mentioned eight sexology books, among the oldest known such texts in the world. All of them disappeared many centuries ago. However, the Han tomb discovery suggests that one day some of these may be unearthed in another tomb.

A note from the compiler of the Han bibliography advises: "If a person regulates his sexual pleasure, he will enjoy tranquility and attain longevity. If he indulges in this pleasure and ignores the tenets set down in these treatises [the sexology classics], he will damage his health and even harm his very life." This reveals the quintessence of ancient China's Art of the Bedchamber: the intimate relationship between sex on one hand, and health and longevity on the other. Good health through good sex was a branch of legitimate medicine in ancient China. For centuries, sex manuals were listed in the bibliographies of Chinese dynastic histories in the category of medicine.

THE EARLIEST SEX THERAPISTS

The three women who are the earliest known sexologists of ancient China were the Elemental Maid, Su Nu, who was the most widely quoted; the Arcane Maid, Hsuan Nu; and the Iridescent Maid, Tsai Nu. Their central theme, like that of their successors, was that health, youthfulness, and longevity can be attained during happy hours in the jade chamber—the boudoir.

The classics named for each of these women, like other major works of the genre, are in the form of dialogues. In these three classics, the legendary Yellow Emperor, Huang Ti, who ascended to the throne in 2697 B.C., converses with his three female consultants in the Tao of Yin and Yang. The Yellow Emperor served as interlocutor because reputedly he pursued health and long life in bed with a total of no fewer than twelve hundred women. This feat, according to Chinese legends, made him an immortal and enabled him to ascend into heaven in broad daylight.

Classics Lost—and Classics Regained

Today we can count at least three dozen Chinese sexology classics written from the second century B.C. to the ninth century of the Christian era. This rich lode is no surprise; for centuries China was the most bookish nation on earth. Its enormous bulk of writing, on every conceivable subject, remains only slightly tapped, even to this day.

The sexology classics have had their ups and downs. At times this normally author-worshipping empire would go through epileptic periods of book-burning and literary purges. Numerous classics, especially those explicitly on erotic techniques, disappeared from China during the past nine centuries, among them the books by the three women sex therapists.

Their existence has been known all along, since they are not only listed in the bibliographies of the several official dynastic histories, but widely cited in Chinese literature. Although the modern Chinese still consume food and herbs that they believe will nurture their sexual vitality and general health, they are only dimly aware of the lost Art of the Bedchamber. They are unaware of the specific erotic techniques used joyously by their ancestors in the ancient bedchamber.

Fortunately for posterity, several of the lost classics were recovered, in part, a century ago. The trail led back to the late tenth century, when Tamba Yasuyori, a distinguished Chinese physician living in Japan, compiled *The Essence of Medical Prescriptions* (*I Shim Po* or *I Shing Fang*). This voluminous work, which cites more than two hundred Chinese medical sources from the third century through the tenth, is a priceless repository of Chinese medical knowledge. Many of the passages quoted would become the only versions in existence when the originals disappeared in China. Tamba was most scholarly in his citing; he left even obvious manuscript errors intact, but added warnings of such errors. Upon its publication, Tamba's book immediately became the most authoritative medical source in and around the Japanese imperial palace.

After many sexology classics disappeared in China, Chinese scholars believed that these literary gems were lost forever. They did not know that Japan, which fortunately always has been interested in things Chinese and acted as a great repository of Chinese culture, had preserved large fragments of many texts in Tamba's enormous medical treatise.

A Chinese scholar learned this fact in 1870—some nine hundred years after the book's publication—when he came upon Tamba's work in Japan's Imperial Library. Early in this century, another Chinese scholar, Yeh Teh-hui, visited the Imperial Library. Using the more extensive quotations from Tamba's book, Yeh reconstructed five of the major sexology classics and published them in China. But he was promptly ostracized by his conservative neo-Confucian colleagues, and his work was studiously ignored. Only in the 1950s were his reconstructed classics republished; today they are being noticed.

At about the same time that fragments of the lost classics were being restored, the French explorer Paul Pelliot discovered an erotic classic of major literary and sexological significance, quoted in the previous chapter. This document had been sealed for nine centuries in the Tun Huang grottoes. The resurrected classics, including those unearthed from the Han tomb, together with the vast body of ancient sexology hardly touched by modern researchers, give us a fascinating view of ancient Chinese sexuality.

A New Dazzle for Ancient Sexology

Since they are quoted from and analyzed in this book, it is worthwhile to take a brief look at the reconstructed classics individually. The best-known of the five books reconstructed by Yeh Teh-hui, *The Classic of the Elemental Maid,* is probably almost as complete as its original. The second book, *Prescriptions of the Elemental Maid (Su Nu Fang)*, is incomplete; very brief, it consists mostly of presciptions for sexually exhausted males. *The Secret Art of the Jade Chamber (Yu Fang Pi Chueh)*, although as long as *The Classic of the Elemental Maid,* is apparently only an eighth of the original, according to notes in the bibliography of the history of the Sui dynasty. *Essentials of the Jade Chamber (Yu Fang Chih Yao)* is a mere fraction of its original length, while *The Mystic Master of the Grotto (Tung Hsuan Tzu)* seems virtually complete. The latter is believed to have been written during the Tang dynasty by the Taoist Chang Ting or by Li Tsung-hsuan, the director of the Imperial School of Medicine. The book features graphic descriptions of passionate foreplay and coitus, and its literary style is similar to that of *The Poetical Essay on the Supreme Joy of the Pleasurable Union of Heaven and Earth, and Yin and Yang,* mentioned earlier.

Most of the classics on erotic techniques were abundantly illustrated, undoubtedly showing the various coital positions described in the texts. Although some illustrations have been reconstructed, the originals are lost forever.

Chinese sexology classics fall into several major categories. The basic and oldest ones are on the art of coitus. They are essentially manuals and describe erotic techniques in dialogues or quoted passages. The originals of most of these classics are lost. Aside from the five reconstructed classics and four discovered in the Han tomb, fragments of others are scattered among many old books.

Another group consists of collections of recipes and prescriptions of food and herbs, aimed specifically at invigorating sexual vitality and broadly at retarding aging and improving health. These recipes were compiled by Chinese physicians and immortality-seeking Taoists over two millennia. Unlike the classics on coital art, most of them were never lost.

One curious group of sexology treatises, written by Taoists mostly during the sixteenth and early seventeenth centuries, concerns mystical sexual alchemy. Many of these have disappeared, but some were preserved in both China and Japan. They will be discussed in chapter 9.

The peripheral categories include such topics as physiognomy, acupuncture, moxibustion (the warming of acupoints with burning herbs), acupressure massage (shiatsu), and mind-body exercises. While all of these practices are sexually oriented, they also aim broadly at general well-being. These classics, though mostly Taoist-inspired, are about health and are by no means religious.

The ancient Chinese sexology classics differ markedly from those of India, the *Kama Sutra* for instance. The Chinese classics, first of all, are health-oriented; the Indian classics are not. The former limit themselves to foreplay, coitus, and sexual health, while the latter examine courtship, and even somewhat mildly violent sexual activity—beating and biting. The sexual positions recommended by the Chinese are all practicable, while many in *Kama Sutra* require the participants to be yogis or contortionists.

Most of the classics of the Art of the Bedchamber were written anonymously or pseudonymously. Their literary style and con-

tent suggest that these works were written by highly educated and sophisticated literary individuals. Indeed, the most respected physicians, essayists, poets, alchemists, and philosophers wrote, edited, commented on, and quoted from these classics. There was no notion of copyright, and some so-called authors were actually editors who collected earlier writings and reworked them into new manuscripts.

Some ancient sexology classics, written in the cryptic, condensed style of most ancient Chinese classical works, leave much to the interpretation of the reader. Others, principally the manuals, are quite explicit. They appear to ignore deliberately any romantic or sentimental feeling between partners. In a few instances, and then only briefly, they describe the passionate effects on partners during foreplay and coitus, but the descriptions are clinical—almost like a modern sexologist's report on sexual activities observed in the laboratory. Still other texts depict erotic passion with poetic fervor.

A feature of the classics that is relevant today is their applicability to both sexes, although much of the writing appears to address specifically the male reader. One section in *The Secret Art of the Jade Chamber,* however, addresses women, telling them that the secret of the legendary Queen Mother of the West's youthfulness lies in her practice of sexual "pluck-and-nurture" with numerous men. Similarly, the Elemental Maid says that "women prevail over men." These comments indicate the Taoist belief that women are sexually stronger than men.

PICTURESQUE NOMENCLATURE

The writings of the Art of the Bedchamber tend to use different terminology for different purposes. What ancient Chinese poets delicately alluded to as the "peony" or "red lotus" was rendered less florally by Taoist sexologists, who referred to the female genitals by such names as "cinnabar grotto," "moon grotto," "Yin gate," and "jade gate." The phallus was usually the "jade stalk," "jade root," "Yang peak," "Yang implement," "hot peak," "jade spoon," "dragon," "duster handle," "tasseled spear," or "heavenly root."

Sex manuals described the vagina—more philosophically than

anatomically—as "that crucial square inch." The mons veneris was the "sand mound," and the clitoris the "jewel terrace" or the "animal in the boat"; this boat was sometimes the "front vestibule." The prepuce of the clitoris was a "dark garden" or "divine field." The upper vulva, where the labia minora meet, was the "golden gulch"; the lower vulva, the "jade vein." The labia minora themselves were "scarlet pearls" or "coxcombs." The female urethral orifice was, understandably, a "vast fountain." "Hidden valley" and "heavenly court" denoted the vaginal vestibule.

The varying depths of coital penetration also were considered in detail in the sex manuals. Poetic terms represented the various measurements: "lute strings" (one inch inside the vagina), "wheat bud" (two inches), "scented mouse" (three inches), "mixed rock" (four inches), "grain seed" (five inches). The "inch" here, a traditional measurement also used in acupuncture, was defined as the length of the second segment of the middle finger of the left hand for a man, and of the right hand for a woman. Beyond "grain seed" came the "flower heart" or "flower pistil," the cervix. The uterus itself was the "scarlet chamber."

Sexual Anatomy

The ancient boudoir artists devoted much research to the size, shape, structure, and "personality" of the genitalia. This research was supplemented by an immense array of literature on sexual physiognomy. The size of genitals is of concern to some people in every culture. The ancient Chinese concocted various recipes for enlarging the penis or shrinking the vagina. As they achieved more erotic sophistication, however, the size of the organ became less significant. Taoist sexologists considered penis size, which is grossly exaggerated in Japanese erotic art and in contemporary Western pornographic books and movies, of minor importance. The Chinese often use a condescending phrase, "big fish, big meat," to satirize a peasant's concept of fine dining: big slabs of fish and meat are mistaken for culinary art. The phrase also has been used for people obsessed with the size of the male organ or the size of female breasts. A sexual gourmand and a sexual gourmet are different.

For the sexually knowledgeable women of ancient China, the

thickness of a jade stalk was more important than its length, its shape more important than its thickness. The shape could be classified as one of three major categories: pagoda, with the base thicker than the head, the most common; cylinder, with the base and the head of the same thickness, less common; and mushroom, with the head thicker than the base, the most valued because it is apt to remain more fulfilling inside the jade gate after detumescence. Even more important than phallic size and shape was phallic performance, the crux of the Art of the Bedchamber.

The Elemental Maid, in explaining to the Yellow Emperor the ideal condition of the male organ for coitus, enumerates the Four Attainments of *chi.* An aroused jade stalk, she says, should pass through four progressive stages: angry, enlarged, rigid, and hot.

Taoist sexologists described the various shapes of the vagina pragmatically; among the self-explanatory terms were "dragon pearl," "monkey," "eagle," "whelk," "dish," "bamboo cylinder," "pheasant," "delta," "duckbill," and "sheep gut." Sexual connoisseurs in China were apt to discuss the topography inside the jade gate the way French oenophiles might discuss their favorite vineyards. Moreover, they relished regional varieties of anatomy. Women from the city of Tatung were prized for their vaginas with "double doors." Women from another locality had practically no pubic hair, and this, according to ancient sexologists, made them extremely wanton in bed.

The sexologists and physiognomists of ancient China must have spent countless days—and nights—researching what was sexually desirable in women, but not in men. When the Yellow Emperor asked the Elemental Maid to describe a desirable woman, his tutor replied: "A desirable woman has a tender, pliable temperament, with a liquid voice, black, silky hair, soft muscles, and small bones. She is neither too tall nor too short, neither too large nor too small. Her vulva is high up front; her mons is hairless; and she is rich in fluids. She is between twenty-five and thirty, and has never been pregnant. While copulating, her fluids flow abundantly, and her body trembles helplessly and is covered with perspiration. She yields to the man whether he wants to raise her high or press her down. If a man can find such a woman, even if they do not follow the proper ways of coition, they would suffer no harm."

Quoting Master Chung Ho, a Taoist sexual alchemist, *The Secret Art of the Jade Chamber* gives a similar assessment for a desirable woman. It describes also a sexually undesirable woman: "Her hair is unkempt, her face coarse, her neck thick, her throat knotted, and her teeth wheat-colored. She has a masculine voice. Her mouth is large and her nose high. Her pupils are unclear. Her lips and cheeks have long, whiskerlike hair. Her elbows and knees are large and protruding. Her hair is yellow, and her flesh is skimpy. Her pubic hair is thick and stiff, and sticks up in the wrong direction. To have intercourse with such a woman will harm the health of a man."

In short, the ancients considered sexually desirable a woman with a profusion of Yin and very little Yang. In modern terms, the sexually desirable woman had an abundance of female hormones.

SEXUAL PHYSIOGNOMY

The Chinese have been refining their study of physiognomy for the past two thousand years. They believe that by comparing the size, location, proportion, shape, color, and movement of an individual's facial features and other body parts with a "norm," a skilled observer can assess the individual's personality, luck, wealth, success, family and social relationships, longevity, health, and sexuality. Whether one considers this science, superstition, or statistical evaluation, the ancient Chinese were deadly serious about it. Physiognomy played an important part not only in making friends, choosing spouses, negotiating commercial deals, but also in waging war, engaging in politics, and maintaining the imperial court in general.

Sometimes physiognomy bordered on the fanciful. The celebrated physiognomist Liu Tsung-yuan had very specific observations. He predicted successful or highly honored sons for a woman with dark nipples and a deep, upward naval. A hairy navel on a woman foretold a son who would be a literary scholar. Skimpy buttocks denoted a skimpy fortune. Liu set forth his wisdom on good female physiognomy, and more: "The anus should be hidden by the haunches and not exposed, preferably with hair. [The woman's] urination should be slow. A fast, spirited rush indicates lack of wealth. A light and long stream is a sign of refinement. If her fecal matter piles up like a coiled ribbon, it is a sign of wealth and high social standing." In the past there were even professional urination auditors, women who, upon listening to an individual's urinating in an adjacent room, could "diagnose" his or her personality and fortune. There are urinalyses and urinalyses.

CONVERSATIONS FROM WILD HISTORY

The most erudite appraisals of genitals in the many centuries of Chinese scholarship are found in a fragment of "wild history" written during the Tang dynasty by Chang Mu. His book, *The Secret Chronicles of Kung Ho Chien,* is lost, but fortunately a work from the Ching dynasty, *Confucius Says Not,* quotes two long passages from it.

One of them reports a conversation between the lascivious empress Wu Tse-tien, whose love life was recounted earlier, and her daughter Tai Ping. (The Kung Ho Chien of the title was ostensibly the office for imperial aides established by the empress; in reality, it was a stable for her favorite studs.) When Tai Ping, sensing that her highly sexed mother is without a satisfactory lover, recommends her own love interest, Chang Chang-tsung, the empress is at first silent. Then Tai Ping whispers into her mother's ear that she has seen the young man taking a bath as her houseguest: "His jade stalk has a full head and a thin root. When it is in repose it droops down and is not long. It is as smooth as a goose egg, and its ridge rises a fifth to a sixth of an inch. It is fresh-red, soft, and mellow."

Smiling, the empress asks whether her daughter has tasted it. Tai Ping says no, but admits that she asked a lady-in-waiting to test him out. The empress turns to the lady-in-waiting and says: "You may tell Her Majesty frankly. Don't be shy about it."

The woman whispers into the empress's ear: "At the beginning of our encounter, it was like a luscious lychee from the South Seas, unusually smooth and tender. Its ridge expanded like an umbrella. After three or four strokes, my flower pistil opened wantonly. My spirit and my soul were borne aloft. What's so good about him was that he did not decide for himself whether to be slow or fast. He tenderly timed himself to my desire."

Empress Wu, overjoyed, exclaims: "I heard that those medi-
ocre women of the outside world crave only muscular hardness
and do not appreciate tenderness. That is the sexuality of peasant
women. . . . The best of male organs are handsome, tender, and
mellow."

PILLOW TALK ON LOVEMAKING

The same chronicle records a conversation between Shangkuan
Wan-erh, the secretary-confidante of Empress Wu, and one of
her own lovers. He is Tsui Shih, the minister of the army who had
to pacify an outraged duke with his own wife. During one of their
trysts, he asks how Empress Wu chose her men. Shangkuan replies that the empress passes over any jade stalk that is "all skin and
sinew." The explanation she gives is a rare gem of Chinese literary
exposition: "Of all the parts of the human body, the tongue has no
skin, so it is able to relish all the tastes; the heels have thick skin, so
they touch only the lowly ground. A woman's cinnabar grotto is
lined with a delicate membrane; so is the best part of a man's jade
stalk. Thus the most tender parts touch during copulation. The
protruding ridge of the jade stalk sensitizes the rubbing and massaging of parts. When the jade stalk is in repose, it is a hidden bud;
when it expands, it is an exposed eggplant. If the more tender parts
are squeezed against other such tender parts, pleasure reigns, as if
all the fecund essences of heaven and earth were being turned into
rich wine. But if the skin of the jade stalk is too thick, it acts like a
suit of armor. This deadens the pleasure while the jade stalk advances and retreats."

Tsui tells Shangkuan that the qualities of female genitals vary
as much as those of male organs. To illustate his point, he extols
her cinnabar grotto for its "pure, clustered flower pistil." When he
enters her, he says, "I felt the tip of my jade stalk pressing against
your tender parts, as if being drenched with melted lard, and I felt
even my hair melting. Sometimes I put my fingers on your rear
opening and felt it contracting and leaping, telling me that you
would soon rejoice. Then I paused until your rosebud stopped
leaping, so that I might renew and redouble your pleasure." He
then contrasts their own connoisseurship to the clumsiness of

sexually illiterate men and women who, "like beggars, having consumed three buckets of lard, pride themselves on achieving the height of sensuality."

Whether literary eroticism from wild history or clinical observation from sexology treatises, the ancient Chinese preoccupation with sexuality is undeniable.

7

Three Peaks, Five Desires, and Nine Essences

Secrets of Love-Play

SOME TWO THOUSAND YEARS AGO, the love doctors of ancient China specifically prescribed foreplay as essential to sexual health. The sexology classics emphasize leisurely and, when desired, lingering foreplay. Such love-play is necessary so that sexual partners "harmonize Yin and Yang." Although this explanation was couched in the context of another culture, it would be understood by any discerning Western sexologist today.

The wise women and men of the East linked male impotence and female frigidity to unsatisfactory foreplay, or its total absence. In *The Classic of the Elemental Maid,* the Yellow Emperor, that ever inquisitive pupil who poses questions most men are afraid to raise, asks one of his tutors about a curse plaguing men in his day as in ours: "Sometimes I want intercourse, yet my jade stalk will not rise up. My face betrays my shame, and my perspiration drops like pearls. My heart and my sentiments are fired by lust, but I have to help with my fingers. How can I be strong? Please enlighten me on this Tao."

The Elemental Maid's reply: "What Your Majesty describes happens to all men. In order to unite with a woman, a man should have ample preparations to harmonize his *chi.* In this way the jade stalk will rise up." By observing the symptoms of erotic pleasure in the woman and acting in a harmonious and wholesome way, she says, a man can strengthen his virility and have an erection at every union. "This way he will be admired by his [bedroom] adversary," she adds. "How could he be ashamed of that!"

In *The Classic of the Arcane Maid,* the Yellow Emperor tells the Arcane Maid that he has learned much of the art of Yin and Yang from the Elemental Maid, but would like further enlightenment from her. The Arcane Maid replies: "Everything between heaven and earth is quickened by the interaction of Yin and Yang. Yang is animated by Yin. Yin is vivified by Yang. When Yin and Yang act harmoniously, the male will be firm and powerful, and the female will open to him."

The emperor says: "Sometimes at intercourse the woman is not moved. Her essences are not stirred, and her fluids do not appear. The man's jade stalk is not strong. It remains small and not angry. Why?" The Arcane Maid attributes unsatisfactory sexual unions to a lack of harmony between Yin and Yang. "Yin and Yang stimulate and respond to each other. Yang without Yin is joyless, and Yin without Yang is unexcited. The man wants to copulate but the woman is not happy; the woman wants to copulate but the man has no desire. When two hearts are not in tune, the essences are not aroused. . . . Love and pleasure are not elicited.

"But if the man woos the woman and the woman woos the man, their sentiments and their minds will merge, and they will delight each other's heart. The woman's passion will be aroused, and she will fondle the man's stalk. She will make it powerful, so it can rap at her jewel terrace, and bring an abundance of secretions for both partners. The jade stalk will be greatly enlarged and will move, sometimes slowly, sometimes rapidly. The jade gate will open, easing the entry of the strong adversary and absorbing its essence to irrigate the scarlet chamber."

The Mystic Master of the Grotto, in the classic named for him, echoes the Arcane Maid on the same subject: "Heaven revolves to the left and Earth rotates to the right. Spring and summer wilt, autumn and winter follow. Man sings, woman accompanies. Action above and compliance below. This is the nature of things. If man rocks and woman responds not, if woman moves and man follows not, their congress will not only injure the man but also harm the woman. For this is counter to the nature of Yin and

Yang, and opposed to the order of events. To unite in such a way gives no benefit to either. Therefore, when man revolves to the left, woman should rotate to the right; when man thrusts from above, woman should respond from below. Only if they unite in this manner will Heaven and Earth be in balance."

Essentials of the Jade Chamber proposes the same theme by quoting the legendary Peng Tsu, who purportedly lived to the age of 800 by taking health tonics and mastering the art of the jade chamber. This Chinese Methusaleh said: "The Tao of sexual intercourse contains no miracle, except that one should act leisurely, evenly, and gradually. Harmony is most valued." *Essentials of the Jade Chamber* also quotes a Taoist sexologist: "The Tao of copulating with a woman starts with lingering frolic and play, and continues until she is harmonious in spirit and moved in thought. Only after extended play should intercourse begin."

In today's terminology, all this philosophizing about Yin and Yang means that partners need to get the juices flowing prior to consummation. They must induce and seduce one another into the proper mood. This leads to a grand and delicious result: the energizing of the man and the satisfaction of the woman, or joyous and healthy sexual union.

The classics prescribe the essentials of love-play and explain how to judge whether a partner has been "harmonized" for the final consummation. They concentrate mainly on male action and female response, probably because characteristically blundering male partners are in greater need of such advice. The Taoists considered the woman not only the repository of life, but also the fountainhead of sexual wisdom.

Thus the Elemental Maid teaches the Yellow Emperor about foreplay: "At the time of sexual union, let the man first ask the woman to lie down flat on her back and bend her legs. The man then gets between her spread thighs. He holds her lips in his mouth and sucks on her tongue. Holding his jade stalk, he strikes the east and west sides of her gate for about a meal's time." In ancient China, it should be pointed out, there was no such thing as fast food.

THE ART OF THE THREE PEAKS

Essentials of the Jade Chamber features a dialogue between Peng Tsu and the Iridescent Maid, one of the three female tutors to the

Yellow Emperor. Sent by the emperor to learn some of the expertise of the ancient master, she hears Peng's instructions to the male partner: "Play with her cinnabar field. Seek what is in her mouth. Press her body deeply and palpate it gently to bring about her essences. When the woman responds to the man's Yang she exhibits these symptoms: Her ears are hot, as if she has drunk rich wine. Her breasts protrude firmly and fill his hands. Her neck moves about; her legs shake agitatedly. She tries to restrain her lascivious motions, but suddenly she clasps his body." Peng Tsu's counsel here is especially intriguing. His words "press her body deeply and palpate it gently" accurately describe a basic technique in ancient Chinese massage aiming at acupoints. The erotic variety of this acupressure can be a most effective aphrodisiac.

The venerable master goes on to extol the benefit of exchanging saliva during foreplay and coitus. The juices from the "five viscera," he explains, flow out under the tongue as saliva, which was considered an elixir by Taoists. Saliva was not the only such tonic. Ko Hung (281–341), a Taoist philosopher, alchemist, and sexologist who contributed much to the development of ancient Chinese scientific thought, mentioned in his book *The Master Who Embraces Simplicity (Pao Pu Tzu)* that the Han dynasty minister Chang Tsang lived 180 years as a result of his ingesting breast secretions of women.

Peng Tsu's idea of sipping saliva at love-play and Ko Hung's tale of sipping breast secretions to abet longevity must have touched off a real fad among sex cultists in later centuries. "Alchemists of sex" proposed the drawing of three fluids from the female body as elixirs for men: saliva from the Red Lotus Peak, milk from the Twin Lotus Peaks, and vaginal secretions from the Purple Agaric Peak. The word "peak" seems inappropriate at least for two of the three bodily locations, and the pluck-and-nurture manuals of the sexual alchemists do not bother to explain this choice of term. It makes sense, however, if we consider a woman's tongue as the Red Lotus Peak, and her clitoris as the Purple Agaric Peak. Purple agaric (the color refers to its stalk) is the most valued of the five varieties of *ling-chih,* or "divine mushrooms"; the Chinese treasure it, believing it promotes health and longevity.

Male aficionados of this Art of the Three Peaks were advised to choose women who had not yet borne a child, so the inclusion of milk is puzzling. In fact, some Chinese concoctions have been known to produce milk in virgins. As for nutritious value in the three elixirs, only breast milk is known to have any. (Should a sexology laboratory seek experimental proof of this ancient nutrition theory, however, it probably would be swamped by volunteers, of both sexes, interested in the ways of science.) What is important here is the erotic efficacy of the Art of the Three Peaks. The sex alchemists' handbooks specify quite clearly that during foreplay and coitus, men should drink the three elixirs directly from their sources.

Saliva, or "water from the heavenly pool," was sipped by both the man and the woman while kissing. In drinking the essence from the Twin Lotus Peaks, also called "coral juice," whether the man actually gets any fluid is not as important as what he does to the nipples and areolas in the process. And as to the absorption of secretions from the Purple Agaric Peak, the handbooks describe the method rather cryptically: The man inserts his jade stalk as a sort of drinking straw, then "crouches down in the manner of a tortoise," using the techniques of *chi-kung* (a Taoist meditative art) to suck or "pluck" the secretions, and finally stores this essence in his cinnabar field.

This description may sound metaphysical, but at least one ancient sex alchemist allegedly demonstrated the technique to an emperor and his ladies in his inner palace. He put his jade stalk in a teacup filled with water, sucked up the water, then expelled it. This probably is a lost art in China. Yogis in India are capable of accomplishing much the same feat through the rectum, and similar but lesser prowess may be observed at Parisian sex shows, where female performers pick up coins or puff on cigarettes with their genitals. Whether ancient or contemporary, whether for health or for entertainment, these feats point to one thing: The smooth muscles of the genitourinary region, controlled by the autonomic nervous system and normally involuntary, can function at will—with enough practice. For centuries Taoists have explored various functions of the autonomic nervous system to enhance health and sexuality. Some of their techniques are detailed in later chapters.

Drinking with the mouth from the Purple Agaric Peak is often described lyrically in bedchamber literature as "drinking at the jade fountain." The sixth-century poet Hsu Ling, in a letter to a friend who had retired and was living in the mountains with a female companion, congratulated his friend on having ample time available to "practice the art of the Elemental Maid." He added enviously: "Why bother with the elixir of immortality when you can drink at the jade fountain!"

Quenching one's thirst at the jade fountain is mentioned less frequently in the literature of later centuries. A few decades ago, however, some linguistic evidence was found. In northern China, a man whose livelihood was pleasing women, the equivalent of a gigolo or a male mistress, was scornfully called a "dish licker." In eastern China, a man adept at pleasing women orally was often teasingly called a "champion melon-seed cracker." The Chinese love to eat roasted watermelon seeds, and some are experts at tossing a seed into their mouth, cracking it with their teeth, separating the broken shell from the kernel with their tongue, swallowing the kernel, and spitting out the neatly broken shell, all within a few seconds—and doing this repeatedly, and in rapid succession. A virtuoso in oral-genital kissing thus was likened to a man who could eat melon seeds with such skill and gusto.

The female activity corresponding to drinking at the jade fountain is "playing the flute." Because of the ancient Chinese taboo against squandering male semen, flute-playing was generally limited to dry runs.

Flute-playing, and drinking at the jade fountain

FOUR ATTAINMENTS, NINE ESSENCES, FIVE DESIRES

The ancient classics, as has been mentioned, place the utmost importance on foreplay. When the Yellow Emperor asks whether he should force himself at the task, if he wants to have intercourse but has no erection, the Arcane Maid warns him: "The only right time to have intercourse is after the man has achieved his Four Attainments. Only then can he bring the woman her Nine Essences."

The tutor then explains to the emperor why the man must await the Four Attainments: "If the jade stalk is not angry, his harmonious essence has not arrived. If it is angry but not large, his muscle essence has not arrived. If it is large but not rigid, his bone essence has not arrived. If it is rigid but not hot, his spirit essence has not arrived." Even if a man has an erection, he cannot perform the act with flying colors unless all four conditions are attained.

The emperor then asks about the woman's Nine Essences: What are they, and how can he tell when they have been aroused? The Arcane Maid answers: "Wait for the Nine Essences in order to learn about them. When the woman sighs deeply and swallows her saliva, her lung essence has been aroused. When she utters little cries and sucks his mouth, her heart essence has been aroused. When she enfolds and clings to him, her spleen essence has been aroused. When her Yin gate is slippery and damp, her kidney essence has been aroused. When she obligingly gnaws him, her bone essence has been aroused. When she hooks her legs around him, her sinew essence has been aroused. When she caresses his jade stalk, her blood essence has been aroused. When she fondles his nipples, her flesh essence has been aroused." (The link between a slippery Yin gate and kidney essence is due to the fact that in traditional Chinese medicine, the term for "kidney" denotes also "gonad.")

Only eight of the essences are enumerated here. The ninth, mentioned in none of the reconstructed editions of *The Classic of the Arcane Maid,* probably is the liver essence. Although it is missing from the literature, this essence, like the others, should never be missing in practice. The Arcane Maid goes on to say that if a man wants to have sufficiently lasting intercourse with a woman, he should first toy with her clitoris and move her spirits until all Nine Essences have been aroused. Anything less than nine will not benefit her.

When the Yellow Emperor asks the Elemental Maid how he might tell whether a woman is enjoying herself erotically, she instructs him to watch for the Five Desires, the Five Symptoms, and the Ten Movements. Here are presented only the Five Desires, which are revealed during foreplay; the Five Symptoms and Ten Movements, observed mostly during actual coitus, will be described in the next chapter.

The Elemental Maid enumerates the Five Desires as follows: "If the woman bates her breath and restrains her energy, her mind wishes it [sexual union]. If her nostrils and mouth are dilated, her vulva wants it. If she abruptly embraces the man, she wants to ejaculate. If her perspiration drenches her clothes, she wants her heart filled. If she straightens her body and closes her eyes, she is near ecstasy."

MYSTIC MASTERY

The Mystic Master of the Grotto, Tung Hsuan Tzu, advises how to meet all the various prerequisites for happy and healthy sex. In the preface to his classic work, he claims that he intended it to supplement and expand the teachings of the Arcane Maid. Written in the typically bold and elegant literary style of Tang classical literature, his work is a poetic essay graced by rhythmic symmetry, graphic imagery, and lyrical ardor. His treatment of love-play is the most detailed among the older sexology classics.

Whoever this Mystic Master of the Grotto was, he left invaluable tips for a healthy sex life, and he had the insight to caution that what he set forth should not be a "single path" for unoriginal lovers, but should open "ten thousand ways" for inventive ones. He was not just a "sex therapist," but a real sage of eroticism.

Master Tung Hsuan cautions that the sexual act from foreplay to coitus should not unfold in a repetitious, predictable manner: "Deep and shallow, slow and rapid, leveling and jerking, eastward and westward. The principle has no single path, but ten thousand ways. It could be as slow as the carp toying with the fish hook, and as swift as a flock of birds encountering the wind. Advance and retreat by dragging or coaxing; follow and oppose up or down; go and return leftward or rightward; withdraw and thrust infrequently or repeatedly: all these actions should be coordinated and devised spontaneously. Never confine yourself to a rigid formula, but choose the style according to the need of the moment."

The master offers a description of foreplay, with four basic positions: Conversing in Loving Entanglement; Whispering Endearments; Exposed Fish Gills (suggesting the open, blood-engorged vulva); and Unicorn's Horn (the male erection). "To start the sexual union, the male sits left, the female sits right. He sits cross-legged, holding her to his chest. He encircles her slim waist and caresses her jade body. They whisper endearments, converse while lovingly entangled. Their hearts and their minds are one. Suddenly they embrace, and just as suddenly resist. Two forms seize at each other, and two mouths nibble at each other. He holds her lower lip in his mouth; she holds his upper lip in hers. They suck at the same time, drink each other's saliva. Each leisurely bites the tongue of the other, or softly gnaws the lips. Each tenderly embraces the head of the other, or boldly fingers the ears. They massage above and pat below; they nibble in the east, kiss in the west. A thousand coquetries are revealed; a hundred worries dissolve. He asks her to hold the jade stalk with her left hand, and he strokes her jade gate with his right. Stimulated by her Yin essence, his jade stalk begins throbbing. It rises precipitously, a lone peak above a distant river. Excited by his Yang essences, her cinnabar grotto oozes with fluids. It drips and bubbles, a secluded spring tumbling into a deep valley."

The master underlines that this stimulation occurs only as a result of the interaction between Yin and Yang: "It cannot be forced through willful efforts. Only when these conditions exist should sexual union begin. If the male is not excited to a zestful erection or if the female emits no fluids, it indicates an outer manifestation of some inner illness."

Next the master describes the initiation of intercourse: "The female is on the left, the male on the right. She first sits, then lies down on her back, spreads her legs, and unfolds her arms. The male kneels between her thighs. He immediately drags his hardened jade stalk lengthwise against the doors of the jade gate, a sloping, luxuriant pine tree nudging at the entrance of an unexpected valley. The jade stalk throbs, pulls, grinds, and bridles. He kisses her mouth and seeks her tongue. Now he gazes at the jade face above, now he looks at the golden gulch below. He strokes and pats the front of her abdomen and breasts, massages the sides of her examination hall. When he is aroused and she is enchanted, he at once uses his Yang peak to assault vertically and horizontally, now impinging on the jade vein below, now pressing at the golden gulch above, now stabbing at the sides of the examination hall, now resting on the right of the jewel terrace."

Here ends the script for love-play, after which the Mystic Master prescribes manners of actual intercourse. His graphic tableaux, like the explicit and sometimes florid instructions for love-play in other classics, are prescriptions for an energetic, passionate, and beneficial sexual union.

8

Clouds and Rain

Positions of Lovemaking

THE FOCUS of the Art of the Bedchamber, sexual intercourse, is termed by generations of Chinese writers more poetically as "clouds and rain." Unlike poets and novelists, the authors of the sexology classics and the love doctors they quote dispense their wisdom more for instruction than for literary beauty. Their language is characteristically explicit and clinical. This does not, however, mean that it is completely without poetry.

Since the purposes of sex in ancient China were procreation, health, and pleasure, the techniques recommended in sexology texts were oriented toward one or all of these goals. Ancient sexologists prescribed specific ways of sexual union for fitness and for conceiving healthy, bright babies. Sex was said to be helpful in sharpening eyesight and hearing; in enriching blood; in curing headaches, drunkenness, and hemorrhoids; and in treating impotence, and frigidity, and of all things, sexual excess.

The bedchamber artists considered tactical maneuvers necessary for harmonizing the mood of the couple. They devised a variety of practices and positions to spice up the connubial act, which could go stale with time. One technique, known as "dead entry, live exit," involved the insertion of a limp jade stalk into the cinnabar grotto, and withdrawal of the now rigid jade stalk before it ejaculated. This was done at times to arouse a languid man, and at times for health benefits. Coital rhythm included a range of thrust patterns (nine-shallow, one-deep; three-shallow, one-deep; three-slow, one-fast, and so on), devised because variation and surprise made them stimulating—sometimes excruciatingly so— to the woman. Early sexologists preferred a brief duration for sexual union, usually only until the woman reached her orgasm. Later sexologists generally let the duration of intercourse depend on male stamina. All ancient sexologists believed in female orgasm and favored infrequent male ejaculation, or its absence altogether. Like some Western sexologists today, they believed that male orgasm and male ejaculation were not necessarily the same. Thus the technique for delaying or forestalling the male climax became all-important. The purpose was ostensibly a serious one aimed at health, but it was also a roguish strategy to heighten erotic pleasure.

The bedchamber sages must have had a rousing time filling out their prescriptions. Some are not very practical for today's lifestyle. One, for instance, states that copulating in a certain position will help strengthen bones and eliminate vaginal odor. The man, however, must make nine thrusts nine times at each of nine sessions per day for nine consecutive days.

To make the large number of complex ingredients of the Art of the Bedchamber more intelligible to modern readers, I present them here in the following sequence: tactical maneuvers; coital positions; coital dynamics and timing; and the delaying, curbing, or avoidance of male ejaculation. The ancients never gave a name to the last practice; I call this mind-body technique "orgasmic-brinkmanship."

Maneuvers in the Dark

In the classics that bear their names, both the Arcane Maid and the Elemental Maid give advice on tactical maneuvers in bed. The Arcane Maid, without any elaboration, enumerates the eight basic movements that will benefit both sexual partners: "Extending and contracting, prostrating and supinating, advancing and retreating, bending and curving."

The Elemental Maid is more detailed in her advice, and she speaks directly to the male partner. The Yellow Emperor, as we saw in the previous chapter, wonders how to tell whether his female partner is enjoying intercourse. The Elemental Maid describes the Five Symptoms in the woman and prescribes the appropriate male responses. "When her face is flushed, gradually begin the intercourse. When her breasts are engorged and her nose perspires, slowly insert the jade stalk. When her throat is dry and she is swallowing her saliva, leisurely rock the jade stalk. When her grotto is slippery, slowly penetrate her to the depths. When her fluids flow to her buttocks, slowly pull out the jade stalk." Although the Elemental Maid appears to be advising the male, her instructions apply only to the early stages of the encounter, before it becomes passionate.

The Elemental Maid also describes the Ten Movements of a woman in the throes of passion, and the urges that impel her: "If she clasps him with her arms, she wants to press their bodies together and have their genitals touch. If she extends her thighs, she wants to rub her upper vulva against him. If she constricts her belly, she wants to ejaculate. If she shakes her buttocks, she is experiencing intense pleasure. If she raises her feet and hooks them around him, she wants to be penetrated deeper. If she crosses her thighs, she is itchy inside. If she rocks to the sides, she wants to be sliced deeply left and right. If she raises her body to press against his, her lascivious joy is extreme. If she stretches her body lengthwise, her limbs and torso are pleased. If her sexual fluids are slippery, she has ejaculated. Observe these movements and you will know how great is her ecstasy."

These words, written some two thousand years ago, might sound surprisingly enlightened to the modern reader. They reveal something about the deepest sexual secrets of women—and they come straight from a woman's lips.

The first known systematic descriptions of human lovemaking positions, with clinical and graphic details, are found in the sexology classics of ancient China. The Arcane Maid's discussion of the Nine Ways, one of the oldest known such texts in the world, in effect offers nine positions for intercourse, with brief descriptions of coital motions and health benefits.

To retain the flavor of the ancient texts, the passages on the nine positions from *The Classic of the Arcane Maid* and on the thirty positions from *The Mystic Master of the Grotto* are rendered here in a translation as close to the original as possible. My own explanations and comments are in brackets.

THE ARCANE MAID'S NINE POSITIONS

Somersaulting Dragons: The woman lies on her back with the man prostrate on top of her, pressing her thighs into the bed. She pulls at her vulva to receive his jade stalk. He thrusts at her grain seed and attacks also the upper part with leisurely, deliberate strokes. Eight shallow, two deep. The jade stalk goes in dead and returns alive, so that he grows vigorous and powerful. She is agitated and pleased, joyous like a singsong girl. He refrains from ejaculating. A hundred illnesses will vanish.

[This position is the traditional no-frills missionary position. "Grain seed" is about five inches into the vaginal canal. "Eight shallow, two deep" means eight shallow thrusts followed by two deep ones. A "dead" jade stalk is limp, a "live" one rigid.]

Stepping Tigers: The woman lies in a crawling position with her buttocks up and her head down. The man kneels behind her, clasping her belly. He inserts his jade stalk and pierces her innermost part as deeply and intimately as he can. They advance and retreat in mutual attacks. Eight thrusts, five times. This should be sufficient. Her jade gate closes and opens. Her fluids seep out. They rest when this happens. A hundred illnesses will not appear, and the man becomes more virile.

[This is the rear-entry position natural to all mammals. The Arcane Maid calls it Stepping Tigers because the participants advance and retreat like a pair of tigers. In this position the jade stalk does not stimulate the clitoris, but it can penetrate to the flower heart. "Eight thrusts, five times" means a total of forty thrusts, with a brief pause after every eight.]

Stepping Tigers

Wrestling Apes: The woman lies on her back. The man supports her thighs, pushes her knees past her bosom, and raises her buttocks and back. He inserts his jade stalk, stabbing her scented mouse. She quivers and rocks. Her fluids are like the rain. He presses into her deeply, without moving, as his stalk grows strong and angry. He ceases when she rejoices. A hundred illnesses will cure themselves.

[A favorite position of the ancient Chinese, this allows deep penetration; in this particular case, however, the man is instructed to reach only the "scented mouse," or three inches deep. When the woman "rejoices" here, she reaches orgasm.]

Cleaving Cicadas: The woman lies face down and extends her body. The man lies on her back and inserts his jade stalk deeply. He raises her buttocks slightly so that he can rap at her scarlet pearls. Nine thrusts, six times. She is excited, and her fluids flow. The inside of her Yin throbs rapidly; the outside spreads and opens. He stops when she rejoices. The seven injuries will eliminate themselves.

[This rear-entry position permits only relatively shallow penetration and limited mobility. "Scarlet pearls" are the labia minora, and "Yin" is the vagina.]

Mounting Tortoises: The woman lies on her back and bends her knees. The man pushes her feet until her knees reach her breasts. He inserts his jade stalk deeply, at times poking at her infant girl. With measured deep and shallow thrusts he reaches her grain seed. She is moved to great joy, and shakes and raises her torso. When her fluids overflow, he pierces deeper. He stops when she rejoices. If he does this without loss of semen, his vigor will increase a hundredfold.

[This position, similar to Wrestling Apes except that the man holds the woman's legs instead of her buttocks, was another favorite ancient Chinese position for deep penetration and high mobility. "Infant girl" refers to the vestibular glands between the labia minora.]

Soaring Phoenix: The woman lies down and raises her legs. The man kneels between her thighs, his hands on the mat. He inserts his jade stalk deeply, piercing her mixed rock. When he guides it in rigid and hot, he asks her to begin moving. Eight thrusts, three times. With their buttocks swiftly attacking each other, her Yin opens and expands, pouring out its fluids. He stops when she rejoices. A hundred illnesses will disappear.

[Note that the coital movements here are carried out mainly by the woman. The "phoenix" in the name refers to the Chinese mythical *feng huang* bird. "Mixed rock" means four inches deep.]

Bunny Licking Its Fur: The man lies on his back and stretches his legs straight. The woman, above him, straddles his body, her knees to the sides. Her back faces his head, while she herself faces his feet. She holds on to the mat and lowers her head. He inserts his jade stalk and pierces her lute strings. She rejoices, and her fluids flow like a fountain. Joyous delight and harmonious pleasure move her spirit and her body. He stops when she rejoices. A hundred illnesses will not arise.

[This position, with the woman above and the man passive, leaves the initiative to the woman. "Lute strings" means one inch inside the Yin. As the penetration is shallow, the woman needs a bit of practice to forestall the dislocation of their organs. The "licking bunny" here is the male organ.]

Fish Linking Scales: The man lies straight on his back. The woman, above him and facing his head, straddles his body with her thighs. She securely and slowly inserts him, stopping when he is only slightly in. He does not penetrate deeply, but instead imitates a baby sucking at the breast. The woman rocks by herself for a long period. He withdraws when she rejoices. This cures all clogging illnesses.

[A variation of Bunny Licking Its Fur, with the woman facing the man's head. Instead of sitting all the way down, here she effects the penetration by moving her loins forward for a moderate penetration but a lengthy union. This position allows the man to enjoy the scenic sight of twin peaks.]

Cranes Entwining Necks: The man squats. The woman rides astride his thighs, her hands holding his neck. She inserts his jade stalk, letting it pierce her wheat bud and stab her seed. He clasps her buttocks to help her rocking and rising. She feels great joy, and her fluids flow and bubble. He stops when she rejoices. The seven injuries will be cured naturally.

[Another position with the woman above, which gives her somewhat less mobility and shallower penetration. "Wheat bud" means two inches deep, and "seed" is the clitoris.]

These nine are all basic postures upon which any couple with a minimum of inventiveness would stumble in their nocturnal play. The last three positions all have the woman above and give her most of the initiative. The cursory, unspecific remarks about curing illnesses at the end of each description, by the way, appear to be decorative, even obligatory, and probably were inserted by later editors.

For all these positions, the Arcane Maid advises the couple to end their union right after the moment of female orgasm. It seems she believed that the man, in order to improve his health and sexual stamina, should not ejaculate at all. Whatever the medical, physiological, and scientific validity of her proposal, she is consistent on one point: At every sexual union, the woman is allowed to "rejoice."

THE MYSTIC MASTER'S THIRTY POSITIONS

Several centuries after *The Classic of the Arcane Maid* appeared, the Mystic Master of the Grotto enumerated thirty coital positions in his own classic. His text would become the basis for later writings on sexual positions, and even modern Japanese schemes can be traced back to it. The Mystic Master intended that his thirty positions amplify the Arcane Maid's original nine. Under the name of each position, he offered a very brief and at times cryptic description. His positions are strictly *tableaux vivants*—still pictures, devoid of motion. Immediately after the positions, however, he set forth separately the dynamic aspects of sexual intercourse in fifteen coital movements. Theoretically, any of the fifteen movements can be applied to any of the thirty positions. The variations, if any pair of sexual partners have the time to experiment, come to 390, excluding the foreplay positions.

The first four (foreplay) positions were described in the previous chapter, so the list here thus begins with the fifth. Perhaps because of errors in or damage to manuscripts, the descriptions of some positions are unclear or puzzling. Only in these cases is the translation less literal; liberties have been taken for clarity's sake. Again, all my comments are in brackets.

Silkworms Entangling: The woman lies on her back, her hands hugging the man's neck and her feet crossing above his back. He kneels between her spread thighs while clasping her neck. He inserts his jade stalk.

[The position is similar to the Arcane Maid's Somersaulting Dragons; here, however, the woman's feet cross above the man's waist.]

Dragons Twisting: The woman lies on her back, bending her legs. The man kneels within her thighs, his left hand pushing her feet forward until they are past her breasts. His right hand inserts the jade stalk into the jade gate.

[This is a variation on the Arcane Maid's Wrestling Apes and Mounting Tortoises.]

Fish Eye-to-Eye: The man and woman lie down facing each other and suck at each other's lips and tongues. She raises one leg above his body while he spreads his legs slightly. With one hand supporting her upraised leg, he inserts his jade stalk into her cinnabar grotto.

[As the partners both lie on their sides, this position frees each of the other's body weight.]

Swifts Sharing a Heart: The woman lies on her back, her legs extended. The man crouches on her abdomen, his hands embracing her neck. She hugs his waist with her hands. He inserts his jade stalk into her cinnabar grotto.

[This is the missionary position, as in the Arcane Maid's Somersaulting Dragons.]

Kingfishers Uniting: The woman lies on her back with her knees raised. The man positions himself between her thighs in a Tartar squat. He embraces her waist with his hands and inserts his jade stalk into her lute strings.

[This position requires very flexible knees on the man's part and is not too comfortable for non-Tartars. The Tartar squat, a customary position of that northern people, here involves the man's putting his knees on the ground while sitting on his left heel.]

Mandarin Ducks Joining: The woman lies on her side, crooking her legs, with her upper leg on the man's buttocks. He faces her back and rides on her lower thigh, raising one knee against her upper thigh. He inserts his jade stalk.

[The instruction in the original manuscript is unclear, perhaps representing an error. Probably the woman lies on her side and raises one leg, while the man faces her spread thighs from the back and with his bent knee supports her raised thigh.]

Butterflies Fluttering: The man lies on his back, his legs extended. The woman sits astride him, facing his head, her two feet on the bed. She uses her hand to insert his Yang peak into her jade gate.
    [This is similar to the Arcane Maid's Fish Linking Scales.]

Butterflies Fluttering

Wild Ducks Flying Backward: The man lies on his back, his legs extended. The woman sits on him with her back to his face, her feet holding on to the bed. She lowers her head and holds the jade stalk to insert it into the cinnabar grotto.
    [This is similar to the Arcane Maid's Bunny Licking Its Fur.]

Sheltering the Reclining Pine: The woman lies on her back and crosses her feet [behind the man's waist]. The man holds her waist with his hands, and she holds his with hers. He inserts his jade stalk into her jade gate.
    [This position also might be called "Sheltering the Missionary."]

Wild Ducks Flying Backward

Bamboos by the Altar: The man and the woman stand facing each other; they embrace and kiss. He pierces her cinnabar grotto deeply with his Yang peak, all the way to her Yang terrace.
    [This, obviously enough, is a stand-up union. It is not recommended for partners who differ much in height.]

Twin Phoenixes Dancing: Two women lie one on top of the other, face to face. The one facing up crooks her legs and the other rides on her, their jade gates facing each other. The man sits cross-legged, exposing his jade object, and attacks both above and below.
    [Another possible error in the original manuscript. The man would be hindered by his own knees; it would be much easier for him if he knelt or stood. This *pas de trois* inspired a Ming position, Gobbling Fish, in which the women were instructed to rub their jade gates against each other before the man joined them.]

Phoenix Holding Fledglings: If the woman is big and fat, she can add a diminutive man to join in her intercourse. This is great excellence!

[Something must have been lost or deleted in this reconstructed manuscript, as nothing else about the position is given. There is the intriguing suggestion of another *pas de trois,* here involving a woman and two men.]

Seagulls Soaring: The man stands near the edge of the bed and lifts the woman's legs high. He inserts his jade stalk into her baby palace.

["Baby palace" here is the vagina; now the term is used only for the uterus. This instruction probably was edited in later centuries: the man could not stand as described and still effect the union on the low bed customarily used during and before the Tang dynasty, when *The Mystic Master of the Grotto* is known to have been written; higher beds came into use only after that era. In a pinch, this position can be used on a desk or dining table.]

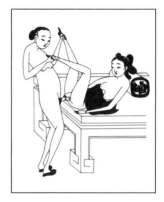

Seagulls Soaring

Wild Horses Leaping: The woman lies on her back. The man lifts her feet and puts them over his shoulders. He inserts the jade stalk deeply into the jade gate.

[This feet-on-shoulders position, a variation of the preceding, was especially popular in ancient China.]

Steeds Galloping: The woman lies on her back. The man crouches, one hand holding her neck, the other lifting her leg. He inserts his jade stalk into her baby palace.

[If the man reclines instead of crouching, he has a more comfortable position while maintaining the unusual angle.]

Wild Horses Leaping

Horse Shaking Its Hoof: The man lifts one of the woman's legs and places it on his shoulder. The woman lifts her other leg herself. The man inserts the jade stalk deeply into the cinnabar grotto. Highly stimulating!

[The leg the woman lifts should be raised unsupported, so that it is like a shaking hoof at active moments.]

White Tiger Jumping: The woman kneels and lowers her face. The man kneels behind her, his hands holding her waist. He inserts his jade stalk into her baby palace.

[This is almost identical to the Arcane Maid's Stepping Tigers, except that the participants do not step back and forth.]

Dusky Cicadas Cleaving: The woman lies on her abdomen, her legs extended. The man positions himself between her thighs with his legs bent. He holds her neck with his hands. He inserts the jade stalk into her jade gate from behind.

[This is same as the Arcane Maid's Cleaving Cicadas, except here the man holds her neck.]

Goat Hugging the Tree: The man sits with legs extended. The woman sits on his lap, her back to his face. She lowers her head to look at the insertion of the jade stalk. He suddenly hugs her waist, bridling and thrusting.

Steeds Galloping

Jungle Fowl Approaching the Arena: The man squats Tartar style on the bed. A young maid servant holds his jade stalk and inserts it into the jade gate of his partner. Then the maid stands at his back, tugging the hems of the other woman's skirts to enliven her legs. Highly exciting!

[A pampered man in those days might require a young maidservant to help him in his hard labor.]

Phoenix Sporting in the Cinnabar Grotto: The woman lies on her back and lifts her feet with her hands. The man kneels next to her, his hands holding on to the bed. He inserts his jade stalk into her cinnabar grotto. Very elegant!

[This is a variation of the Arcane Maid's Wrestling Apes and Mounting Tortoises.]

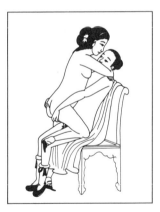

Humming Ape Embracing the Tree

Roc Soaring over Dark Sea: The woman lies on her back. The man puts her feet on his upper arms. He stretches his hands down to clasp her waist, then inserts his jade stalk.

[This is a variation of Seagulls Soaring and Wild Horses Leaping.]

Humming Ape Embracing the Tree: The man sits with his legs extended. The woman straddles his thighs, embracing him. He uses one hand to hold her buttocks, and the other to hold on to the bed. He inserts his jade stalk.

[This is a musical variation of the Arcane Maid's Cranes Entwining Necks.]

Cat and Mouse Sharing a Hole: The man lies on his back, his legs extended. The woman crouches on top of him, thighs spread, with his jade stalk deep inside her. Another man lies on her back, also inserting his jade stalk into her jade gate.

[The original manuscript is extremely cryptic, but unless it contains an error, this position involves two men and a woman.]

Donkeys of Spring: The woman holds on to the bed with her hands and feet. The man stands behind her, embracing her waist with his hands. He inserts the jade stalk into the jade gate. Very elegant!

[This position is quite stimulating to the woman who, however, requires some balance to crouch on all fours.]

Dogs of Autumn: The man and the woman both hold on to the bed with their hands and feet, back to back, their haunches pressing against each other. He lowers his head and uses one hand to push his jade object into the jade gate.

[This is the only bizarre position in this classic text. It is possible only if the woman's moon grotto is low-slung, if the man has a very long jade stalk, and if both partners have lean buttocks.]

Donkeys of Spring

Since the days of the Mystic Master, several additional sexual positions have been invented by other sexologists. Notable among them are *Spider Trapped in Its Own Web,* in which the woman dangles from a set of ropes that hang from the ceiling, as if on a swing, or rides on a horizontal bar, with her thighs spread; and *Feast of Peonies,* in which the man lies on his back with one woman riding him and another sitting on his face. The trio position, it should be pointed out, was in those days a respectable family union in traditionally polygamous China.

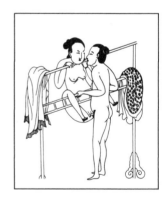

*Spider Trapped
in Its Own Web*

THE DANCE OF LIFE: THE NINE MANNERS AND SIX STYLES OF THE MYSTIC MASTER

The static poses of the Mystic Master listed above are enlivened by his coital dynamics. These are divided into two categories and listed immediately after the positions. The first category includes the Nine Manners of moving the jade stalk:

> The jade stalk may strike left and right, like a fierce warrior crashing through the enemy line.

It may climb up and jump down, like a wild horse leaping across a mountain torrent.

It may emerge and submerge, like a flock of gulls frolicking over crystal-clear waves.

It may tamp heavily and stir lightly, like birds pecking in a grain mortar.

It may penetrate deeply and skim shallowly, like a big rock thrown into the sea.

It may stir gradually and push slowly, like a chilled snake crawling into a cave.

It may loosen rapidly and pierce suddenly, like a frightened mouse dashing into a hole.

It may lift the head and hook the feet, like a green falcon teasing a tricky hare.

It may rear its top and dip its base, like a large sail bucking violent gusts.

The second category comprises the Six Styles of penetration:

In sexual unions, the jade stalk may be pressed firmly, sawing the jade gate back and forth, in the style of cutting open an oyster for its bright pearl.

It may tug at the jade vein below or shove into the golden gulch above, in the style of splitting a rock to search for beautiful jade.

The Yang peak may ram against the jewel terrace, in the style of an iron pestle pounding in an herb mortar.

The jade stalk may thrust and withdraw, assaulting left and right of the examination hall, in the style of five hammers pounding on heated iron.

The Yang peak may move to and fro, grinding and plowing between the divine field and the hidden valley, in the style of a farmer plowing his autumnal soil.

The dark garden and the heavenly court may grind against each other, in the style of two mighty peaks crushing together.

Here "dark garden" means the prepuce of the clitoris; "heavenly court," besides referring to the jade stalk, is the name of a high peak of the Kun Lun Mountains.

FURTHER DYNAMICS

It should be noted that the apparently specific instructions in this and other texts were not intended to turn sexual partners into technicians. Some classics inject brief but graphic descriptions of passionate coital scenes, which not only inspire lovemaking but lift the texts to the level of art.

The Elemental Maid, after advising the Yellow Emperor on how to arouse a woman with foreplay lasting "about a meal's time," goes on to instruct him:

> If the jade stalk is thick and large, insert it one and a half inches. If it is weaker and smaller, insert it one inch. Do not agitate or rock, but withdraw slowly, then insert it again. This will eliminate a hundred illnesses. Do not let the fluids seep out [between the connection]. When the jade stalk is thrust into the jade gate, it turns hot and urgent. The woman by her own will stirs and rocks her body, and presses herself upward against the man. When this happens, thrust deeply. A hundred illnesses will be eliminated for both the man and the woman. The jade stalk should pierce shallowly to the lute strings. Then the man should close his mouth and begin thrusting. One, two, three, four, five, six, seven, eight, nine. Penetrate the jade stalk deeply to the mixed rock. The man should put his mouth on the woman's and suck in her breaths. Perform the Tao of Nine Nines [eighty-one thrusts]. After this, stop.

After discussing foreplay, the Mystic Master of the Grotto instructs:

> When the woman's lubricious juices are bubbling in her cinnabar grotto, the man should at once put his Yang peak into her baby palace, and quickly make her ejaculate her essence. Her secretions will surge upward to the divine field and irrigate downward into the solitary valley [vestibular fossa]. He makes the jade stalk go back and forth, pressing and attacking, advancing and retreating, rubbing and grinding. She is bound to plead for death and for life. He wipes her dry with a piece of silk, then again inserts his jade stalk deep into the cinnabar grotto, all the way to the sun terrace [vestibular glands], a lofty cliff pressing into a deep valley. Then he practices the art of nine-shallow, one-deep. He rams vertically and jerks horizontally, pulls to the side and strokes slantingly. Suddenly it is slow, and suddenly it is rapid. It is either deep or shallow. Keep on for twenty-one inhalations and exhalations to await the exit and entry of *chi*. When the woman rejoices, the man swiftly loosens himself and suddenly pierces, using his hands to pull and restrain her hips, while elevating her legs high. Wait for her to move and rock.

Then, in time with her slow or quick movements, attack her grain seed with the Yang peak, then stab deeply into her baby palace, rubbing and grinding left and right, without bothering to pull out. Her fluids now are flowing and overflowing. The man must withdraw alive, not dead [without ejaculating]. It would greatly harm the man for his jade stalk to die. Beware of this!

Although the exact identity of the Mystic Master of the Grotto is shrouded in the mists of antiquity, his vivid writing makes him more than a sexologist. While the author of *The Classic of the Elemental Maid* and other anonymous writers wrote pithily and often cryptically, the Mystic Master was less restrained. He presents details in a phantasmagoria of light and sound. The choreography is animated. Especially vivid are his delicate arabesques, swift pirouettes, and various juxtapositions of *pas de deux*—and occasionally *pas de trois.* The music of his brush ranges from pianissimo to fortissimo, with moments of flowing largo and frenetic staccato. Whoever this Mystic Master was, he was a maestro of erotic orchestration and a gifted choreographer of lovemaking.

His descriptions may seem to suggest sexual encounters at which the man behaves like a perpetual pumping machine, capable of operating at any angle, bringing his partner to one orgasm after another and drowning her in her own secretions. These might be wishful tales of heroic erotica if one basic technique of the Art of the Bedchamber is not taken into account: namely, for the man to engage in coitus but delay or avoid ejaculation. This fundamental practice of ancient Taoist sexology, when practiced with self-discipline and finesse, became a delightful and useful art. According to the ancient sages, a man who mastered it could satisfy up to ten women in a single night sexually. And the practice, common in ancient and medieval China, was not limited to young men.

EJACULATION AND ORGASMIC BRINKMANSHIP

In *The Classic of the Elemental Maid,* the Iridescent Maid asks Peng Tsu a very natural question. How, she wonders, since the joy of sexual intercourse lies in ejaculating, could a man enjoy sex without discharging his semen? The old sage replies that after a man ejaculates, his ears ring, his eyelids droop, his throat dries up, and his joints ache. Whatever pleasures he takes in ejaculating are only momentary. But if he reaches the brink without ejaculation, he can preserve his energy and will thirst perpetually with love and passion for his partner. The Elemental Maid tells the Yellow Emperor about the benefits of reaching the brink without ejaculating. She is the same therapist who warns the emperor that celibacy is harmful.

The Mystic Master recommends that when the man wants to ejaculate, he should wait until his partner reaches orgasm. The Tang dynasty physician Sun Szu-mo (601–682), author of the medical classic *Prescriptions of a Thousand Goldpieces,* took a similar stand. He wrote that if a man has great sexual stamina, he should not hold back from ejaculating for too long, or he will suffer congestion and illness. Frequency of ejaculation, Sun said, should depend on a man's age and general health, and the season.

The ancient classics agree in general in their recommendations for male ejaculation schedules. Some of them give alternatives for the more vigorous and the less so. *The Classic of the Elemental Maid* says that virile young men between the ages of fifteen and twenty may ejaculate once a day, or several times a day if they are strong. At thirty a man may ejaculate once a day if he is strong, every two days if he is not. Men of forty may ejaculate once every three to four days; men of fifty once every five to ten days; men of sixty once every ten to twenty days; and men of seventy once every thirty days—or not at all if they are weak. *Prescriptions of a Thousand Goldpieces* gives these recommendations: At age twenty, men may ejaculate once every four days; at thirty, once every eight days; at forty once every sixteen days; at fifty, once every twenty-one days; and at sixty, once every month—or not at all if they are weak. *The Secret Art of the Jade Chamber* gives this advice: At age twenty, men may ejaculate once every two days; at thirty, once every three days; at forty, once every four days; at fifty, once every five days; and at sixty, not at all. *The Essentials of Nurturing Life,* quoting the Taoist Liu Ching, recommends an ejaculation once every three days in spring, twice a month in summer and fall, and none at all in winter. In the spring, Liu reasoned, a man's sexual essence is strong, while in winter it is weak. The book gives no recommendations according to age, so presumably these prescriptions are for the middle-aged.

Orgasmic brinkmanship—going to the brink but not over—as taught in ancient Chinese classics employs both psychosomatic and purely physiological techniques. The former are recommended when the man feels the approach of orgasm; the latter are applied as an emergency measure when ejaculation is imminent. Below is a summary of the recommendations in various classics:

In his *Prescriptions of a Thousand Goldpieces,* Sun Szu-mo teaches that whenever a man feels he is near ejaculation, he can control himself by opening his eyes wide, closing his mouth, and breathing through his nose with his diaphragm. Then, using his index and middle fingers, he should press firmly the *ping i* acupoint (found one inch above the right nipple) and gnash his teeth a thousand times.

Essentials of the Jade Chamber, quoting *The Classic of the Immortals,* teaches that a man may surmount the crisis by pressing his fingers on the *hui-yin* acupoint (found on the perineum between the anus and the penis) while breathing deeply and gnashing his teeth several dozen times.

The Secret Art of the Jade Chamber, quoting the second-century B.C. sexologist Wu Tzu-tu, says that a man may control himself by raising his head, stopping his breathing momentarily, shouting, and glaring left and right while contracting his abdomen. The text also prescribes pressing "below the genitals" with the left hand.

The Mystic Master of the Grotto advises the male partner to wait and time his own orgasm to coincide with that of the woman. He suggests these delaying tactics: The man should withdraw his jade stalk so that the insertion is only one or two inches deep—"like a nipple in an infant's mouth." Then he should close his eyes and concentrate while pressing his tongue on his palate, hunch his shoulders and stick out his head, dilate his nostrils and inhale deeply. This will not only delay his ejaculation but limit it to twenty to thirty percent of the normal emission when it does take place.

A Ming dynasty sexual-alchemical treatise with the formidable title *Interpretation of the Cultivation of Truth by the Great Immortal of the Purple-Gold Glory* echoes Wu Tzu-tu's recommendations. During copulation, it says, when the man is making three-shallow, one-deep thrusts and feels he is about to emit, he should withdraw his jade stalk so that it is only one or two inches deep, and wait until he calms down. Then he may resume his thrusting. The man is advised further to adopt a deliberate attitude of indifference toward his partner in order not to excite his passion.

Acupressure methods are very effective, but they should be only as an emergency measure, since apparent nonejaculation may mean an internal ejaculation into the bladder. This defeats the purpose of the exercise and may harm the man.

The ancients practiced orgasmic brinkmanship for two purposes. One was health—which included preserving the man's life essence and promoting longevity. The other involved the sex act itself—prolonging male activity and bringing the woman to her climax, repeatedly if desired. Which purpose was more important was—and is—a matter of personal choice. What is significant is that this technique is workable, even though it takes some practice and plenty of self-discipline. For modern lovers this opens new vistas on the erotic horizon. If a man is skilled in this art, with the cooperation of his partner he can create ecstatic pleasure for both of them in their lovemaking.

Sexologists in ancient China believed that blood and semen were different manifestations of *chi,* or life-energy. To their minds, semen was a much more concentrated form of life essence than blood. Any indiscriminate squandering of semen, and to a lesser extent, blood, would bring ill health, even death. Significantly, they used the terms "return alive" to describe the unejaculated phallus after coitus, and "return dead" to describe a spent phallus. Most earlier sexologists advocated limited male ejaculation, certainly for improved procreation, generally for health, and often for pleasure. The consensus of ancient Chinese sexologists was that both men and women must have sexual intercourse regularly for health and longevity, but that limited male ejaculation was essential. Female sexual essence was inexhaustible, according to the Taoists, and thus female orgasm and ejaculation would not harm a woman's health.

In light of this theory, rabid dogmatists, especially later sexual alchemists, took the extreme view that every ejaculation of male semen was a dire catastrophe. Out of this belief was born the bizarre—and at times hilarious—sexual practice of "pluck-and-nurture," described in the next chapter.

9

The Sexual Duel of Pluck-and-Nurture

Battling for the Elixir of Life

LIKE AN UNDULATING DRAGON, *the white wall with its wavy, tiled top encloses the secluded garden. On the far side, bamboos sway in the refreshing breezes of a summer evening. Goldfish swim languidly in an irregularly shaped pond fringed with greenery and spanned by a narrow, arched bridge of brilliant vermilion. On one side is a low, rambling house with curved eaves and upswept roof corners. The fragrance from a clump of jasmine bushes lends an intoxicating sensuousness to the air.*

A man and a woman sit by a table near a giant boulder. They sip warm rice wine from little porcelain cups and sample delicacies from several plates. The maidservant who brought the dishes has promptly disappeared. The man and woman converse in hushed tones. As the man continues talking, one of the long, loose sleeves of his muslin robe brushes against a pair of chopsticks, sending them off the table. He stoops down and crouches under the table to retrieve them. Instead his hand touches her small, dainty foot.

"Oh!" The woman gasps in apparent consternation. The man begins to fondle her feet. Her face blushes a shocking pink. He stands up and walks to her side. Holding her cringing shoulders with his hands, he puts his nose next to the nape of her neck to sniff-kiss her.

"Please! Please! Don't!" She whispers weak protestations. Then, as

his sniff-kisses reach her cheek, she suddenly turns her face and kisses him full on the mouth.

She always has appeared demure and ladylike, but he knows better. These women are all alike, with their cold shoulders and hot lips, their soft glances and hard nipples. Often he has sensed a hidden voluptuousness in this beautiful young widow, and he has worked for months to trap her. Their mating dance has been protracted. Veiled with traditional etiquette and expressed in subtly coded words, their time-consuming exchanges of signals finally made her consent to this dinner in his elegant garden.

After he made a pilgrimage to a Taoist mystic high in the mountains a few years ago, his life has never been the same. He has been transformed from a decorous, book-wise scholar to a master in bedroom kung fu—the kind that makes women die without killing them. The mountain recluse taught him the secrets of Taoist sexual alchemy, priceless for health and a delight to practice. The most potent elixir of life, he learned, is the essence that the opposite sex secretes at the height of sexual ecstasy. If one can pluck this essence at the crucial moment, one can nurture one's own sexual potency and longevity—perhaps even become an immortal.

The secret of pluck-and-nurture, the mystic told him, lies in exciting a woman sexually and bringing her to a climax, more than once if possible, then absorbing her orgasmic fluids. But he was warned: "Most important: Never emit yourself. It would be a great calamity."

Since then he has used his skills on women of various vintages. He plays with them; leads them on; pushes them over the brink. While the women enjoy their ecstasy, he gets their elixir. He has succeeded with all the women he has taken to bed, driving them wild with his nearly perfect self-control. This has given him a certain reputation. He is no lecher, just a zealous lover of the ultimate health food.

The man and the woman walk into the house, murmuring to each other all the way. Soon they enter a bedchamber. Dominating it is an enormous traditional bedstead, almost a miniature room by itself. An intricately carved ebony latticework frame guards three sides of the bed. Inside the latticework hangs a wraparound muslin curtain; its two front flaps are secured with a pair of large silver hooks, from which dangle beads and semiprecious stones.

As soon as they sit on the bed, the man and the woman resume their kissing. He slowly disrobes her—the sash around her waist, her silk gown, her chemise, her bodice, finally her trousers. The woman's half-resisting, half-yielding responses only excite his ardor.

When they are both naked, he casts his eyes on the luscious feast of tonic food spread before him: her almond eyes, her cherry mouth, her bare arms that remind him of clean-scrubbed lotus roots. Her breasts are like two mounds of newly congealed tofu, each topped with a freshly peeled lotus seed. Now he is about to sample the delicacies. In so doing, he will enrich her essence for his purpose. This will be the most sumptuous dish of his feast of longevity.

He pays homage to every part of her delectable body with a hundred fingers and a thousand lips, alternating subtle tenderness with brazen boldness. She retreats like a fleeing animal, but every once in a while stops to tease and taunt him. For a long time their whole world is a tangle of legs and loins, of soft warm flesh and dripping tongues.

He pauses to look at this amazing woman. Her translucent, porcelain skin, moist with perspiration, exudes a delicate female aroma. She is breathing deeply, giving little sensual tremors to her dimple of a navel and her willow waist. Just beneath these, her cinnabar field bulges ever so slightly with its abundant essence. She spreads before him a freshly opened pomegranate with crimson pulp.

Now that Yin and Yang are in perfect harmony for a joyous union, he begins his sacred mission into the grotto of love—the mystic grotto out of which babies come, and into which grown men strive to enter. As he begins his journey, her dark eyes, up to now half closed in a velvety languor, suddenly open with a glazed stare of sharp desire.

His swordsmanship has been called magnificent. His thrusts, parries, and ripostes have vanquished the deadliest of boudoir adversaries. Soon she responds—"No! No! No! No!"—and gasps to his rhythm. The silver hooks of the bed curtain tinkle ever so faintly as the dance of life goes on.

To him this is an exercise in pleasure, but one of supreme importance. It is even better than ginseng, and much more fun. He tumbles her around in various positions taught by the masters, to bring the desired effect on her. He recites silently to himself the secret passages from that amazing book on sexual alchemy: "The white tiger swings hither and yon. The blue dragon moves up and down. The moon grotto closes and opens. The heavenly root thrusts and strums. . . . I must contract my rectum, hold my breath, close all my orifices. Now the dragon seizes the tiger buttocks, presses the tiger bosom, sucks the tiger tongue, clasps the tiger waist, and raises the tiger knees. . . . Let the tiger move. Let it sway. Let it emit. When the tiger's golden eyes float upward in ecstasy, it is emitting."

It seems to work well, he tells himself. The sedate chrysanthemum is turning into a dew-drenched peony quivering helplessly in the wind. When the tiger's golden eyes float upward, he can pluck her elixir. Soon. Very soon. She will drown in her own juices. She must be the most wanton woman this side of the Great Wall.

The peony is dripping with dew, but it is not yielding its elixir. This delicate, lovely woman is stronger than he thought. The battle might be a long one. The best repertoire of his bedroom kung fu must be invoked. He moves on to the devastating technique of variegated thrusts. From nine-shallow, one-deep he shifts to eight-slow, two-fast.

It must be working. Her voice and movements betray a string of tiny sensual ripples in her, but the big explosion does not come. She remains at the edge of the precipice but does not fall off. He must work harder. The harvest will be bountiful.

Suddenly, shrill alarms sound throughout his body. He himself is on the brink. Immediately he stops and holds on to her to check her motions. Now they are like two statues frozen in a weird dance. He will resume the battle after this respite and, in the next round, surely push her over the cliff.

Her body, like his, is now perfectly still, but he feels some little tremors in her moon grotto. The tremors grow into spasms. The cinnabar grotto of this lascivious woman seems to have a life of its own. It is opening and shutting and squeezing in a most unnerving manner.

In seconds, the Yellow River is breaching its dikes. He finds himself ejaculating. His jade stalk, hitherto an invincible conqueror in the arena of pluck-and-nurture, is being milked helplessly by the pulsating wall of her moon grotto, while the flower heart deep inside her is voraciously draining his essence.

His defeat is total—and humiliating. He collapses onto the bed, feeling like a fly sucked dry by a voracious spider. Weakly he moans: "What have you done to me! Years of cultivation and nurture, all gone!"

She replies quietly: "As a man, sir, you have a reputation for plucking us women. For more than two hours you did your best to extract my nectar. Instead, I got yours."

He groans in despair.

She continues: "So what's wrong for a woman to pluck a man? In the battle of pluck, my dear friend, one must accept defeat as well as victory."

"You've ruined me," he whimpers. "You—you wanton fox demon!"

"Nonsense! Don't you believe those shamans. You're not ruined—unless you do it too often. We both enjoyed what has happened. And it will keep us both young."

As she puts her clothes back on and darkens her eyebrows with the charred tip of a willow twig, she smiles beatifically. She is once more a demure lady.

PLUCK-AND-NURTURE

The above re-creates a popular sexual practice that took place in countless bedrooms in China from the fourteenth through the sixteenth centuries. In this deadly serious health practice, called *tsai-pu* (pluck-and-nurture), one partner tried to "pluck" the orgasmic secretions of the other to "nurture" his own sexual potency and health, while refraining from reaching orgasm.

The idea of extracting nutrients from one's bedmate was believed eagerly but practiced surreptitiously in China; attempts at pluck-and-nurture had results ranging from the farcical to the tragic. Although this sexual vampirism was performed mostly by men on female partners, willing or not, some women were known to be virtuosas. When both partners were practitioners, intercourse became a sexual duel, in which the unsuspecting "plucker," usually the man, might end up the "pluckee."

The cult of pluck-and-nurture, however, was an aberrant outgrowth of the vast repertoire of Chinese sexual practices advocated by various ancient Chinese sexology schools. The mainstream Art of the Bedchamber taught of health benefits from the *mutual* absorption of sexual secretions and sexual energy by *both* partners during frequent but prudent sexual unions.

Thus the classics of the Art of the Bedchamber advocated joyous sexual union to benefit the health of both partners. It frowned on sexual abstinence as it did on sexual indulgence. It cautioned against excessive emissions of male semen, which was believed to be limited. During the Ming dynasty, centuries after the principal sexology classics disappeared in China, a new bedroom "science" flourished among certain sectors of the leisure class: sexual alchemy. This had nothing to do with the ancient Taoist alchemy that aimed at creating the elixir of life, and it had no connection to the pursuit of immortality. It was not an integral part of the ancient Art of the Bedchamber, but a perversion of it. This later sexual alchemy, which also recognized the health benefits of absorbing one's partner's sexual secretions, was based on an obsessive fear of male emission.

This fear probably reflects feedback from the ancient Chinese sexology, modified by Lamaist practices popular in the second half of the fourteenth century, under the last Mongolian emperor. At that time, Tantric debauchery both inside and outside the royal palaces pushed the Taoists and all their theories on health and sexuality to the background.

After the Mongolian dynasty fell, in 1368, and the Yuan dynasty gave way to the Ming, Taoist priests staged a comeback. To compete with Lamaist practices, the Taoists developed the arcane theory of pluck-and-nurture, which was based on the ancient Art of the Bedchamber's plausible premises of good health and good sex. Pluck-and-nurture cultists created a sexual practice with a mystical health goal and elaborate, sometimes ritualistic techniques.

Although a cultural renaissance took place under the Ming dynasty, some of the crudity and oppressiveness of the ousted Mongolian regime rubbed off on the rulers of this new dynasty. Many literati were persecuted for real or imagined sedition. Neo-Confucianism, which exaggerated Confucian concepts of loyalty to the emperor and of female chastity, became stronger. By the second half of the sixteenth century, European missionaries visiting China reported that the seclusion of women in the cities was virtually total. The militant neo-Confucian bureaucracy appeared in complete control. China became a nation of prudes—at least on the surface.

By then books of ancient sexology had disappeared. Any sexual texts originally contained in both Buddhist and Taoist canons had been expurgated. Pluck-and-nurture treatises, once written in plain language, now read increasingly like essays on military strategy or alchemy, to avoid the possible wrath of the neo-Confucian guardians of public morals. This did not deter some brilliant writers from producing pornography on the sly, however, or members of the leisure class from practicing *tsai-pu* behind closed doors.

The theory of pluck-and-nurture appears to have a believable foundation, the linking of sex with health. But it had also an obviously fallacious minor premise—its obsession with nonejacu-

lation by the male. Adherents of the Taoist pluck-and-nurture school believed that when a man emitted semen during orgasm, he suffered a catastrophic loss. A woman, it was believed, also ejaculated a fluid at orgasm. The fluids emitted by one partner would be absorbed by the other as ambrosia through the genitalia, and refined and stored in the cinnabar field. Taoists of the Ming era considered this absorption the most effective form of rejuvenation.

The theory supposedly worked both ways, so a woman too could rejuvenate herself by indulging in such practices. Hsi Wang Mu, the mythological Queen Mother of the Western Heaven, where the Peach of Immortality grows, was the supreme example. This Taoist immortal attained the stature of goddess through the divine ways of nurturing her *chi*. Every day she ate yogurt, and played the five-string lute; she kept her serenity, never letting any extraneous thoughts distract her meditation. Her best secret of youth was her sexual union with many men. Her extraction was so effective that after a single encounter with her, a man would fall sick and become sexually withered, while she became ever younger and healthier. Ancient Chinese chronicles cite numerous women, both historic and fictional, who reportedly practiced these techniques and reaped similar benefits.

Although the Taoists traditionally considered female orgasm harmless, some pluck-and-nurture advocates believed that it would benefit a woman more if she could refrain from orgasm while absorbing a man's semen. The woman thus would try titillation and arousal to bring her partner to climactic ecstasy, while holding herself back from reaching orgasm.

Pluck-and-nurture was practiced ostensibly for two respectable purposes. One was to sire a healthy son. By repeatedly extracting female orgasmic secretions without himself ejaculating, cultists believed, a man's sexual essence could be so refined that when he did emit, his supercharged semen would produce a superior baby boy. The other purpose was for health and rejuvenation.

HOW TO PLUCK, HOW TO NURTURE

Though short-lived and limited to a small percentage of the population, *tsai-pu* was a virtual subculture, with its own theories and esoteric vocabulary, unintelligible to the uninitiated. A woman to be plucked, for example, was called a "crucible."

Connoisseurs were meticulous in picking their crucibles and used many tests to select candidates. Once a crucible was chosen, she went through a complex training procedure to prepare for the plucking. The men trained too. While the pluckee was being groomed for the grand encounter, the plucker disciplined himself with the techniques of "sealing" and "refining" semen, so that at the actual plucking he could extract the female essence effectively, and store this elixir of immortality inside himself.

Among the pluck-and-nurture aficionados, the really rich and decadent usually got their nutrition from young concubines or stables of well-nourished young women kept especially for this purpose. Such playmates were assured a pleasant lifestyle—fine clothes, comfortable living quarters, nutritious food and herbs. They were treated like pampered milk cows, so that the essences they yielded would be of a superior grade. Nurture lovers who could not afford stables of their own had to pluck whenever opportunity presented itself.

The art of pluck-and-nurture, which was all technique, could be performed in several ways. In one method, a sort of "inner copulation," an individual derived benefits through exercises, self-massage, solitary meditation, and sexual intercourse in the mind. This method was, understandably, not too popular. A second method sought the benefits through an exchange of sexual *chi,* by sleeping with and fondling young members of the opposite sex, and even drinking their sexual juices—but without actual copulation. This was practiced mainly by old and middle-aged people who were not strong enough for *mano a mano* combat. A third way, for men, was to bring one's sexual partner to an intense orgasm and "extract" her secretions. For such a purpose the partner was preferably young and, even better, virginal.

This last technique was most popular with apprehensive middle-aged men. They believed their waning sexual stamina would be rejuvenated—the experience would be like grafting a new branch on an aging tree. If a man could discipline himself not to ejaculate, every session of sexual intercourse would add

vigor and years to his life. The basic thinking, although it was carried by some to extremes, was not all nonsense.

A major element in pluck-and-nurture is "suction" of female essences by the plucker. Cultists believed that male nonemission by itself was not enough. The man must absorb the woman's orgasmic secretions to nurture himself. Treatises on pluck-and-nurture use thinly veiled alchemical or military terminology to instruct the plucker how to tell the exact moment of orgasm of the partner; they describe in detail a wealth of physical and auditory symptoms just before and during the female climax. The male plucker is instructed to inhale the breath and drink the saliva of the woman in passion, and to siphon the precious female fluids with his jade stalk at the moment of her orgasm, then to move them upward mentally, "like a reverse river," to an acupoint in the brain. From here the precious essences will descend down into the cinnabar field, where they are stored as life-force.

Pluck-and-nurture, then, was a serious practice. In one treatise the plucker is instructed to meditate in a quiet room for no fewer than a hundred days, and to train himself with various exercises for thirty hours immediately before the encounter. When the time of plucking arrives, the participants are to harmonize by arousing each other sexually to the highest pitch.

One treatise on pluck-and-nurture concentrates on female saliva as a favorite elixir for men. The man is instructed to excite the woman with deep kissing and copulation. Through various coital techniques he makes her climax, then drinks her saliva while inhaling the air she breathes out. The man should repeat this at least three times in one night, and if he can keep himself from emitting, he can bring the woman to one orgasm after another, each time drinking her saliva.

During the heyday of *tsai-pu,* one variation called *shuang-hsiu,* or dual training, was quite popular. In it, both partners trained in the pluck techniques so that they would receive equal benefits. Usually, married couples took part in this dual discipline, which encompassed the entire spectrum of bedroom techniques.

Tsai-pu is no longer practiced in China as it was in medieval times, but in a sense it does live on. Some mainstream erotic techniques originally developed for the Art of the Bedchamber were refined by pluck-and-nurture enthusiasts. However naive their theories may seem, some of their practices might be of immense value in modern bedrooms.

10

Food and Herbs for Love

Aphrodisiacs and Sexual Nutrients

IN CHINA, aphrodisiac tonics have been pursued diligently and continuously for millennia—openly in the remote past, less so in recent centuries. The discussion of erotic techniques from the Art of the Bedchamber was lost centuries ago, and recovered only relatively recently; but information on aphrodisiac tonics survived even the most puritanical periods because the search for them has been discreet, even camouflaged, and because, for the Chinese, foods and herbs for sex are intimately linked as well with health and longevity.

The Chinese quest for aphrodisiacs long ago shifted from ingredients that supposedly created instant lust to those that were said to cultivate and nurture sexual vigor for the long term. The latter type are not orthodox aphrodisiacs for immediate physical arousal, but rather aphrodisiac health tonics, sexual nutrients that, ever so slowly but persistently, promote sexual potency, and indirectly heighten sexual desire.

From the vantage point of modern knowledge, the ancient Chinese search for aphrodisiac tonics may seem a mix of quackery, mysticism, and uncanny empirical experience. The last deserves the attention of modern researchers, and this chapter will therefore concentrate on that empirical experience. Some ancient Chinese practices and substances have been proven in today's laboratories; others may not even have been tested.

A profusion of anecdotal testimonials from this ancient culture still is unsubstantiated in the laboratory. But some ingredients that people have relied on for centuries have been confirmed by modern science. This is of interest not only to lovers but also to sexologists and scientists.

For the traditional Chinese, it is virtually impossible to draw a line between food and medicine. On the one hand, they attribute specific medicinal properties to specific foods, and on the other, all medicinal ingredients in Chinese pharmaceutical encyclopedias are listed with not only their known health effects but a description of their taste as well. For centuries the Chinese have taken herbal prescriptions for maladies. Likewise, they have created dishes for their gustatory delight and their tonic effects—facilitating circulation, strengthening the spleen, energizing the gonads. Some dishes are prepared with medicinal herbs. Often such herbs, whether in food or in medicine, are taken preventively as health tonics rather than as cures for specific diseases. And some of these herbs offer a bonus—enhancement of sexual vitality.

APHRODISIAC HEALTH TONICS

The Chinese have known and taken advantage of the beneficial effect of herbs for health and sexual vigor for centuries. The health tonics they have created are in various forms: powders, boiled solutions, culinary dishes, medicinal wines and liquors, as well as ointments, rinses, suppositories, and skin patches for specific acupoints. The ingredients of these tonics are animal, vegetable, and/or mineral.

Minerals in aphrodisiacs were popular in earlier centuries. One famous recipe, Five-Mineral Mix, consisted of ground amethyst, quartz, kaolin, stalactite, and sulfur ore. During the third century the formula gained great popularity when a high imperial official claimed positive results from taking it. The minerals themselves, listed in old Chinese pharmaceutical books as toxic, were to be used in minute amounts, but many eager consumers overdosed and died horrible deaths. Even during the enlightened Ming dynasty, charlatan Taoist alchemists still concocted their dubious elixirs with minerals. One well-known Ming prime minister was so severely poisoned that at his death his whole body allegedly resembled a roasted fish. Most minerals eventually were rejected as ingredients for aphrodisiacs, and plant and animal ingredients have been used much more frequently during the past four centuries.

The ancient Chinese chose particular ingredients for reasons ranging from the naively obvious to the mysteriously prescient. Some were chosen because of their shape. A favorite ingredient in aphrodisiac health recipes is *jou-tsung-yung,* or broom rape (*Orobanche ammophyla*), a fleshy parasitic fungus that grows wild in the shade of trees. Its stem is about five to twelve inches long and is covered with tiny scales, its upper end slightly thicker than the rest of the stem. The plant resembles an erect phallus. Another parasitic plant, *so-yang* (*Balanophora*), found in northwest China, is similar in form to broom rape. Legends say that when wild horses mate with dragons, their sexual secretions drip into the soil, and then *so-yang* emerges from the soil. Passionate Tartar women would squat on *so-yang* to console themselves, and the plants then would zoom up with gusto. A close relative of this plant that grows in North America is nicknamed "squaw root." Both *jou-tsung-yung* and *so-yang* are important ingredients in aphrodisiac health tonics for both men and women.

The Chinese always have believed that what one eats fortifies what one already possesses. Thus the dried penises, and testicles, of deer, tiger, seal, and beaver are treasured tonic ingredients for males. These high-priced items are found in Chinese herbal pharmacies throughout the Orient and in Chinatowns around the world. Two other animals known for their copulative energy furnish ingredients for aphrodisiacs. One is the red-spotted gecko. This lizard, only several inches long, is normally quiet, but during the mating season geckos bark incessantly through the night. When they mate they remain locked together all day long; nothing can separate them. Their abundant sexual secretions, white in color, dry on their bodies and look like snow. The lizards are often captured in pairs, one male and one female, and soaked in wine or liquor. They make a potent green medicinal drink. Dried, they are used in various prescriptions and recipes.

The other animal is the male silkworm moth. Silkworms were domesticated in China more than five thousand years ago. They are fed with mulberry leaves, and the cocoons they spin are unreeled into strands of silk. When moths emerge from the cocoons, their only mission is to mate before they die. Mating takes an inordinately long time, during which the moths flutter their wings ecstatically for hours. For this reason male moths are used in sexual tonics. Moths that have never mated are considered superior in potency.

Many other animal ingredients are believed to give potency to men and women, including the gallbladders of dogs, bears, and pythons; elephant semen; donkey embryos; and ambergris from the sperm whale. The Chinese also find sexual possibilities in such creatures as "vinegar turtles"—actually tiny snails with spiral shells, which when put in vinegar revolve until the shell is completely dissolved. The most celebrated animal element for health tonics and aphrodisiacs is newly sprouted "velvet" deer horn.

The Chinese search for aphrodisiac health ingredients does not limit itself to nonhuman animal products. The human placenta, the maternal organ that links the fetus to the uterus during pregnancy, has been valued for health tonics in China. Midwives often made fortunes smuggling out the placentas they collected at the birth of babies, especially of firstborn boys. Families guarded jealously against such thefts, in the belief that if others consumed the placenta, the infant might not survive. Certain human body fluids have been used in medicines or aphrodisiacs. Charlatan Taoist elixir-makers of the Ming dynasty were notorious for their use of menstrual blood in rejuvenating tonics. The Ming emperor Shih Tsung (1522–1567) conscripted 460 virgins under the age of fourteen, then accommodated them in his palace and collected their menses as his health-giving cocktail. Little boys' urine was drunk, sometimes mixed with wine, as a medicine.

Elixirs from the Three Peaks, described in chapter 7, were favored by Taoist pluck-and-nurture enthusiasts. Saliva was considered a great energizer. Human milk was a favorite in ancient China among rejuvenation-minded elders. It was taken with herbs or consumed more imaginatively. When the Han dynasty prime minister Chang Tsang left his post, he was already in his nineties. Yet at that age he reportedly had more than a hundred concubines, some of whom bore him children. His secret: He employed a number of wet nurses in his home and drank their milk—directly from the source. Male semen and female sexual juices also have been considered potent aphrodisiacs and health tonics.

The Popular Quest for Potency

The desire for rejuvenation and sexual potency was prevalent among the royalty and upper class, who could afford expensive concoctions, but it was no less characteristic of humble craftsmen and peasants. The water of the so-called Fountain of Lust, in southeast China, could make even the most chaste women wanton, so the story went. Peasants sometimes scraped lime plaster from statues of the Buddha and ate it, in the belief that it would build sexual stamina.

In Shantung province a rumor once spread that some "stone suet" (a mineral formation) found on the famous Mount Tai, if consumed as a powder, would make one an immortal as well as a great bedroom hero. Thousands of peasants rushed to the mountain to dig for the mineral and ingest it, until the government banned the digging.

When the use of aphrodisiac health ingredients was at its height in China a few centuries ago, people not only created recipes of their own, but spent fortunes on commercially prepared ones. The commercial preparations bore names ranging from prosaic and obvious to fanciful and elegant: one could try, among others, Gold Lock and Jade Chain, Enduring Passion, Golden Recipe of the Upside-Down Beauty, Pillow Elixir, Ointment of Thirsty Seedlings and Happy Rain, Iron Hook, Ten Thousand Moans of Princess Tai Ping, Night-Blooming Princess An Loh, Imperial Concubine Yang's Bidet, Elemental Maid's Immortal Pill, Imperial Concubine's Coyness Night After Night, and Beauty's Quivering Moans. No record is available as to what went into these preparations and what specific effects they had.

Recipes for Sexual Nutrients

Their lengthy pursuit of health and pleasure, sexual and otherwise, has left the Chinese with countless recipes, some spurious, some effective. In the past, palace recipes were top-secret, jealously guarded by the royalty and known only to them, sometimes only to the emperors. Upper-class Chinese kept many of their recipes as family secrets. The lower classes also had their favorite concoctions, however. Today, some of the old recipes are lost, while many once secret ones are known.

Recipes for the three most celebrated ancient Chinese aphrodisiac health concoctions are given below. They and thousands of others have been taken avidly by men yearning to improve their bedroom performance or recapture lost vigor, and by women seeking to enhance their general health as well as their sexuality. The recipes are offered here as a matter of historical record and for possible study by interested researchers. They are presented without any warranty of safety or effectiveness. Ingredients are identified by their Chinese name and a common name in English or a description; for accuracy, the botanical name in Latin is also given. All "parts" are by weight, unless indicated otherwise. The Chinese usually take their sexual nutrients in small quantities, daily for several weeks or months, then stop, then resume. Their interpretation of body metabolism bids them to take nutrients most of the year, but seldom in the summer.

Bald Hen Mix

In his classic, the Mystic Master of the Grotto tells of Lu Ching-ta, a third-century magistrate of a prefecture in Sichuan (Szechuan) province who took a herb powder at age seventy—and sired three sons. As he continued to take it, the old man's persistent sexual exertions caused pain in his wife's moon grotto. One day the distressed woman intercepted a new supply of herbs for his recipe; she angrily threw them into the courtyard of their house. A rooster ate the herbs and became so aroused that it mounted a hen and copulated for several days without letup. In its throes of passion the cock kept pecking at the hen's head until it was bald. Thus the recipe earned the unlikely name Bald Hen Mix.

The Mystic Master gives the recipe as follows: Combine three parts each of *jou-tsung-yung* (broom rape, or *Orobanche ammophyla*), *wu-wei-tzu* (five-flavor seeds, or *Schizandra chinensis*), *tu-szu-tzu* (dodder seeds, or *Cuscuta chinensis*), *yuan-chih* (Siberian milkwort, or *Polygata tennuifolia*); and four parts of *shao-chuang-tzu* (the seeds of an aromatic biannual grass, *Cnidium monnieri*). In a mortar, pound the five ingredients into a powder. Take a square-inch measure (a heaping tablespoon) of the powder with warm rice wine on an empty stomach three times a day. The Mystic Master warns: "Do not take it if you are without a [sexual] adversary. After taking it for sixty days, you can tame forty women.

I To Mix

This recipe is found in the dynastic records of the Sui emperor Yang, the seventh-century canal-builder and tyrant whose toys included a defloration couch. A noblewoman who had been convicted of murdering one of her servants addressed a petition for clemency to the emperor. She explained that her eighty-year-old husband, Hua Fou, had found himself incapable of bedchamber activity. A close friend gave him a recipe for a marvelous herb powder, but Hua died before he was able to use it. So out of pity, his widow gave it to a family retainer named I To. The seventy-five-year-old servant was sickly and arthritic, white-haired and bent with age. After twenty-odd days of taking the powder, the old man's body straightened, his hair turned black, and his face took on the ruddy glow of a man in his thirties.

The widow gave her two maidservants to the rejuvenated I To as wives. They bore him four children. I To took to visiting the corner wine house and often returned home inebriated. It happened that one of the maids normally slept in an alcove off the widow's bedchamber, and when I To came home, he sometimes crept into this maid's bed. The widow, pretending to sleep, watched and listened to their lovemaking. This old man, she found, was full of energy, different from others.

"Although I was already fifty, I suffered from my unfulfilled desires," the widow confessed in her petition to the emperor. "Soon I also began a relationship with I To and bore him two children. Although I To had us three women, he was still full of energy." Eventually she felt such shame for carrying on an affair with a lowly servant that she killed him. She then discovered that his shinbones were full of yellowish marrow, which the ancient Chinese believed was a sign of superior health. Evidently trying to trade her recipe for the emperor's pardon, the noblewoman concluded her petition: "If Your Majesty wants to tame many women, this mix will give you yellow marrow throughout your bones. I humbly offer it to Your Majesty."

History does not record the fate of the woman, but here is her recipe, known to posterity as I To Mix: Combine three parts *sheng-ti-huang* (*Rehmannia glutinosa,* a fresh plant similar to foxglove), soaked in rice wine for a week; two parts *kuei-hsin* (debarked cinnamon twigs, or *Cinnamomum cassia*); five parts *kan-tsao* (licorice root, or *Glycyrrhiza glabra*); two parts *pai-shu* (the root of the perennial grass *Atractylis alba*); and five parts *kan-chi* (dried lacquer, or *Rhus vernicifera*). Pulverize the mixture and take a tablespoon of the powder three times a day, after each meal.

The Plant of Lustful Sheep

Ancient Chinese herbal encyclopedias record that in northern Sichuan province, after eating leaves from a certain plant, some sheep fell into a lustful frenzy, copulating a hundred times a day. For many centuries the Chinese have used this "plant of lustful sheep," or *yin-yang-huo*, in various concoctions. (In the plant's name, *yin* means "lustful"; *yang* means "sheep." While the Chinese characters are different from *yin* meaning "female," and *yang* meaning "male," their transliterations into English are identical.) The dried leaves of this plant are soaked in wine or liquor in various proportions for two months, and then filtered. About a jigger of this is taken every night.

The "plant of lustful sheep" is mentioned in *Shen Nung's Medical Herb Classic* (c. 550) and in Li Shih-chen's *Materia Medica* (1578), the two most prestigious Chinese herbal medicine encyclopedias. Modern medical scientists in Japan, China, and Korea are analyzing and experimenting with this mysterious herb, which is known botanically as *Epimedium sagittatum* or *Aceranthus sagittatus*. A perennial found in many parts of China, it grows to more than a foot tall and has egg-shaped leaves with serrated edges. Scientists have determined that the plant contains a number of unidentified alkaloids and flavonols, and is rich in manganese, an antioxidant essential for sexual potency. Chinese physicians have used the plant to treat nervous disorders, chronic bronchitis, and menopausal ailments.

As a sexual nutrient, its key ingredient is epimedin (or icarin, in plants found in Japan and Korea), which has an aphrodisiac effect. Laboratory dogs fed epimedin exhibited increased sexual activity, and male dogs injected with a solution of this ingredient began to secrete semen five minutes after the injection; the secretion continued for ninety minutes. A Japanese scientist theorized that increased semen production indirectly stimulated the central

nervous system, and thus the aphrodisiac effects. The lustful sheep of Sichuan were the inadvertent victims—or happy beneficiaries—of what they ate.

A RECENT DISCOVERY

The Chinese seem to find aphrodisiac health ingredients or sexual nutrients everywhere. One of the latest discoveries was made in mainland China only a few years ago. Near his field a farmer had a pond in which he hatched carp, as is often done in China. One day he turned the carp-feeding chore over to his son, who unknowingly gave the fish the wrong feed: green oats (*Avena sativa*). After some time the error was discovered, but the farmer was stunned to see hundreds of young carp—double the expected number— and livelier old carp in his pond. Carp are slow breeders; but after this farmer's fish had eaten the "wrong" feed, they became very sexually active. Something in the green oats must have had an aphrodisiac effect.

Soon the news attracted agriculture and aquaculture scientists in China. After studying the fish and the feed, they confirmed that the green oats had raised the carp's sexual hormone level and caused them to mate more often. Understandably, the scientists began to eat the stuff, and after a few months they were ecstatic to find themselves as lively as the carp.

The news touched off a flurry of activity in the Institute for Advanced Study of Human Sexuality, a nonprofit graduate school in San Francisco. Its researchers conducted a double-blind study of 160 male and female volunteers. According to Dr. Raymond McIlvenna, the Institute's dean of students and a member of its board of trustees, the results of the study were "phenomenal." Both male and female test subjects claimed an increased interest in sex, and some ninety percent of the men claimed improved performance.

Researchers at the Institute subsequently found that a certain ingredient in the young oats could release the testosterone that is bound with globulin in the bloodstream. Testosterone is the hormone responsible for sexual arousal in both men and women. The portion that is bound to globulin is biologically inactive, and its percentage increases as people age. By freeing the bound testosterone into the body, the oats apparently increased the biologically active percentage of this hormone, thereby heightening sexual desire. As a result of this study, a commercial product consisting of extracts of green oats, nettles, and vitamin C is now available in the United States.

THE MYTH AND SCIENCE OF GINSENG

The pièce de résistance of ancient Chinese aphrodisiac health tonics is ginseng (*Panax ginseng*); it is surrounded by legend and mystique, and little-known modern scientific data. This humble-looking root is among the best known and least understood in the West. Most Westerners think of it vaguely as a panacea, an aphrodisiac, or an expensive nonsense steeped in superstition.

For centuries the Chinese have revered it as the plant of life, the root of rejuvenation. They call it *ginseng,* or "human root," because it often resembles a human figure. They have claimed enthusiastically that it invigorates the mind, rejuvenates the body, promotes longevity, prevents many diseases, and restores sexual vitality.

In the past, Western scientists have been skeptical, ignoring or ridiculing the value of ginseng. To the "rational" West, which demands laboratory proof, anecdotal claims are subjective, unscientific, and therefore to be discounted. Can modern science fully analyze a substance valued so highly by the Chinese for thousands of years? In this century, a few non-Chinese scientists have made isolated probes, but a serious assault began in 1961, when Japanese and Soviet scientists independently studied the root and found similar results. Today scientists in China, Japan, Korea, Taiwan, Hong Kong, Germany, Great Britain, and other countries have greatly augmented their data.

In carefully controlled tests, laboratory mice and dogs given ginseng were found to swim twice as long before exhaustion, to increase their sexual activity, to minimize the trauma of stress, and even to incur less radiation damage to the body. In human beings, ginseng has been found to increase the overall efficiency and accuracy of radio operators and proofreaders. In both humans and laboratory animals ginseng "tunes up" the central nervous system (the brain and the spinal cord), normalizes blood pressure, and alleviates incipient diabetes.

Scientists have determined that ginseng contains numerous complex organic compounds. Of these, the most significant were at least fifteen saponins, substances found in various plants which produce a soapy lather. Some water-soluble saponins stimulate the central nervous system, while some alcohol-soluble saponins sedate it. The latter also act like sex hormones for both males and females. Besides the saponins, ginseng contains essential oils, fatty acids, mucilaginous resins, sugars, alkaloids, and silicic acid; ginsenin, which resembles insulin; enzymes for digesting starch and protein; flavonoids, which increase capillary elasticity; and phytosterols, which promote hormone production. Ginseng also contains traces of numerous minerals, including manganese, magnesium, copper, cobalt, vanadium, iron, zinc, potassium, calcium, sulfur, phosphorus, and germanium, which is known to attack cancer cells. In addition, ginseng has vitamins B_1, B_7, B_{12}; biotin; pantothenic acid; choline, which lowers blood pressure; panaxic acid, which reduces cholesterol; panacene, which relieves pain; panaxin, which tonifies the central nervous and cardio-vascular systems; panquilon, which stimulates the secretion of pituitary, thyroid, and adrenal hormones; and maltol, an antioxidant now recognized for its antiaging effects. It is very likely that other components of the humble-looking root have yet to be isolated and identified, and that the properties and functions of those already identified are not entirely known.

Ginseng's action is unique. It has ingredients that stimulate the central nervous system and others that sedate it. It has ingredients that lower blood pressure and others that elevate it. According to a careful study conducted in an American university, however, long-term use may result in a steady lowering of blood pressure, as blood vessels in certain parts of the body are relaxed. Ginseng also lowers blood cholesterol and normalizes blood sugar. Ginseng conditions and soothes the central nervous system, thereby regulating and normalizing major body functions. It shields the body from harmful inner factors such as stress, and detoxifies the body from damaging outside elements such as climatic extremes, drugs, and even radiation. Not only does it stimulate the secretion of certain hormones, but some of its components behave like sex hormones; it has, for instance, an effect like that of estrogen on menopausal women and prevents vaginal atrophy. Although ginseng is not an instant aphrodisiac in the narrow sense of the word, it is a top sexual nutrient, which preserves and restores sexual well-being in middle-aged and older people. And it has no harmful side effects if taken regularly and in small doses.

No other single plant—no single item, in fact—is known to have such properties. Scientists coined the term "adaptogen" to describe a substance's ability to help the body adapt itself to different conditions—if and when this is needed. This modern term affirms what the Chinese have long known about the root, and the uses to which they put it. They have reserved it for middle-aged and older people, for convalescents, for the physically and mentally exhausted. Ginseng is not a tonic for the young and healthy.

Is ginseng really the root of rejuvenation, as the Chinese have claimed? With modern laboratory results incomplete but suggestive, the answer seems to depend on where one's prejudice lies. No wonder Chinese emperors and polygamous husbands took it. No wonder Soviet cosmonauts and Olympic athletes have taken it. No wonder its prices have been pushed sky-high today through avid purchases by many newly rich Japanese businessmen.

Although North American ginseng (*Panax quinquefolium*) is a close relative of the Oriental variety, it is less potent and different in various properties. It has been used by the Chinese as a nutrient, but not a sexual nutrient.

THE PLANT OF IMMORTALITY

When the term "adaptogen" was coined, ginseng was the only single substance known to help the body regulate its functions as it did. Since then, modern researchers have discovered other adaptogens. Among the latest to be tested in the laboratory is *ling-chih,* the "divine mushroom" (*Ganoderma lucidum*). As mentioned earlier, it provides a favorite motif in Chinese art, represents a felicitous sign, and is a symbol of female sexual essence. Major Chinese medical treatises rank it with ginseng as the best of "superior medicines." Legends claim that *ling-chih* brings eternal youth and assures longevity. It was said even to resurrect the dead, and hence is sometimes called the "plant of immortality." So fabulous was its reputation and so rarely was it found that when a large growth of *ling-chih* was reported to Emperor Wu of the Han dynasty in the second century B.C., he declared a national celebration and ordered a general amnesty.

Earlier efforts to cultivate *ling-chih* failed, but in 1972 researchers succeeded in doing so in Taiwan. Subsequently it was planted successfully in Japan, South Korea, and China, and intensive research and experimentation became possible. Because *ling-chih* has the same capability as ginseng to normalize blood pressure and blood sugar, it too is classified as an adaptogen. In clinical tests in China and Japan, it has been found effective in lowering blood cholesterol and fat. It is believed effective in preventing or alleviating some two dozen ailments or diseases, including bronchial asthma, chronic hepatitis, diabetes, hemorrhoids, varicose veins, rheumatoid arthritis, strokes, and deficiency of steroid hormones secreted by the adrenal cortex.

More recently, reports that *ling-chih* can combat certain types of cancer (of the breast, uterus, and digestive tract) have been attracting attention in Asian medical circles. Precisely why *ling-chih* may be effective is not known, although one Japanese scientist suspects that the rich amount of the anticancer mineral germanium it contains may be the answer. *Ling-chih,* ginseng, and garlic have the highest amounts of germanium known. No large-scale research on *ling-chih* is being done by Western researchers.

FROM HORN TO NUTS: OTHER FAVORITE TONICS

One treasured Chinese aphrodisiac tonic that has met with skepticism in the West is velvet deer horn. On a visit to Hong Kong, when a British royal was told that the Chinese consumed ground-up deer horn for health and longevity, he was said to have commented laughingly that if deer horn was good for health, ground-up table legs would be too.

The young plum blossom deer (also known as the spotted or sika deer) sheds its antlers in the fall and grows new ones in the spring. The newly grown horn is soft, fuzz-covered, and rich in blood vessels. In the summer, before the new velvet horns harden into bony antlers, the Chinese collect them; they process them and slice them into paper-thin wafers, which they sell at high prices in herb pharmacies. The Chinese use velvet deer horn as a sexual tonic and as a general tonic for debility and impairments related to age. In Siberia, where deer are plenty, scientists have experimented with an extract from the deer horn, pantocrine. They found that it enhanced physical stamina in mice in certain laboratory tests. Then they tried it on human beings. It increased endurance in volunteers on a bicycle ergometer, and in fifty young men running three-kilometer races. As these experiments were preliminary, much more data are needed for a complete evaluation.

A fiery, medicinal-tasting liquor has been consumed for centuries in China as a general nutrient, a booster for male potency, and an antidote for debility, nervousness, depression, menopausal blues, rheumatism, and other ailments. Called *wu-chia-pi,* it takes its name from *wu-chia (Eleutherococcus senticosus; Acanthopanax spinosum),* a thorny bush that grows in many parts of China and Siberia; the bark (*pi*) of its root is used as a tonic. Scientists of the Academy of Sciences of the Soviet Union took a great interest in Chinese claims about this bush and spent years researching it. Their experiments not only substantiated many of the Chinese claims but also found that *wu-chia-pi* regulates blood pressure and blood sugar, just as ginseng does. Although *wu-chia-pi* has some properties similar to those of ginseng, calling it "Siberian ginseng," as is sometimes done, is inaccurate.

Yet another ancient Chinese aphrodisiac health tonic receiving an enthusiastic nod from modern researchers contains *huang-chi,* or yellow vetch (*Astragalus hoangtchy*). The root of this herbaceous plant has been popular among the Chinese as a tonic and versatile medicinal ingredient for more than two thousand years. Chinese physicians and nutritionists have claimed that *huang-chi* nurtures life-force, and they have used it to treat many wasting diseases, as well as prolapses of the uterus, night sweats, and diabetes. It is often helpful to people recuperating from surgery, and as a defense against cold and flu.

The latest discovery about its immune-boosting qualities appears to confirm age-old claims. Two scientists have found that doses of *huang-chi* taken over a two-month period greatly strengthened the human immune system by bolstering defensive T cells and restoring damaged ones, both in test tubes and in cancer patients. *Huang-chi* also lowers blood pressure and inhibits harmful free radicals. Reseachers in Japan found that laboratory mice, normally in heat for one day, became sexually active for as long as ten days after eating the root.

The oldest surviving tree on earth is said to be the gingko or ginkgo (*Ginkgo biloba*), and China is the source of transplants to Europe and the Americas. Once a favorite of Chinese emperors, gingko nuts are actually the seeds or pits of fruit grown on tall gingko trees. The pulp of the fruit is toxic and corrosive, but the "nut" inside is rich in vitamin B_2, beta-carotene, and minerals.

Gingko nuts have been used by the Chinese as a cure for frequent urination, asthma, and vaginal irritation or infection. Shelled gingkos, after soaking in vegetable oil for a hundred days, have been used to treat tuberculosis in China for several centuries. Chinese scholars placed gingko leaves in their books to prevent damage by bookworms. Buddhists monks often ate a gingko nut just before their Zen meditation to facilitate deep breathing and forestall coughs. Gingko nuts are always roasted before being eaten, as they are toxic when raw. Even roasted nuts must be eaten in a limited number at a time.

Most of the positive properties of gingko nuts have been confirmed by modern research. Laboratory experiments have isolated an antibiotic ingredient in the nut that in the test tube effectively attacks tuberculosis, typhoid, diphtheria, and dysentery. The nuts are known also to have anticancer properties. An extract from the gingko leaf is now used widely in France and Germany as an anti-aging treatment for senile dementia and memory loss. This is because of its ability to improve blood circulation in the brain.

If an extract from the gingko can improve blood circulation in the brain, can it do so elsewhere? According to a study in *The Journal of Urology,* gingko restored erections to half of sixty men suffering from impotence due to decreased blood flow to the penis.

SEXUAL NUTRITION

Popular food and herbs in China include not only such celebrated items as ginseng, velvet deer horn, spotted lizard, and *ling-chih,* but also other mushrooms, bird's nest, silvery tree ear (a fungus), sea cucumber, jujube, tortoise, and snake—to name a few. Food and herbs as sexual nutrients always have been consumed avidly by the Chinese, who consider this nutrition inseparable from *yang-sheng,* or life-nurture. This is of supreme importance in Chinese health practices, as it enhances primeval life-energy, from which people derive their sexual vitality.

Someday we might find a genuine, safe aphrodisiac, one that brings instant sexual arousal without unwanted side effects. Up to now, however, all known aphrodisiacs that create the illusion of arousal have been found to be harmful. Some—such as Spanish fly, and perhaps the palace grapes eaten by the official in the story recounted earlier—may momentarily heighten "arousal" of the sexual organs, but they do not enhance genuine sexual desire. They stimulate the body in ways not intended by nature and drain it of its limited vitality, and their long-term side effects may include eventual impotence and even death.

The answer does not lie in a pill that instantly gives people overworked sex organs and later rewards them with impotence and ill health. Perhaps the real aphrodisiac is something that first boosts sexual health, then in turn naturally arouses sexual desire.

Up to now little has been studied in the modern laboratory, not even the long-term side effects of aphrodisiacs as defined in the classical sense. The ultimate laboratory is the human body itself. The ancient Chinese, with their fervent though discreet pursuit of sexual vitality, have been at it more or less for several thousand years. Perhaps their interest in sexual nutrients can give us some hints in our own quest for the perfect aphrodisiacs.

11

Sexual Vitality from the Sea of *Chi*

The Taoist Fountain of Youth?

IN THEIR SEARCH into the art of lovemaking, the ancient Chinese Taoists went beyond food and herbs, even beyond erotic techniques. The quintessence of their Art of the Bedchamber was to generate and maximize sexual vitality by consciously maneuvering the human body's *chi,* or life-energy. They did this to enhance sexual arousal, control orgasm, and intensify ecstasy for both men and women.

Was this pure mysticism? Or can it be reconciled with modern science? The answer may come more easily from the modern bedroom than from the modern laboratory. Scientists have, it is true, stumbled on some intriguing findings in the laboratory, but in doing so they have come up with more questions than answers. This chapter, which examines Taoist ideas of sexual enhancement, touches on both the mystical and the scientific.

In modern terms, the Taoists' *chi* maneuver is a form of mind-body interaction in which the mind consciously attempts to direct the body. It is intriguing first to survey what ancient physicians and sexologists theorized and practiced, on their terms and with their rationale, and then to learn about discoveries in this area by contemporary scientists, East and West, and finally to see specifically how the ancients used mind-body interaction to boost their sexual vitality.

The notion that there is powerful, albeit elusive, life-force in the human body has been maintained firmly and continuously in China for more than three thousand years. Chinese traditionalists believe that this primeval force of life can be controlled and manipulated not only to intensify sexual prowess, but also to reinforce martial arts strength and improve health and longevity.

According to the ancients, *chi* is generated and stored in a mysterious reservoir inside the lower abdomen between the navel and the pubic region. This reservoir, the *tan-tien,* or cinnabar field, however, is not an anatomical structure that can be found in surgery or by autopsy. It is rather an energy field whose role is indicated indirectly and tenuously by many medical and health practices. Ancient Chinese meditation is aimed directly at the cinnabar field, as suggested by the colorful though inaccurate expression "contemplating the navel."

As long as a person is alive, his *chi* circulates ceaselessly in his body in a network of energy channels called meridians, which are linked to specific organs or physiological functions. Dotting these meridians like pumping stations are acupoints. The acupoint nearest the cinnabar field is called *chi-hai* (sea of *chi*) and is believed a key point connected to the cinnabar field.

By selectively manipulating specific acupoints with needles, burning herbs, or fingers, one can sedate or stimulate a particular organ or physiological function. According to the ancients, acupuncture cured diseases because it regulated the flow of *chi* and restored the balance of Yin and Yang for life-energy.

Chinese physicians and acupuncturists, Zen Buddhists, Taoists, kung fu masters, acrobats, dancers, and sexologists all have considered the cinnabar field of supreme significance in their respective domains. They use various forms of physical exercise and mental therapy to cultivate and train it.

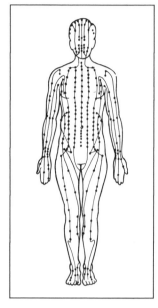

Contemporary acupuncture chart

CHI-KUNG

Among the various Chinese practices to manipulate life-energy, the most potent is *chi-kung,* or *qi-gong* (life-energy skill), a combination of meditation and diaphragm breathing that consciously harnesses vital energy. The practitioner sits on a stiff chair or in the lotus position on the floor, or stands, breathing slowly, while directing his mind on the circulation of life-energy to and from the cinnabar field. This becomes more complex as the practitioner progresses through half a dozen stages, including reverse diaphragm breathing, throat breathing, rectal breathing, and the most advanced, cinnabar field breathing.

The catatonic appearance of *chi-kung* practitioners belies the powerful results of this purely internal exercise. Usually the first noticeable result is improved digestion; the next, enhanced sexual vitality; and finally, blooming health. The Chinese consider *chi-kung* a rejuvenation exercise because it is believed to energize internal organs and thus to aid digestion, facilitate blood circulation, and stimulate hormone secretion. It is a potent exercise—so potent that those practicing more advanced stages must be trained by a *chi-kung* master to avoid possible serious injury.

In recent years, Chinese scientists have been conducting experiments on *chi-kung* that border on the mystical. By consciously directing their *chi* toward specific acupoints of patients, medical technicians trained in *chi-kung* have been successfully anesthetizing patients for thyroid and stomach surgery—without using drugs, acupuncture, or even human touch. Physicians with the proper training are popular in China for *chi-kung* treatments in which they direct their energy at patients, without touching them, to cure certain ailments. How such seemingly outlandish practices are appraised by some scientists will be discussed later in this chapter.

Chi-kung is the basis of all higher forms of Chinese martial arts. Tai chi chuan (great ultimate fist) is a mind-body exercise very popular for health and for self-defense. Its graceful, balletlike movements reinforce the flow of *chi,* so that when the practitioner does strike, the blow can be devastating. It also epitomizes the Taoist philosophy of softness conquering rigidity: one uses the opponent's own force to attack him. Japanese judo and jujitsu are simplified self-defense systems derived from tai chi chuan.

An esoteric branch of martial arts known as *tien-hsueh* (pointing acupoints) is a deadly art in which a kung fu fighter can temporarily paralyze, or render unconscious, or even kill an opponent by pressing a specific vulnerable acupoint with a finger while directing the *chi* from his *tan-tien* to his finger. These paralysis and death points are carefully catalogued in kung fu manuals. It is be-lieved that some martial arts masters in China can still practice *tien-hsueh.*

MIND OVER BODY?

Can a person really direct his own mind to control some of his bodily functions? Curiously, quite a few mystical-sounding an-cient mind-body practices are being confirmed in the modern laboratory, either directly or indirectly. A few examples are en-lightening.

In recent centuries, Western scientists have sharply separated the body from the mind. During much of this century, the physi-cian took care of the body, and the psychologist took care of the mind. Each kept to his own territory, and neither realized that what was happening in his own realm could strongly affect what was happening in the other. Physicians have traditionally consid-ered the human body like a machine, functioning mechanically, with the main causes of disease as bacteria, viruses, and other out-side agents.

This paradigm is changing. For some decades physicians have known that a few diseases are psychosomatic (affected by the mind), but their scope was thought to be limited. Recent re-search, however, indicates that at least ninety percent of diseases are affected by the patient's mind.

The most exciting development in contemporary health sci-ences is the growing recognition of mind-body interaction. Since the 1960s, American scientists have become increasingly inter-ested in a phenomenon called biofeedback. Monitoring it in-volves hooking a person to an array of electronic devices that record brain waves and physiological condition, then feed the in-formation back to him.

The electrical potential of the human brain varies according to different mental states, as is shown clearly by electroenceph-alography. Scientists have found four principal types of brain waves: alpha (during deep relaxation), beta (during awake and alert states), theta (while dreaming), and delta (in deep sleep, or while under anesthesia). Biofeedback instruments enable a per-son to keep himself in profound relaxation, when his brain emits mainly alpha waves. He can watch the monitoring instruments and, with a little practice, keep himself on alpha waves for long stretches of time.

It has been found that while in the alpha state one can consciously control the autonomic nervous system, which regulates the normally automatic functioning of internal organs. This means that with the help of biofeedback, a person can learn to control or at least influence his normally involuntary functions such as heartbeat, blood pressure, and skin temperature. Patients on biofeedback programs have been able to "think" their way out of the symptoms of many ailments, including migraine headaches, irregular heartbeat, and high blood pressure. Biofeedback researchers believe that people who have mastered the alpha state can keep in good physical health with little medicine.

The findings on biofeedback, gathered from laboratories all over the United States and elsewhere, fly in the face of orthodox physiology, which claims that we cannot control our autonomic nervous system voluntarily. The evidence to the contrary was quite a discovery, but was it really? For many centuries Chinese Taoists, Chinese and Japanese Zen Buddhists, Tibetan lamas, and Indian yogis have been exercising extraordinary mental control over their bodies through transcendental meditation, without using any instruments.

As a matter of fact, the techniques of biofeedback were invented after a Japanese scientist, intrigued by the remarkable mental state of Zen meditators, monitored their brain waves. As has been pointed out, Zen Buddhism originated in China, with its meditative practice inspired by Taoism. For thousands of years Chinese Taoists and Zen Buddhists have been using meditation as a mind-body means to improve their health and longevity.

The firm link between the mind and the body has been established further by contemporary scientists. In the 1980s a new science was born: psychoneuroimmunology, which studies the interplay among the mind, the nervous system, and the immune system. Among its findings are that the mind and body are in constant dialogue. The many billions of neurons (nerve cells) of the human brain are endlessly whispering and shouting to each other, and to cells elsewhere in the body. Our emotions can cause the brain to produce any of the fifty known neuropeptides, or brain chemicals.

Numerous laboratory experiments have shown that when a person becomes depressed or elated, angry or loving, when he is stressed or relaxed, when he meditates or prays, his brain releases specific neuropeptides into the bloodstream. These signal to defense forces in his immune system, such as scavenger macrophages and defensive "killer cells," and may strengthen or weaken his immune system. Spontaneous remissions from a fatal disease may be the work of the mind through neuropeptides. A person's health may be subtly, or even powerfully, affected. The ancient Chinese believed firmly that the body-mind approach could bring good health and longevity.

Modern scientists are proving what Eastern mystics always believed: The mind is a powerful thing. For many centuries the ancient Chinese have advocated the use of the mind to control, discipline, and nurture the body for various purposes. In traditional China the mind-body approach was popular and highly respected. Physicians emphasized mental hygiene and moderation in lifestyle as a means to good health. Philosophers preached the tranquility of the heart and the cultivation of the mind. Taoists and Zen Buddhists used meditation and deep breathing to elevate their consciousness and enrich their life-force. Martial arts masters have performed incredible physical feats through intense mental concentration. These feats, according to the ancient Chinese, were manifestations of all-important *chi*.

EXPERIMENTS ON *CHI*

Direct evidence of *chi* was collected in the late 1970s by Chinese scientists in Hong Kong. Researchers conducted experiments on two groups of people engaged in the conscious manipulation of life-force. The first group included Chinese physicians who treated patients with mental concentration of their *chi,* without touching their patients. The second group consisted of kung fu masters who employed their *chi* to perform powerful feats of internal strength.

The first group was made up of eight teams, each consisting of a physician and a patient. During the physicians' treatments, for every one of the teams, the temperature of the tip of the physician's nose lowered a degree or two, while that of the patient was raised correspondingly. This temperature shift suggested an exchange of energy between physician and patient, and hinted at a flow of some form of energy from physician to patient. The findings were confirmed and measured by infrared instruments.

The same instruments, when employed to detect energy from the martial arts experts, failed to measure any change in the case of a practitioner of *chi-kung*. Instead, scientists detected that one acupoint between his eyebrows was sending out an electrical charge measured at 1×10^{-14} coulomb. Such an electrical charge has never been detected in ordinary people. Another martial artist was found to give off a magnetic force measured at 10 to 15 gausses, several hundred times that of the highest known emanation from a normal person.

The researchers were puzzled that the energy generated by the test groups appeared sometimes as heat and other times as electromagnetic waves. These detectable but unexplained phenomena brought the scientists engaging in the research to coin the term "human body field"; this force field of the human body has yet to be explained by modern science. Whether one calls it emanation, bioplasma, or life-force, it seems that the ancient Taoist concept of *chi* is not all hot air.

CHI AND SEXUALITY

Almost all the classics and manuals of the ancient Art of the Bedchamber directly advocate or subtly suggest the role of *chi* in sexual activities, the erotic and health value of certain bodily secretions, the benefits of physical contact and simple proximity between opposite sexes. Although some of these concepts were cloaked in ancient superstition and the explanations couched in metaphysical terms, the basic approach seems quite valid to the modern observer. In fact, during the past few decades, medical scientists and sexologists have, through experiments and tests, lent indirect support to some concepts of ancient Taoist sexology.

Today we know that sex hormones are essential to sexual activities, which in turn stimulate and increase the secretion of sex hormones. Scientists are aware that we secrete many enzymes and and hormones, in varying quantities. Perhaps the production of these substances in the body can be increased or decreased not by taking harsh chemical drugs but through the ingestion of food and herbs, and even more through physical and mental therapy, including sexual activity. Continuing sexual activity in middle and old age appears crucial in keeping people healthy and youthful.

In light of the latest scientific findings, it is worthwhile to look at some points raised by ancient Chinese physicians and sexologists. As has been mentioned, they believed that certain body fluids contained ingredients of life essence, and they recommended a generous exchange of fluids between sex partners. In the Art of the Three Peaks, for instance, the male was advised to drink or absorb the saliva, milk, and vaginal juices of a female sex partner. Women likewise were advised to reap the benefits of male saliva and genital emissions.

Taoist life-nurture experts, incidentally, prescribed several exercises by which a person can increase the secretion of his own saliva, and then swallow it as a "tonic." The one to two quarts of saliva we secrete each day not only help digestion, enhance the taste sensation, and kill bacteria, but also guard teeth against decay and combat cancer-causing agents. Three Japanese scientists recently isolated from saliva a sex hormone that is abundant in the young; they believe it may help retard aging.

A male secretion, semen, is rich in protein and contains many chemical substances, some of which benefit a woman's ovaries as water nurtures flowers. Since this effect lasts four or five months, biologically speaking, it might suggest that semen should "irrigate" female sexual organs at least once every four or five months; otherwise her organs will slowly atrophy, and she will age faster. Modern researchers have found that women who have sex weekly are more regular in their menstrual cycles than those who have it less frequently or not at all. It was the Taoist belief in the abundance of life essence in sexual fluids that led Empress Chia, mentioned earlier, to nourish herself with cocktails of semen collected from a stable of young men.

THE EXCHANGE OF LIFE-ENERGY

Ancient Chinese beliefs about sex, health, and longevity involved not only the exchange of body fluids but also the even more mystical interaction of *chi* between individuals. The custom of

polygamy enabled affluent old men to have several young wives and concubines—an undesirable sexist practice, it is true, whose biological consequences should nevertheless be separated from its ethical implications. Sharing the vital energy of young women, it was believed, gave new life to hopeful elders. Such "rejuvenation" was achieved through copulation and sometimes mere physical contact, even proximity. So convinced of the interaction of *chi* between people are many elderly Chinese that they decline to sleep in the same bed with their very young grandchildren, because they believe they will sap the children's life-energy.

Conventional Western knowledge of physiology might dismiss such a belief as simply an old wives' tale from an ancient culture. Some of the latest findings of modern biochemists and endocrinologists, however, should make us hesitate to pass judgment that quickly.

Both men and women secrete the male hormone testosterone and the female hormone estrogen, although in different quantities. It is the former that fires *both* men and women with sexual desire. The level of testosterone in individuals fluctuates in daily and seasonal cycles.

A team at the University of Pennsylvania studied the cycles of testosterone and sexual activity in eleven young married couples and thirty older married couples. The researchers found that each partner had come to adjust his or her hormonal cycle so that the sexual desires and activities of each partner became synchronized. Even more fascinating is another experiment, conducted by the Monell Chemical Senses Center in Philadelphia. The experiment showed that women who menstruated irregularly became regular when exposed to male underarm odor (samples were attached to their upper lips and renewed regularly) for a period of three months.

In some cases physical contact may not even be necessary. Scientists at the Sonoma State Hospital Brain Behavior Research Center in California found that female roommates in college arrived each fall with their own individual menstrual cycles. At the end of an academic year, however, cycles often had become synchronized. Tests indicated that the young women gave off odor signals to each other and thus their menstrual cycles began to coincide.

Through intimate contact or even proximity, then, and whether through exchange of body fluids, odor, or other signals, two individuals, especially of opposite sexes, may affect one another physically. Such mutual influences tend to benefit both parties physiologically, and probably also mentally and emotionally. But the benefits may not be equal if there is a large gap in age or health between the parties. This is suggested by a study conducted at the University of Oklahoma. Using data from the U.S. Census Bureau and a national mortality survey, the study showed that men between the ages of fifty and seventy-nine with much younger wives had a death rate thirteen percent below average, while the death rate of those married to older women was twenty percent higher.

This analysis lends support, albeit indirectly, to the ancient Taoist belief in the interaction of *chi* between two individuals: The person with more abundant life-force may boost the relatively lower life-force of the other. In so doing, the individual's own life-force is of necessity decreased to a certain extent. This flow of vital energy seems to be affirmed by recent experiments on *chi.*

The analysis of individuals married to much older spouses gives only part of the picture, however. On the basis of Taoist beliefs, people married to much older mates should fare better than people who are not married at all. This is due to the so-called harmonizing of Yin and Yang, which in modern terms corresponds to the biological and psychological benefits derived from the sexual stimulation enjoyed between spouses.

SEXUAL EXERCISES

In keeping with their concept of *chi,* ancient Chinese Taoists advocated therapy and a bewildering number of mind-body exercises for better sex and better health. Some of these look dubious, while others are quite rational. They believed, for example, that during urination, hair follicles and capillaries were utterly vulnerable to outside influence. When a man urinated, he should grit his teeth and stand on tiptoe to guard himself against outside harm; a woman should do the same while squatting or sitting. This protective maneuver would not only guard a person's health but also

preserve his or her sexual strength. A man could strengthen his genitals by alternately warming and chilling his scrotum in a bathtub.

Traditional Chinese physicians often check their male patients' big toes. Full and firm big toes indicate sound health. If it is pressed, the tip of the toe normally bounces back; if it does not spring back, but stays like a partially deflated ball, it means a problem not only of health but also of potency. A man suffering from impotence can be helped by massaging the big toes, which are linked by meridians to his glans.

Both men and women can benefit from regularly exercising the pubococcygeal muscles, those of the pubis and coccyx. A woman can activate her vagina indirectly, and thus bring her partner to orgasm without moving her body; she also can induce intense orgasms in herself. A man well trained in the same exercise can will an erection, vivify his organ, and give great pleasure to his bedmate. Such exercises are often euphemistically called *hui-chun* (recapture the spring; "spring" in classical Chinese implies youthfulness and sexual vigor). Several simple exercises aiming at enhancing sexual vitality are described in chapter 13.

Both tai chi chuan and *chi-kung* are used for health and sexuality. The latter has been practiced in China for more than three thousand years, by Taoists, Buddhists, and Confucians. Specially geared to sexuality are *chi* exercises of the southern Taoist school, which rely on pluck-and-nurture techniques, and the eastern Taoist school, which aim at dual training for shared pleasure.

After diligent and sufficient training, a *chi-kung* practitioner of either sex often discovers that sexual arousal is heightened and quickened, and sexual vigor greatly increased. Anecdotes testify to the disappearance or diminution of such problems as impotence, premature ejaculation, and frigidity. And many men claim to have achieved total orgasm control; if required, they could carry on sexual intercourse as long as they want without emitting. Of course, dogged endurance for a man does not necessarily mean sexual pleasure for his partner, but it is useful if needed.

Many of the amorous emperors of the past learned these aspects of the Art of Bedchamber, to their delight. And quite a few ancient Chinese royal women were known adepts of mind-body control for sexual pleasure. Two among them were Chao Fei-yi, who successfully masqueraded as a virgin for three nights for the

Han emperor Cheng, and Hsia Chi, the femme fatale whose lovers flaunted her underwear in the royal court. By devotion to *chi-kung* practices such as contracting the rectum while breathing in, and mentally willing the *chi* to sink into the sea of *chi* and the cinnabar field for regeneration and enrichment, they and others reaped bountiful rewards in bed.

For sexual purposes, *chi* also can be manipulated externally with various techniques. Ancient Chinese erotic massage, for example, combines traditional therapeutic massage with acupressure, to treat frigidity and impotence, strengthen sexual stamina, or arouse sexual desire. The theories of *chi* and acupressure are intriguing. The ear, for instance, is said to have 120 acupoints. Theoretically, a lazy person can avoid all those exhausting gymnastics and still enjoy the benefits of whole-body exercises by simply pressing and massaging specific points on his ear.

By massaging the top and middle cavities and the front wall of the ear canal with a finger daily, one can strengthen sexual vitality. A woman who massages her breasts daily stimulates production of sex hormones, thus heightening her sexuality and facilitating her milk production if she is nursing. Massaging the groin at the juncture of the lower abdomen and thighs is a recommended mind-body sexual therapy. Male masturbation, however, has always been discouraged in Chinese sexology, because of the loss of semen.

There is yet another esoteric but effective practice of manipulating *chi* for sexual purposes. A number of acupoints, when stimulated in the proper way, can effectively treat impotence, premature ejaculation, insufficient erection, frigidity, menstrual irregularity, and other dysfunctions. Most of these points are involved also in strengthening sexual stamina and arousing desire.

These sexually sensitive areas might be termed "sex points," or better, "love points." Some of them are in the so-called erogenous zones, while others are not; most are on the lower torso and legs. The more effective ones, including the sea of *chi,* are immediately adjacent to the cinnabar field. When they are stimulated with adroit acupressure and massage as part of love-play, a consummate bedchamber artist can do wonders with these love points. These are not simple push-buttons of lust, however: if some of the love points are pressed too heavily, or jabbed forcefully, serious injury or even death may result. Specific instructions on love points are given in chapter 15.

All ancient Chinese mind-body practices to invigorate sexuality are intimately linked to the life-energy stored in the mysterious cinnabar field and the elusive sea of *chi*. This inner region of the lower torso is the fountainhead of life-force which benefits health and longevity in general, and sexual vitality in particular. Ancient Chinese physicians and sexologists emphasized the importance of health tonics and mind-body practices. They believed they had found the Fountain of Youth somewhere in the cinnabar field. Whether this was wishful thinking or not remains to be seen. Either way, in the spirit of scientific experiment, it is enjoyable to contemplate the navel and exchange *chi* with a beloved partner in a bedroom.

Part Three

ANCIENT SECRETS
FOR MODERN LOVERS

THE COLORFUL SEXUAL MANNERS AND MORES of a bygone age and the mystique of the ancient sexology classics deserve more than casual attention. Their universal themes may contain valuable hints for modern men and women. It should be noted that many of the "revolutionary" ideas of contemporary sexologists, including Masters and Johnson—so different from the traditional ones in the West only decades ago—appear to echo some of the tenets advocated by ancient Taoists.

The relentless pursuit of sexual vitality in ancient China was inspired by the Taoist belief in physical immortality, and sustained by a pragmatic desire to satisfy all the spouses of a polygamous husband. These are not the goals of our times. The Art of the Bedchamber does, however, have a message for us. To nurture our life-energy and sexual *chi* with certain foods and herbs, to train our sexual muscles and nerves with exercise and therapy, and to use mind-body erotic techniques to make sexual unions beneficial and pleasurable: these purposes and practices are universal and timeless.

Modern lovers with a monogamous lifestyle can spice up their sex life immensely if they borrow some of the erotic techniques taught by the Taoists. These ancient secrets can be used directly or modified for one's own lifestyle. They need no proof in the modern laboratory. To sophisticated modern lovers, every bedroom is a laboratory for love.

12

The Mystic Master of the Grotto, and Masters and Johnson

Where Ancient Taoists and Modern Sexologists Meet

SOME OF THE LATEST THEORIES of modern sexologists agree with those propounded by Chinese Taoists one to two thousand years ago. This is all the more remarkable when we compare the evolution of the two groups. The Taoists advanced their theories in a tolerant milieu for a thousand years; then they were swept away by the neo-Confucian tidal wave which covers China to this day. In the West, early sexologists had to contend with the Victorian social-religious attitude, which was extremely uneasy about human sexuality. Only in recent decades have sexologists been able to conduct their studies with relatively more science and less social pressure.

It is enlightening to view the similarities and differences between the observations of the ancients and those of the moderns. The basic premise of the Taoists was that good sex promotes health and longevity. Regular and enjoyable sexual activities bring health and long life to men and women. The Taoists advocated the golden mean, frowning on both celibacy and sexual excess. Early

Taoists may have linked sex to immortality, and later pluck-and-nurture extremists may have been obsessed with one partner's extracting orgasmic secretions from the other without ejaculating, but mainstream Taoists advocated another golden mean—sex for health, youthfulness, and longevity. Their intuitive attitude appears to be confirmed by the latest findings of modern scientists about the link between sex on the one hand and health, aging, and longevity on the other.

Admittedly, there is little direct laboratory proof, but proliferating indirect evidence has shown a strong correlation between sex and healthy longevity. Increasing numbers of sexologists and gerontologists today are aware of such a correlation.

Sex and Aging

In 1635, when the English longevity champion Thomas Parr died at the reputed age of 152, the celebrated English surgeon William Harvey performed an autopsy on him. Harvey reported that Parr had unusually heavy, well-developed testicles for his age. The twentieth-century Swiss gerontologist Paul Niehans had advocated that the secretions of endocrine glands, especially the gonads (sexual glands), were related to longevity. Niehans claimed that Parr's long life was due to his unusually abundant and durable genital secretions from his oversized testicles.

Serge Voronoff, a Russian aristocrat, was physician to the Egyptian khedive early in this century. The large harem in the royal palace was guarded by eunuchs, and Voronoff reported that these unfortunate castrates as a rule were quite sickly and aged rapidly. None of them was known for longevity or creative achievement.

Voronoff successfully transplanted testicular tissue of young animals, some rams and a bull, to the testicles of older creatures of the same species, and found apparent rejuvenation. By the 1920s he was ready to attempt human testicular transplants. Since for legal and ethical reasons he could not obtain human tissue, he tried to graft testicular tissue from chimpanzees on men. Today we know why he failed, as transplantation between different species without an effective immunity-suppressing drug does not work.

A man begins to grow old once he reaches his twenties. His secretion of testosterone, the principal male sex hormone, declines gradually—but not abruptly—throughout his life. A man ages, and his sexual power wanes steadily yet gradually. In contrast, a woman's secretion of estrogen, the principal female sex hormone, declines abruptly during menopause, when menstruation ceases. She experiences a host of dramatic physiological and psychological changes at menopause. The abrupt decrease of estrogen production causes her ovaries to atrophy, her vaginal lubrication to dry up, and her arteries to harden—in short, she ages faster than a man.

Such conditions in a woman, if severe, can be remedied with estrogen hormone therapy. Similarly, a man can be "rejuvenated" with chemically synthesized testosterone hormone. But hormone therapy discourages the production of natural hormones; the body's feedback mechanism makes the glands "lazy," and once hormone therapy stops, the body's natural production of hormones will be even less than before. Persistent hormone therapy, some fear, increases the chances of cancer.

The production of sex hormones can be increased and maintained at a higher level naturally. As was pointed out earlier, in recent years an increasing amount of evidence has shown that sexual activity among healthy men and women tends to boost the secretion of sex hormones as well as other substances, such as beta-endorphine, the hormone responsible for "runner's high" and other euphoric feelings. An experiment conducted at the famed Max Planck Institute in Munich in 1974 showed that even visual arousal in the form of a sex movie can raise the level of testosterone in male test subjects.

All these findings suggest that various forms of sexual arousal, ranging from visual stimulation to sexual intercourse, tend to encourage the production of sex hormones, which improves sexual stamina and probably helps keep people more youthful and live longer. Here modern sexologists and gerontologists have had an unexpected encounter with ancient Taoists.

SEX AND ENJOYMENT

Whether the goal of sex is procreation only or pleasure depends on deeply entrenched religious and social attitudes in each culture. Although the idea that the sole purpose of sex is to propagate the human race may seem a medieval concept few people now believe, it survives in some cultures. The idea that sex itself is immoral and dirty lurks within certain segments of Western society, and perhaps in the subconscious of many who consider themselves sexually liberated. For many years this attitude toward sex, found often in the United States, has amazed and amused people from other lands. While Hollywood and Madison Avenue endlessly dish out titillating and suggestive images of voluptuousness, the laws of some states treat any sexual activity other than conventional heterosexual intercourse as a crime. These laws, which vary somewhat from state to state, have labeled sodomy—an umbrella term covering anal intercourse and genital kissing—a crime even in the marital bed. In certain states, technically it is unlawful for a husband to kiss his wife on Sundays.

In spite of such laws and the attitudes behind them, however, many Americans have been practicing what they do not preach. They have experimented and diversified their sexual practices, albeit not with the relish of the French or ancient Chinese. This experimentation was revealed not long after World War II by the pioneering sexologist Alfred Kinsey, director of the Institute for Sex Research at Indiana University. His findings, based on interviews with some five thousand men and an equal number of women, disconcerted many when they were published. He reported that many Americans practiced masturbation and homosexuality, had premarital and extramarital relations, and engaged in other sexual activities then considered shocking. One of his more interesting findings was that heavy petting, oral sex, and prolonged foreplay were all common among college-educated and high-income respondents, whereas those on the lower rungs of the education and income ladders tended to skip such preliminaries and go directly to intercourse. Kinsey stirred up a furor. He was denounced by church leaders, even members of the press, as offensive, amoral, and antifamily.

The momentum created by Kinsey paved the way for the celebrated team of William Masters and Virginia Johnson, with their revolutionary approach to sexology. Their admittedly controversial techniques of studying sex in the laboratory shed much light on hitherto murky areas of human sexuality, at least from the physiological angle.

The ancient Chinese considered food and sex as essentials to life; by themselves they were neither moral nor immoral. Procreation was emphasized because of the need for heirs, but there were still many ways to increase enjoyment in bed, just as there were many ways to increase enjoyment at the table. Modern Western attitudes about sex are in this respect not so different from ancient Eastern attitudes.

Early Western sexologists did not believe that women enjoyed sex. Sir William Aston, a prominent English Victorian physician and the author of several books on sexology, wrote: "The majority of women (happily for them) are not very much troubled with sexual feeling of any kind. . . . A modest woman seldom desires any sexual gratification." He called the attribution of sexual feeling to a woman a "vile aspersion." Even the German psychiatrist Richard von Krafft-Ebing, considered the founder of modern sexology, says in his *Psychopathia Sexualis* (1886) that the sexual desire of a normal woman was small; if it were not, "the whole world would become a brothel."

This Victorian dogma was shattered by Sigmund Freud, father of psychoanalysis, who boldly disagreed with the idea that "good" women had no sexual desire. More recent sexologists, including Kinsey and Masters and Johnson, have listed many symptoms of female sexual manifestations before and during coitus. These include sexual flush, nipple erection, breast engorgement, muscular contractions, hyperventilation, increased heartbeat, elevated blood pressure, sweating, and lubrication of the vagina.

These symptoms were observed and recorded more than a thousand years ago as the Arcane Maid's Nine Essences; as the Elemental Maid's Five Desires, Five Symptoms, and Ten Movements; and as the manifestations described by the Mystic Master of the Grotto, all cited in earlier chapters. Ancient sexologists were convinced of the existence of female sexual desire and consequently devised bedroom techniques for men to satisfy women at every sexual union. After all, some of these sexologists were women; they did not need men to tell them whether women had any sexual desire.

Love-Play

Love-play includes a variety of well-known and little-known sexual practices. It has been accidentally discovered, practiced, and refined by lovers from time to time here, there, and everywhere. Some never engage in such foreplay because they consider it taboo

on religious or moral grounds. Others feel the same, but engage in it anyway—and enjoy the forbidden fruit. Still others do not practice it, out of ignorance or unimaginative sexuality.

Modern sexology has evolved considerably from Krafft-Ebing, who lumped sexual deviation with sexual crime, to Masters and Johnson, who recommend sex play to treat impotence and other sexual dysfunctions that come between partners. Today's sexologists and sex therapists place increasing importance on sex play as part of healthy sexual union.

Masters and Johnson introduced "sensate focus exercises"—carefully regulated, progressive love-play designed to arouse the sexual desire of each partner. An important feature of their therapy for the male's temporary impotence is the nondemanding nature of the exercise. No matter how aroused partners are, they are not to have intercourse until the man's erections have become regular and reliable. This assuages the male fear of performance, the principal cause of this form of impotence.

Masters and Johnson changed the term "foreplay," which has been used popularly, to "noncoital sex play." As they and their cowriter, Robert Kolodny, explain in *Masters and Johnson on Sex and Human Loving,* such activities need not precede actual intercourse. Sex play can be enjoyed before, during, or after coitus—or even without it. This last possibility is indicated by a recent American poll in which many women responded that they found love-play essential in sex, and in many cases even preferable to intercourse.

While today's sexologists' ideas on love-play might have shocked early Western sexologists, they are in broad agreement with the teachings Taoist sexologists propounded centuries ago. The ancients put great emphasis on love-play, and came up with various means to harmonize the Yin and Yang embodied in the partners. This is evident in the graphic instructions in many an ancient sexology classic. As is stated explicitly at the opening of *The Classic of the Elemental Maid,* sex play was not only pleasurable by itself, but essential to avoid sexual dysfunction.

Sexual Muscles

In the 1940s, the gynecologist Arnold Kegel introduced a revolutionary treatment for urinary stress incontinence (inability to control urine) in his patients. Instead of performing surgery, as was traditional, he taught the women to strengthen their pubococcygeus muscles with exercise. These muscles, found between the pubic bone and the coccyx, are controlled in a complex manner by the pudendal nerve, which is linked to the genitals, and the pelvic nerve, which is linked to the uterus (the prostate in men) and the bladder.

The exercise, which involved contraction of the muscles, not only helped Kegel's patients control urination, but as a surprise bonus enabled some of them to have orgasm for the first time in their lives. Sexologists Beverly Whipple and John Perry claimed in 1980 that their research confirmed that this exercise, when done by both male and female partners, greatly enhanced their sex lives, improving male erection and female orgasmic capacity.

How "revolutionary" was this discovery? For more than ten centuries, adherents of the Art of the Bedchamber had been exercising their genital area, including the pubococcygeus muscles, to enhance their sex lives.

Female Orgasm

In the West, until the mid–twentieth century, many people still believed the Victorian myth that women were neither interested in nor capable of orgasm. Even some physicians and medical scientists shared this belief. Contemporary sexologists, including Kinsey and Masters and Johnson, have found that women can have orgasm, and multiple orgasms.

In the politically more authoritarian but sexually less inhibited East, female orgasm has been taken for granted for centuries; indeed, earnest efforts to bring it about resulted in the Taoist Art of the Bedchamber. As we have seen, the art revolves around the major technique of male orgasmic brinkmanship; such control by the male is necessary because, according to the Taoists, the female is the stronger sex. Since the male is temporarily incapacitated by orgasmic ejaculations, and the female can "come, and come again," brinkmanship is essential to buttress male endurance, at least until the female "rejoices," and at most so she can have repeated orgasms.

MALE ORGASM AND EJACULATION

There has been a considerable difference between the East and the West in the assessment of male orgasm as well. In the East, the various schools of Taoist sexologists were always cautious about male ejaculation; this caution might be extreme, as in the pluck-and-nurturists' "never," or moderate, as in the mainstream advice for ejaculation regulated according to age and health. In the West, until recent years male ejaculation at orgasm was taken for granted as the logical denouement, and often the sole purpose, of sexual intercourse. The second-century Greek physician Galen advised men to ejaculate at every coitus; he believed the retention of sperm was harmful. This view was echoed adamantly by the gynecologist Theodore Van de Velde in his 1928 bestseller *Ideal Marriage.* He criticized another doctor, Alice Stockham, for recommending male nonejaculation in her late-nineteenth-century book *Karezza,* and yet another, Marie Stopes, for mentioning but not condemning it in her book *Married Love.* "Karezza," also known by its Latin name, *coitus reservatus,* is a method mentioned also in Tantric literature, which, as was pointed out earlier, may have been inspired by Taoist sexology. It has been practiced by Arabs—including Aly Khan, whose sexual staying power was legendary—and by members of the Oneida Community, a group engaging in communal polygamy in upstate New York during the second half of the 1800s. The Oneida technique was a pale and listless version, involving only occasional movement of the male organ. The Taoist version is much more dynamic.

Van de Velde's "urgent warning against Karezza" was probably responsible in part for the consensus among Western sexologists that coitus without the man's orgasmic ejaculation was harmful to him. Masters and Johnson disputed this opinion. They also recognized that male orgasm and male ejaculation may not be the same. They not only suggested that a man need not ejaculate every time, but even introduced their own technique to delay male ejaculation. Their "squeeze technique," probably Tantric in inspiration, requires the man to withdraw when he feels his climax is near, and then the woman to pinch his penis frenulum (under the glans ridge) with her thumb and two fingers.

The best Taoist method differs from the "squeeze technique"—

and perhaps is superior to it—in that it does not require with-drawal, or any effort by the woman, or—if the man wants to be discreet—even the woman's awareness. The art of male orgasmic brinkmanship will be described in detail in chapter 16.

The mainstream Taoist concept of sexual health may have gotten support, however tenuous, from a recent experiment conducted at the National Institute of Mental Health. Dr. Nancy Ostrowski and other researchers found that male golden hamsters allowed to have sex on demand showed a weakening of defensive "killer cells" in their immune system. As this experiment was only tentative, it must be augmented by further tests. For now we can only assume from its findings that since the male hamsters probably ejaculated every time, the weakening of their immune system was a result of ejaculation. We might extrapolate further and apply this to ejaculation in men. It is conceivable that experimentation on human beings will conclude that while sexual activities strengthen health in the long run, ejaculation lowers immunity, at least temporarily.

THE G SPOT

Now that they agree that women do have orgasm, contemporary sexologists have found themselves in a controversy about its exact nature. Freud distinguished clitoral from vaginal orgasm, calling the former immature and neurotic. Masters and Johnson, like Kinsey before them, stated that all female orgasms involved the clitoris directly or indirectly.

The debate on clitoral versus vaginal orgasm, started by Freud and put to an end—for a while—by Masters and Johnson, was rekindled by sexologists Beverly Whipple and John Perry in 1980, when they announced the findings of their research on the G spot. In the early 1940s, while doing research on birth control, the German gynecologist Ernst Gräfenberg claimed to have discovered a bean-size spot on the front wall of the vagina, about two inches from the entrance. The well-hidden spot was difficult to locate in self-examination or during missionary-position intercourse. Gräfenberg found this spot extremely sensitive to deep pressure; when stimulated, orgasm resulted. Whipple and Perry termed this little erogenous area "Gräfenberg spot," or "G spot." Of the approximately four hundred women volunteers their team examined, all were found to have the G spot.

Whipple and Perry announced that stimulation of the G spot by deep pressure led to a deep "cervical" orgasm in the female, dissimilar to the usual clitoral orgasm, and that during such deep orgasm many women ejaculated a fluid, sometimes abundantly. In the past this ejaculation may have embarrassed some women because they thought, incorrectly, that it was urine.

Whipple and Perry were joined by Alice K. Ladas, a psychologist and sexologist, and her husband, Harold, who had been on a similar track researching clitoral and vaginal orgasms. The findings of the four are still controversial today, but they seem to confirm some older beliefs formerly ignored or rejected by the scientific community. It will be interesting to see their confirmation by future research.

While the existence of the G spot and its function in relation to deep vaginal orgasm still have not been accepted by all sexologists, the ancients seem to have made use of the G spot either through experience or by instinct. The Taoists never described a specific feature that might be the G spot, but there is evidence they understood it all the same. The optimum intercourse positions for intense stimulation of the G spot, as pointed out by Gräfenberg, Whipple and Perry, and other sexologists, are rear entry and woman's feet on man's shoulders. These two lovemaking positions happened to be among the most popular in China for centuries. When one considers a major goal of the Art of the Bedchamber, to excite and please women sexually, an empirical knowledge of the G spot seems confirmed.

Masters and Johnson, perhaps the most renowned among modern sexologists, exploded many sexual myths long held in the Western world. They claimed, for example, that the size of a man's penis has nothing to do with his sexual satisfaction or that of his partner; that the male-on-top, face-to-face position in intercourse is not necessarily the most natural and satisfying; that sexual abstinence for long periods may not be beneficial; and that older people can continue sexual activity well into their eighties and nineties. Masters and Johnson's successful treatment for sexually dysfunctioning couples, instead of hunting for Freudian ghosts in the subconscious, has relied mainly on normalizing natural erotic feelings through extensive use of "noncoital sex play," or love-play.

These ideas, which might have seemed radical to earlier Western sexologists, were advocated long ago, and for centuries, by the ancient Taoists. When one compares their thinking with that of modern sexologists, what is most surprising is not how they disagree—as might be expected with the great differences in historical time, culture, and scientific knowledge—but in how much they agree. Concepts of those ancient mystics appear finally to have earned the blessings of the latest researchers.

13

Recapture the Spring

Exercises for Sexual Vigor

THROUGHOUT THE CENTURIES the Taoist Chinese have discreetly but avidly sought for the magic to enhance their sexuality. Among their efforts are a variety of therapeutic mind-body exercises to invigorate them sexually. Erotic exercises and therapy, as noted before, are known as *hui-chun,* or "recapture the spring." (In classical Chinese, as has been mentioned, the word for "spring" not only denotes the season, but also alludes to youth and sexuality.)

Contrary to what many Westerners and even many Chinese believe today, the ancient Chinese were concerned with physical culture, and engaged widely in dancing, sports, and martial arts. Some ten centuries ago, however, when the imperial system of literary competition dominated the aspirations of educated Chinese, many of them began neglecting physical activity. By the tenth and eleventh centuries, scholars virtually scorned physical exercise as uncouth. Some Taoist and Buddhist priests, acrobats, kung fu masters, practitioners of life-nurture, and devotees of sexual enhancement, though, continued to practice and develop various forms of physical culture with the mind-body approach.

Sexually oriented exercise and therapy are believed to tune up sexual organs, fortify sexual stamina, sharpen sexual sensations, and generally increase pleasure in the bedroom. Because these mainly Taoist exercises and therapy were often jealously guarded secrets, revealed only to family members and trusted disciples, many of them are lost. Others have been preserved and now are public knowledge. These, numbering in the hundreds, are useful and within reach of everyone. If they are practiced properly and faithfully, one may feel the effects after several months.

As mentioned previously, two of the best exercises, tai chi chuan and *chi-kung,* are aimed broadly at life-nurture but can strengthen specifically sexual stamina. Instructions for tai chi chuan, a combination of shadowboxing, gymnastics, and therapeutic ballet, are too complex to be covered here. This art is best learned from a tutor. *Chi-kung* is so potent, and its effects so little understood by modern science, that unless it is practiced properly under an experienced master, it can injure the body internally. But its elementary stage, consisting of meditative deep diaphragm breathing, can be learned safely without a teacher. Instructions are found in the following pages.

The erotic exercises recommended here include gymnastics, therapeutic massage, acupressure, and others. They have been practiced for centuries to train the sexual muscles; to improve blood circulation in the pubic region; to stimulate the autonomic nervous system, which controls many sexual functions; to promote gonadal secretions; and to heighten sexual sensations. Faithfully practiced, these exercises may enhance and prolong a man's erection, and increase his sexual stamina by promoting the secretion of semen. They may increase the elasticity and liveliness of a woman's vaginal orifice and canal, and heighten her orgasmic response. Such results help bridge the gap between male and female capabilities, and improve sexual health and pleasure for both.

Some Western-style exercises that involve chest, arm, and leg muscles can be done while one reads, watches television, or ponders over the stock market. The exercises described here are more or less internal: they require some degree of mental concentration or meditation to be effective. Almost all of them involve directly or indirectly deep diaphragm breathing.

Taoist purists believe that the best times to practice these sexual gymnastics are 11:00 p.m. to 1:00 a.m.; 5:00 to 7:00 a.m.; 11:00 a.m. to 1:00 p.m.; and 5:00 to 7:00 p.m. People with a busy lifestyle may do them anytime, except within fifteen minutes before a meal and within an hour after it. The best time to do them is right after getting up in the morning, or just before retiring at night—but not soon after a heavy meal or drinking. Most of the exercises may be done in loose-fitting clothes such as pajamas; it is better not to do them in tight clothes that may impede breathing and circulation. Some of the exercises are best practiced in the nude in the privacy of one's bedroom.

The following exercises were selected from Taoist kinesitherapy, which has been practiced for centuries in China. Most of them are taken directly from the Taoists, while some are slightly modified. Unless designated otherwise, they are for both sexes.

Warning: The recommended exercises, beneficial as they are, come with no warranty. Avoid overdoing any of them, as too much of a good thing could be harmful. If you have any physical or mental health problem or are taking any special medication, check with your physician before doing any of the exercises.

DEEP DIAPHRAGM BREATHING

Deep diaphragm breathing is the key to all Taoist mind-body activities, from health therapy to meditation, from martial arts to the Art of the Bedchamber.

Unlike thoracic deep breathing, which involves expansion of the upper chest, Taoist deep breathing is done by moving the diaphragm, the powerful sheet of muscle separating the chest cavity from the abdomen. In this form of breathing, the chest moves very little, while the abdomen alternately bulges and collapses. The advantage of abdominal or diaphragm breathing over chest breathing is known to every opera singer in the West, and every kung fu master in the East. It should be known to every bedroom sportsperson, East or West.

Chest breathing, even deep chest breathing, involves the expansion and contraction of the rib cage. This empties the lungs partially, leaving much stale air inside. Diaphragm breathing is far more powerful, in that it enables the lungs to take in an amount of air—including oxygen—four to five times that inhaled in shallow chest breathing. Besides this aerobic advantage, the pulsing diaphragm gives a sort of internal massage to the vital organs in both the chest and the abdomen. Studies published by the Chinese in 1958 revealed that respiration therapy actually enlarged patients' internal organs.

You may practice deep diaphragm breathing indoors, or outdoors in mild weather; wear loose clothing, without any tightly restraining belt around the waist. Sit on the front portion of a stool or stiff chair (not an upholstered sofa or armchair); a slightly padded dining chair is suitable. Avoid any distraction or noise, even music. Keep the body straight but relaxed. Put your hands on your knees, spread about a foot apart. Close your eyes or look at the tip of your nose. Close your mouth and breathe through your nostrils, with the tip of your tongue touching the palate or the roof of your mouth. Expel all extraneous thoughts.

Exhale as much stale air as possible by moving your diaphragm upward and your abdominal wall inward. Keep your lungs emptied for a few seconds; then inhale by moving your diaphragm downward and your abdominal wall outward. Breathe as slowly as possible in a gentle, steady, silent stream. Concentrate your mind on the respiration. While inhaling, imagine a stream of life-force entering your nostrils, then your lungs, and going all the way to the cinnabar field. While exhaling, imagine the vital stream leaving the cinnabar field and exiting your nostrils. Normally a man breathes about 10 to 18 times a minute; a woman slightly faster. After enough practice, one can slow breathing down to two times a minute during the exercise. This should be done naturally, not forced.

After months of practice, any of the following symptoms *may* occur during the exercise: quivering of skin and muscle at certain spots; feeling of radiating warmth in the cinnabar field; sexual arousal; and even out-of-body sensations. Taoists masters believe these possible mind-body phenomena are normal reactions; but they are more likely to emerge—if at all—only during the later, more advanced stages of *chi-kung.*

Practice deep diaphragm breathing for a minimum of 15 minutes daily—again preferably right after arising or before retiring, never after a big meal or heavy drinking, and never with anger or grief. If you do this exercise faithfully and correctly, you will feel a noticeable difference in a few months. Eventually you may develop diaphragm breathing as an unconscious habit—and a big boost to your health.

THE PUBIC SQUEEZE

Centuries ago, the life-nurturing eroticists designed an exercise to increase marital happiness. The pubic squeeze, intended to inject more life into the genitals, is one of the most valued and effective erotic exercises. The Taoists claimed that with sufficient practice of this exercise, a man could will an erection, increase his coital endurance, and bring his partner to orgasm without any bodily movement; a woman could "nip" or "milk" her partner to ejaculation and intensify her own orgasm. There are two versions: a quick and a slow.

First, the quick squeeze: This can be done in any kind of clothing, anytime, anywhere. Contract as much as possible the pubococcygeus muscles (in the genital and anal region), as if trying to hold back or interrupt urination or defecation. You will feel the anus tightening and the genitals moving slightly. After a few seconds, relax the muscles completely. Alternately squeeze and relax, squeeze and relax, 50 times at first. When you are used to it, increase this to 100 per session. Each day do a minimum of 300 squeezes-and-relaxes—better still, 700.

Now, the slow squeeze: This version, much more powerful than the quick one, not only is done much more slowly but is combined with deep diaphragm breathing and requires mental concentration. Contract the pubic muscles while inhaling slowly. Hold the squeeze and the breath for several seconds. Then relax the muscles while exhaling. Do this 300 times daily, but not more than 100 times per session. If you feel dizzy, stop the exercise and resume later.

The effectiveness of either version of this ancient exercise is supported by modern knowledge. Although male and female genitals consist mostly of involuntary (smooth) muscles, they are surrounded by and intimately linked to voluntary (skeletal) muscles in the pubic-coccygeal region. This complex network of muscles not only supports the genitals and other, internal organs, but is directly or indirectly responsible for sexual health and pleasure. Among the muscles benefitting from the pubic squeeze are the ischiocavernosus, which helps in the erection of the penis and the clitoris, and the bulbocavernosus and ischiobulbosus, which have a central role in male erection and ejaculation, and in female compression of the vaginal orifice and sphincter. This web of muscles, centering around the perineum (the area between the anus and the genitals), is linked to several sacral and coccygeal nerve trunks. The nerves control the motor activity of these muscles, communicate sensations to the brain, and are responsible for the rhythmic contractions of sexual organs during orgasm.

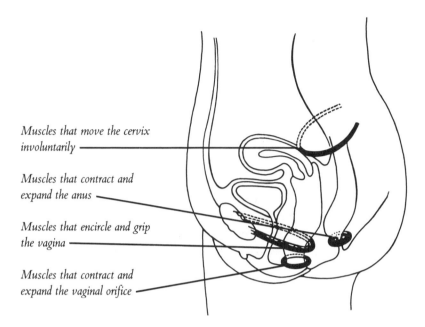

Muscles that move the cervix involuntarily

Muscles that contract and expand the anus

Muscles that encircle and grip the vagina

Muscles that contract and expand the vaginal orifice

In many men and women, the sexual muscles are weakened by chronic tension or atrophied through disuse. As a result, the pleasure these individuals get from sex is reduced and they may face more serious problems, such as urinary incontinence, hemorrhoids, lower back pain, displacement of the uterus or bladder, and painful intercourse.

CINNABAR FIELD MASSAGE

The ancients used this exercise to invigorate the cinnabar field, the fountainhead of *chi,* and to stimulate the digestive organs. It is a favorite therapeutic self-massage for both men and women.

The exercise is done either lying on the back or standing. Uncover the front torso. Relax the abdominal and chest muscles. In cool weather rub the palms together vigorously for several seconds, until they are warm, to avoid chilling the cinnabar field; warm palms facilitate the circulation of *chi.* Put the right palm on the cinnabar field (between navel and pubic hair). Press the palm down with moderate force while moving it clockwise, first up to a point between the navel and the breasts, then back down to the cinnabar field, and around. Use the navel as the center of the circle, and move the palm at a rate of 4 seconds per circle. After 50 circles with the right palm, rub the palms together vigorously again. Then, with the left palm, start from the cinnabar field in a counterclockwise motion, for another 50 circles. Be careful to use only moderate pressure and to press with the palm, not the fingers. When you have found the optimum pressure and your abdomen is used to the exercise, in about a week or two, increase to 100 circles for each palm.

The exercise may be done in a vertical rather than a circular version. Put the right palm at the same starting point, with the left palm pressing on top of it. Move both palms vertically upward with moderate pressure to the area between the navel and the breasts, and then move them downward. Switch the positions of the palms and repeat.

GROIN MASSAGE

This exercise, intended to stimulate secretion of gonadal hormones, is especially beneficial to men and women past age forty. This is really a self-massage, but it can be done as partner massage as well. There are two versions, one for males, one for females.

First, the female version: With the fingers of both hands, gently rub up and down along the left and right groin, where the legs meet the abdomen, from the sides of the vagina to the vicinity of the hips—and back. Massage 36 times each session.

Next, the male version: Using the left hand to keep the genitals out of the way, massage the right groin with the right fingers 36 times. Then change hands and massage the left groin with the left fingers 36 times.

SACRAL-COCCYGEAL PRESS

If the name of this exercise is too much of a jawbreaker, you may simplify it to "Tush Push." At the lower end of the backbone are five vertebrae fused into the sacrum, below which are four vertebrae fused into the coccyx. You can feel the sacrum and coccyx in the lower back adjoining the buttocks.

Ancient sexologists used acupressure to stimulate the eight "love points" located in the sacrum and coccyx area to heighten sexual energy. In this same area modern anatomists have found five pairs of sacral nerves and one pair of coccygeal nerves, which control movements and monitor sensations throughout the lower limbs as well as in the genital and anal areas.

To do the exercise alone, disrobe below the waist or wear underpants of a thin material. Stand with your feet slightly apart, or sit on a stiff chair. With the fingertips of both hands, press and rub this area up and down with moderate pressure 50 times. This acupressure may be performed more effectively by one partner on the other; in that case the recipient lies stomach down.

PERINEUM PRESS

The perineum, the area between the genitals and the anus, is crucial in Taoist sexology; one of the most important love points, *hui-yin,* is inside the perineum. In acupuncture terms, the front midline meridian, the conception vessel, meets the back midline meridian, the governing vessel, at this point. Today's anatomists tell us that three pairs of sacral nerves monitoring the genital-anal area are centered here. As will be shown in the following chapters, *hui-yin* acupoint is a key for sexual arousal as well as orgasmic brinkmanship. Acupressure here should enhance sexual stamina.

To do the exercise alone, lie on your back with your pants off, your thighs spread apart, and your knees bent. Use the middle fingertip of either hand to press on the perineum with moderate force for about 3 seconds. Repeat the acupressure 100 times. Partners may perform this exercise on one another.

CHEST MASSAGE

This massage aids circulation. Put your left palm on the center of your chest, directly on the sternum (midway between the nipples), and your right palm on top of the left. Press down moderately 3 times. Move your palms downward to the waist, then circle clockwise, with the sternum as the center of the circle. Use moderate pressure all the time while circling. After 50 circles, return your palms to your chest. Change palms and do 50 circles counterclockwise.

BREAST CIRCLES

This exercise for women is designed to beautify the breasts, promote the secretion of female hormones, and facilitate milk production in nursing mothers.

Wear a thin T-shirt or disrobe above the waist. Stand, sit down, or lie on your back. Rub your hands together to warm the palms. Put your right palm on the lower portion of your right breast without touching the nipple, and do likewise with your left palm on your left breast. Gently massage the breasts, the right palm circling clockwise, the left palm counterclockwise—symmetrically and simultaneously. After 36 circles, reverse directions and do another 36 circles. Inhale deeply while moving the palms up, and exhale while moving them down. If you massage directly on the skin, a bit of scented herbal oil may help.

SCROTUM RUB

For men, this may be the best massage for sexual energy and health. The principal male sex hormone, testosterone, is produced by the testicles. The Scrotum Rub is designed to enliven the male organ in general and stimulate the secretion of testosterone in particular. This exercise may be done with one hand while the other does the Cinnabar Field Massage.

Disrobe below the waist. Lie on your back with your thighs spread and your knees bent, or stand with your feet about 24 inches apart. Rub your palms together until they are warm. Press the right palm on the scrotum with a lifting motion, so that the limp penis is up against the pubic region and the tip of the middle finger just over the perineum. With gentle pressure, massage the scrotum up and down 50 times; then change hands and do another 50 times. When your scrotum becomes used to the exercise and you know the optimum pressure to apply, increase the massage to 100 times for each hand. Be sure to do this very gently, as the scrotum is very delicate and can be injured easily.

PILLOW NIP

This exercise for women aims at promoting the elasticity of the vagina wall.

Lie on your back with your knees bent and held slightly apart. Put a bed pillow, folded double, or a stiff sofa cushion between your thighs. Close your thighs tightly against the pillow, nipping it with as much pressure as you can. Release after a few seconds. Nip and release in this manner 50 times.

HIP SWIVEL

This exercise stimulates both the internal organs and the cinnabar field.

Stand with your feet about 24 inches apart, your knees slightly bent, and the cinnabar field slightly protruding. Put your hands on the side of your waist, with thumbs in front and fingers at the back. Imagining a vertical axis from the center of your head, all the way down, swivel your hips to the right, back, left, and front in a clockwise direction. Move at about 3 seconds per circuit. Inhale and contract your anal-genital muscles while moving your hips forward; exhale and relax the muscles while moving them backward. Move in smooth, continuous circles 10 times. Then reverse and move in a counterclockwise direction another 10 times.

BODYQUAKE

This exercise, as the name implies, wakes up internal organs. Like any other active exercise, it should not be attempted by anyone with a heart condition, high blood pressure, or a slipped disc. You should wear loose clothing so that your scrotum or breasts can bounce up and down freely and vigorously.

Stand upright with your entire body weight on the right leg, your left toes lightly touching the floor, and your left arm raised. Shake up and down rapidly 36 times, at about two quakes per second. Relax the unoccupied left leg and right arm while shaking. Then switch arms and legs, and shake another 36 times.

KITTEN STRETCH

This is a longevity exercise that benefits the central nervous system and the *chi* meridians.

Stand with your feet slightly apart and your arms stretching out horizontally to left and right. Relax and exhale, while moving your arms slowly toward each other and slantingly downward until they are parallel and pointing forward at a 45-degree angle to the floor. Inhale and move your arms back to their original position. Do this 8 times. Next kneel down, lean forward, and support your upper body on your palms, with your arms stretching down vertically. Bend your elbows so that your head almost touches the floor while your buttocks are raised high. Move your head forward while inhaling, as if trying to lick the floor with your tongue—don't actually do it! Move your head backward, exhaling. Stretch forward and backward a total of 64 times. Then stand up and repeat the arm movement 8 times.

Although it looks relaxed and smooth, the kitten stretch could be quite strenuous, especially when you first practice it. Do not strain for the required number of stretches, but stop whenever you feel tired. After a number of days, increase the stretches gradually until you can do 64 without strain.

SALIVA FOUNTAIN

This is a drinking exercise—you will be drinking your own saliva.

Close your lips but not your teeth. Use the tip of your tongue to explore and sweep everywhere inside your closed mouth—palate and floor, gums, between gum and cheek. The tongue sweep stimulates the saliva glands. Sweep for 3 minutes, or until a large quantity of saliva has been collected. Then swallow it in three gulps. The exercise may be practiced between partners. As a love game it will be described in chapter 15.

Alone, you may do this from time to time during the day. It not only aids digestion and alleviates bad breath, but irrigates your system as well. Saliva is still not fully understood; what ancient Taoists called the elixir of the Red Lotus Peak has been found by modern scientists to contain various enzymes and antiseptics and a sex hormone.

Teeth Chatter

This practice strengthens the teeth and gums, and gives some of the benefits of the Saliva Fountain.

Close your mouth and chatter your teeth resoundingly 36 times. Next hold the forehead with one hand and the jaw with the other. With firm but gentle force of your hands, move the jaw to the left and right of the forehead 36 times. After a while this should produce a mouthful of saliva. Swish the saliva inside your closed mouth; then swallow it in three gulps.

It must be noted that all these sexually oriented exercises—like all Chinese exercises for health purposes—are gentle, slow, and aimed at long-term results. The traditional Chinese concept of health and fitness is different from the Western version. Instead of pumping iron, lifting weights, or jogging to exhaustion to "shape up" the body and strengthen external muscles, the Chinese prefer to work on their internal organs. They believe that healthy, strong vital ogans mean smooth, trouble-free circulation, respiration, digestion, excretion, and procreation. Only professional acrobats and kung fu devotees punish their bodies with strenuous, "no pain, no gain" exercises. But even they must strengthen themselves internally before they feel safe to build themselves up externally.

Judging by modern standards of physiology and sexology, these erotic exercises and therapy appear to benefit sexual muscles, sexual nerves, and even hormonal secretion. The Taoist belief in energizing sexual *chi* through meditative deep breathing, whether it can be proved in the laboratory or not, may be an added benefit.

14

The Alchemy of Desire

Enhancing Love-Play

SOPHISTICATED LOVERS OFTEN ENJOY a refinement of sexuality, which depends largely on what may be called the alchemy of desire. The ancients intended for this alchemy to achieve the ultimate harmony of Yin and Yang, in which the dual elements endlessly energize each other with sexual *chi*. Like the alchemists who experimented with a wide variety of substances in the crucible, ingenious lovers are ever creative in their love-play. But mere creativity and experimentation are only part of the picture: love requires sentiment, passion, and affection; and play the ability to tantalize, seduce, and frolic whimsically.

Ancient sexologists such as the Elemental Maid, the Arcane Maid, and the Mystic Master of the Grotto all advised fun and frolic before intercourse, so as to energize the partners for a rewarding sexual union. For people today, with a stressful lifestyle and accompanying sexual problems, modern sexologists increasingly recognize that love-play is essential to satisfactory sexual intercourse. The "sensate focus" exercises devised by Masters and Johnson to treat sexual dysfunctions between partners now are recommended by most contemporary sexologists.

BRIDGING THE SEXUAL GAP

The love-play suggested by ancient and modern sexologists has several essential functions. One is to bridge what may be called the sex gap. While men and women are very much alike in having basic sexual urges, they are quite different, physiologically and psychologically, in their sexual responses. If we ignore this and other differences, we may pay a terrible price in bed.

For example, men are at their biological sexual peak between the ages of sixteen and twenty, but women peak between twenty and thirty. Sexual arousal patterns are also different between the sexes. Although there are always exceptional individuals, and exceptional times for the same individual, the general patterns for men and for women are consistent: Other factors being equal, a man normally is aroused easily, and can get an erection in a few seconds. But as a rule it takes longer for a woman to be aroused. She needs a longer and wider variety of stimulation, both physical *and* emotional.

Alfred Kinsey found that of the husbands he surveyed, three out of four ejaculated within two minutes during coitus; a more recent American study reveals a longer time of ten minutes. This is definitely an improvement but is still no blessing for many women who in active intercourse require more time to reach orgasm. In other words: The average man comes on strong, but soon falls off the cliff. The average woman climbs slowly to her peak and, once she is there, wafts down slowly or goes from peak to peak.

Men often have considered themselves the stronger sex because of their physical prowess and apparently greater muscularity, their love of combat, and their highly visible phallus. Because of hormonal and other differences, however, women are more resistant to pain and disease; they live longer than men; they are the survivors in life. The ancient Taoists, prizing resilience over rigidity, inaction over action, and insisting that the weak can conquer the strong, considered women the stronger sex not only in life but also in bed.

As far as sexual activity is concerned, there are at least two approaches to bridging the dismal and often neglected gap between the sexes: The languid female sexual response may be accelerated with love-play, or the hair-trigger male response may be decelerated with orgasmic brinkmanship. Better than either approach, of course, is a combination of both.

According to ancient Chinese sexologists and some recent researchers, erotic love-play and prudent coitus promote healthy longevity. Scientists today believe that if a person is relaxed and happy, and engages in or even thinks about sex, his body sends nerve signals to the brain and produces a host of body chemicals—neuropeptides and hormones—that can alleviate illness, improve health, and even prolong life.

SEX AND THE SENSES

When love-play is practiced as foreplay to coitus, it helps pace the partners for a satisfactory union; it can be enjoyed also as an end in itself. Love-play runs, or should run, the gamut of our senses: sight, touch, smell, taste, hearing. Just as a gourmet enjoying a delicacy not only inhales its aroma and savors its flavor, but delights in its presentation, luxuriates in its texture, and notices the crunch and snap as he chews, we enjoy sex best with all our senses. The art of such enjoyment, which must be learned—and even more precisely, cultivated—elevates mere mechanical groping to erotic love-play.

Visual images are very powerful for human sexuality. They can act as a sophisticated shorthand in arousing us, for what we see suggests what we may get.

Touch, the basic language of sexuality, is far more developed in human beings than in other animals. Our fingertips tell us whether something is firm or soft, rigid or pliable, cold or warm, dry or moist, rough or smooth or slippery. In fact, our skin is our largest sensory organ, with varying degrees and types of sensitivity. The slightest touch on an erotically sensitive area by a sexual partner can cause an immediate response, whether it be ticklishness or sexual flush or phallic or clitoral erection.

Caressing, fondling, and kissing are favorite pastimes between lovers. A well-known folk song from southwest China entitled "Eighteen Fondlings" is a favorite of cultural anthropologists, who have enshrined it in the scholarly archives of Beijing University. Lyrically, but in rather uncouth graphic terms, the song describes one after another the eighteen female anatomical terrains a male peasant explores on his woman. The fifth fondling, for example, involves "a triangular field," "a shuttle pointed at both ends," and "a mustache that points in two directions." Whether in the form of boorish petting, or subtle tactile flirtation between sophisticated lovers, touching is certainly the most direct and instinctive form of love-play.

The sense of smell is vital to most animals, which are powerfully influenced by pheromones, the chemical messengers secreted by animals to signal creatures of the same species. A principal means of communication for them, pheromones also contain an attractant for the opposite sex. Our distant ancestors developed an acute sense of smell in order to survive in their hazardous world, but because of disuse our olfactory sense has degenerated. We have mastered speech, so we no longer need rely on smell as a major means of communication.

In close personal relations, however, we are influenced very strongly by our sense of smell, though in great part subliminally. When we say we "instinctively" like or dislike someone we meet, our judgment may well reflect how that person's scent fits with our own olfactory preferences. There is no question that smell plays a significant though often unconscious part in sexual relations. Whether we realize it or not, we are attracted or repelled by the body odor of a member of the opposite sex. Some men are able to detect the particular scent that may be emitted by menstruating women.

Because of genetic and dietary factors, different races emit distinct types and degrees of body odor. The body scents of most Orientals, for instance, are much subtler than those of Caucasians. In general, Orientals have a very faint musky odor, while that of Caucasians resembles ambergris. (Both of these scents, musk and ambergris, it should be noted, are animal scents, and both have been used in aphrodisiacs and perfumes. Musk, which comes from a sac within the abdomen of the male musk deer, in its concentrated form has a persistent, penetrating odor. Ambergris, a secretion from the intestines of the sperm whale, is soft and black and has a disagreeable odor when fresh, but is hard and lighter-colored and emits a pleasant scent when it has been exposed to sun and seawater. It is known as "dragon saliva" in China; the ancient Chinese believed it to be the saliva left by these creatures—which they considered benign and auspicious—while sunning themselves at the seashore. When used in perfumes, musk or ambergris is sometimes blended with floral, woody, mossy, and herbal scents.)

A look at several thousand years of Chinese history and literature reveals how significant was the role of the olfactory. When the first-century B.C. Han emperor Cheng became enamored of two sisters, for example, his infatuation was due partly to their natural body fragrance. He once remarked that he was drawn more to the younger one because she was even more fragrant than her sister. And then there was the story, also related earlier, of the Ching emperor Chien Lung and his tragic Fragrant Imperial Concubine.

Female body aroma has been a favorite subject in erotic writing and in other literature as well—in fiction, essay, drama, poetry, and song. The most famous Chinese literary gem about female scents is an eleventh-century poem entitled "Ten Fragrances." In delicate and tasteful classical verse, it enumerates and describes the scents of a woman: the fragrance of her hair, her bosom, her cheeks, her neck, her tongue, her lips, her fingers, her feet, her vulva, her entire body. The fragrance of the vulva is introduced thus:

> *Loosening her trouser-cord, she shivers in shame.*
> *His hand touches her body, and her heart beats so,*
> *Not realizing that within her skirts*
> *Comes a soul-melting fragrance.*

This poem is famous for causing the tragic death of an empress of the Liao dynasty in the late eleventh century. A top imperial aide deviously tricked the empress into copying the poem in her own hand; he then planted it as evidence of adultery between her and a palace composer. The emperor, Tao Tsung, fooled into believing his wife's infidelity, ordered her to commit suicide.

Although less prominent than visual, tactile, and olfactory senses, the sense of taste often has an important role in foreplay. The gustatory sense is not just an empty image for poets when they sing of drinking nectar from a loved one's lips. There is a physiological basis for such poetry. The taste buds sensitive to sweetness are near the tip of the tongue, which acts as the vanguard in erotic kissing. Fortunately for lovers, taste buds for bitterness and sourness are far back on the tongue. The Taoist Art of the Three Peaks, which involved savoring three bodily fluids, is mainly taste-oriented. For many, the taste of love juices is a potent aphrodisiac.

The sense of hearing, like the sense of sight, is largely cerebral. Some individuals blessed with a sexy voice might excite members of the opposite sex merely by speaking. Music, from romantic strings to hard rock, often has erotic overtones for those attuned to it. Unabashed erotic whispers, murmurs, moans, or aerobic breathing are strong aphrodisiacs during lovemaking. Women from two places in China—Tatung in Shansi province, and the Tientsin suburb of Yangliuching—were famous for their love calls in bed.

Lovemaking—like eating—can be enjoyed as a feast when we employ fully our five senses, and satisfies an instinctive need in life. When the mood or circumstance calls for it, we can enjoy an occasional quickie or an impromptu snack. To forestall bedroom problems, to harmonize Yin and Yang, erotic wooing by both partners before, during, and after coitus is not just desirable but essential. The most erotic stimulus in love-play, the most powerful aphrodisiac for all the senses, is the human mind: the brain, for all else it is, may be called a sex organ.

A Two-Way Game

A lover who is good in bed knows which are the body's erogenous zones and where the love points are, and understands how to decode the sexual responses of a partner and how to excite, seduce, and satisfy that partner. Love-play is an erotic language for lovers who enjoy sex and all its sensual ramifications as natural pleasure. It is played in privacy by a couple as a reciprocal game.

Fulfilling sex does not depend entirely on specific techniques or even successful performance of the Art of the Bedchamber. Sexual happiness between partners in a monogamous relationship depends on a host of other factors—physical, psychological, emotional, even financial. The art of lovemaking can enhance pleasure and thrill in a happy relationship, but it cannot create them in an unhappy one. Above all, personal alchemy between lovers is a unique mind-body interaction, unprecedented in experience and unpredictable in result.

Many couples, especially those long married, tend to stay in a well-worn lovemaking rut. They become captives of routines, from initial love-play, if there is any, to orgasm. Lovemaking, especially love-play, becomes exciting when it is improvised occasionally. Improvising enables each partner to adapt to whatever responses are observed in the other, and concentrate on whatever best excites the latter. People exhibit a wide variety of reactions to erotic stimulation, whether it be external stimulation of the body or internal stimulation of the mind—or both. Some moan, some whisper, some talk a blue streak, some ululate like banshees. Others, instead of vocalizing their reactions, express them in body language, from epileptic thrashing to apparent rigor mortis. A sensitive lover can gauge a partner's reactions to love-play.

The various reactions, or symptoms of arousal, range from physiological, reflecting the sensory input experienced by the body, to cerebral, reflecting thoughts and emotions exciting the mind. Men often react readily to physical stimulation, while most women are put in an erotic mood more easily by psychological stimulation of thoughts and emotions. The relative power of physical and psychological stimuli, however, varies among individuals and over time within the same individual.

Love-play starts, or should start, long before a kiss or an embrace. It may begin with a subtle innuendo, an erotic code word, a brazen sexual invitation. Or the body may speak with a glance, a smile, a toss of hair or heave of bosom. Or the opening signals may begin amid an erotic ambience of low lights, sensual music, the scent of flowers or natural perfume of the body. Familiar partners, especially long-married spouses, often telescope or even skip love-play, but an occasional return to romance could banish bedroom blahs and lend a piquant touch to lovemaking.

The physical phase of love-play should be approached with caution. Since love-play and coitus are the most intimate acts shared by two individuals, personal hygiene is of paramount importance.

As men are more genital-oriented than women, a man might tend to go directly to his partner's genitals at the start of love-play. This may dampen the ardor of a sensitive woman. Since any sudden sexual act could be either elixir or poison to a sensitive partner, especially a female, one should respect all the dos and don'ts, and watch for the various traffic signs—"slow," "yield," "stop," "soft shoulder," "curve ahead," "slippery when wet." If one wants to venture into uncharted territory, a good tactic is to zip in tentatively and zip out immediately, to test the partner's reaction. If the reaction is clearly negative, change course. If the resistance seems halfhearted or a mere ritual, use the Taoist tactics of two steps forward, one step back. With this strategy in love-play, one may discover untold delights that both partners secretly yearn for but are reluctant to admit verbally.

Anytime and anywhere could be good for love-play. Although some lovers, out of either inventiveness or desperation, are attracted to unconventional, even dangerous, locales, most prefer a more romantic environment—a secluded, moonlit beach, or a cozy, dimly lit living room, with the flowing cadences of a piano in the background, or a candlelit bedroom, perhaps with the bed strewn with rose or jasmine petals.

LOVE-PLAY HAS A PRELUDE

The prelude to love-play may be deliberately programmed or entirely spontaneous. A nervous laugh, significant glance, double entendre, or similar gesture or comment from either partner could touch off a train of delightful events—whether a brief exchange of sensual affections or lengthy lovemaking in the form of repeated, passionate coitus.

The signals may be romantic. By stroking the partner's palm very lightly with a finger or sucking a fingertip, one can ignite an all-night conflagration. Occasional butterfly kisses—quick, light, flirtatious—here and there on the partner's arm, face, and neck titillate. Nibbling an earlobe is one way to excite a partner. After all, some of the acupoints on the ear are love points. The natural fragrance of a clean woman is intoxicating to some men, especially during an erotic encounter.

Olfactory sensitivity is a major element in Chinese erotic poetry, as seen in the celebrated poem "Ten Fragrances," mentioned earlier. It is also important in the West. The French, for instance, use the term *cassolette* (perfume pan) to describe the fragrance from a woman's body—lips, hair, skin, armpits, vulva—as well as her lingerie. This natural feminine fragrance is best enjoyed with the sniff-kiss, or so-called Chinese kiss, done by putting one's nose next to the selected area of the partner's body and sniffing away soulfully. The Chinese use the nasal kiss mainly as an affectionate gesture with little children and as a flirtatious act between sexes. Lip-kissing is strictly an erotic bedroom act in China.

If partners are dining privately, perhaps with candlelight and

soft music, feeding one another may be stimulating. The feeding can progress from spooning food into one another's mouth, to mouth-to-mouth transfer of soft food. Ideal erotic foods for this purpose include peaches, jelly, raw oysters, and clams. Mouth-to-mouth feeding of wine is an age-old sensual act that tantalizes many lovers. Some people delight in pouring a little champagne into the navel of the partner, and drinking from—as well as licking and kissing—the fleshy cup. The chilled, fizzing champagne stimulates the partner onto whose navel it is poured. Warm rice wine, such as Chinese Shaoshing or Japanese sake, is a good alternative.

One of the great preliminaries to sex is dancing—touch dancing. Many forms of dancing, in fact, are evolved from stylized, symbolic representations of the sexual act. Touch dancing may permit one to sense a lot physically about one's partner through rhythm, movement, and body contact—even with the clothes on. A discerning individual can appraise intuitively the sexual style of the dancing partner. Dancing in private while half dressed or undressed is a spicy prelude to love-play.

Signals of this prelude are often playful. Sporadic, fleeting gestures carried out in a seemingly accidental or absentminded manner have a built-in safety cushion in case of resistance, yet they may be very tantalizing to a receptive target. Some signals are especially effective, whether one is dealing with a sexually inhibited partner or a familiar but hitherto platonic friend. One is the "dead hand," by which a person "absentmindedly" and lightly places a hand on another's upper arm, shoulder, waist, or thigh. If the reaction is negative, the hand is promptly withdrawn; if there is no negative reaction, it remains there without any movement, as if dead; if the reaction is positive, the dead hand comes to life and becomes progressively friskier.

Another playful ploy is a pinch, applied on some firm, fleshy part of the body such as the shoulder if one is shy, or the thigh or buttocks if one is bolder. The surprise smack, administered in the form of a single resounding slap on the recipient's rear, is a great ice-breaker at an opportune moment, for instance when the person targeted is picking something up from the floor. Tickling, popular with teenagers, is also great for grown-ups, because the sensation is definitely sexual. The armpits, the undersides of the knees, the soles of the feet, the nape of the neck, the sides of the torso, and the inner thighs are most sensitive to tickling. An infallible erotic prelude is friendly wrestling. Since this playful tussle requires neither a referee nor rules, a handcuff hold by the stronger partner may easily lead to more interesting activities.

A preliminary with great physical potential is the pillow fight. This bedroom game may dissipate any latent sexual hostility and at the same time bring partners to enjoy erotic playfulness. Down pillows with no buttons or other hardware attached are the ideal weapons. One can hit the opponent at various strategic spots with great gusto, without causing any real injury, as long as no heavy blows reach the face, breasts, or genitals of either partner. As a vigorous pillow fight may result in a mess of flying feathers, one might want to consider pillows with synthetic or rag stuffing.

As for clothing, a couple may start their love-play dressed, partly dressed, or undressed, according to their personal taste and the whim of the moment. Disrobing oneself rapidly bespeaks either great urgency or lack of finesse. Sometimes partners' undressing each other can be a potent source of erotic arousal, seductive and titillating. This can be done slowly, in for example a game of strip poker, in which the loser of each round must divest one or more articles of clothing.

Pressing On at Love-Play

Whether the prelude lasts the wink of an eye or an hour, or even days, the unmistakably sexual love-play that follows often evokes all the senses of both partners. This phase of lovemaking consists mainly of kissing, hugging, and caressing. These activities can be enjoyed with endless variations. They involve the entire body, and eventually focus on the genital area.

Kissing is an effective and essential part of love-play. The mouth, lined with soft, pliable tissues including keen tactile and taste sensors, is an erotic organ. It is extremely responsive to sexual stimulation. The sensitive nerve endings on the lips and tongue and elsewhere inside the mouth can react erotically to the touch of a lover's lips, tongue, and in moments of passion, teeth. The tactile sensation varies with the amount of suction used. Since the olfactory nerve cells in the nose are near the mouth, the scent of a partner's breath, mouth, and the surrounding skin is highly arous-

ing, especially when combined with the very personal taste of lips and tongue. In erotic mouth-to-mouth kissing, one touches, tastes, and smells a member of the opposite sex; this intimacy is analogous to coitus.

The erotic kiss may be as light and fickle as a flitting butterfly, or as deep and enduring as the celebrated French kiss, indulged in by the young people of Pays de Mont in Brittany, in which lovers use their tongues to penetrate and explore one another's mouth, sometimes for hours on end.

Deep kissing is usually the first undeniably erotic act between lovers. Depending on the degree of intimacy and the mood of the moment, it often leads to other forms of touching, namely caressing. Experienced lovers who want to arouse and pleasure their mates have quite a store of information on this: modern sexologists have enumerated erogenous zones, and ancient Taoists mapped various love points on the body. Any part of the body, actually, could be an erogenous zone. Stroking the nape of the neck lightly, kissing the sides of the neck, probing the ear opening with a stiff tongue, nibbling the earlobe might bring a partner to a high pitch. Other erogenous zones are the armpits; inside the elbows, thighs, and knees; at the lower spine; and of course, in the genital areas. Some of the love points identified by the ancient Taoists coincide with the erogenous zones, while others do not. Love points are discussed further in chapter 15.

The sensitivity of the commonly accepted erogenous zones differs among individuals; some people, in fact, are completely without sensitivity in certain areas. Some women's breasts are so sensitive that when caressed the woman may reach an orgasm; other women may be unarousable when so caressed. In zones generally less sensitive than the breast, the reaction is even more unpredictable. But most people's erogenous zones are erotically sensitive. A careful lover first explores and experiments on these areas in love-play to find the most effective way to arouse and pleasure the partner. Sensitivity to erotic caresses usually increases from the extremities of limbs to the torso, and from the peripheral parts of the torso to its middle. Caressing a partner in the peripheral areas and progressing to more sensitive areas tends to create a crescendo of desire.

Kissing naturally merges with caressing in love-play. With some exceptions, a good lover does not zero in on the partner's genitals in the beginning, sometimes not even on the breasts. An inexperienced or inconsiderate lover, usually the male, is often guilty of heavy-handed love-play. A rough squeeze or two of a woman's breasts, a firm grab of her buttocks, and he is ready for penetration and discharge. Such a crude style turns many women off. What turns them on, at least in the beginning, are gentle and tender caresses. Energetic, vigorous love-play is effective when the partner has been highly stimulated already. Even many men are aroused more by love-play that titillates and tantalizes. And it should be remembered that the sight, sound, and scent of an aroused mate are often potent aphrodisiacs.

Most women are highly stimulated by having their breasts caressed and kissed. There is an important nerve link between a woman's lips and her breasts, and another between her breasts and her genitals; thus mouth-to-mouth kissing often makes her nipples become erect, and stimulation of her breasts by a lover often causes her clitoris to become erect and her sexual juices to flow. A good kiss is, therefore, the start of a delightful "downhill" journey.

In some passionate women mere psychological reactions may make their nipples erect. But most are aroused by a combination of psychological factors and the physical love-play at their breasts. A good lover therefore, after kissing and caressing his partner's face, neck, and shoulders, will go on to her breasts. When done with tender passion, this will greatly arouse his partner.

Most women enjoy having their breasts cupped and hefted with the palms, lightly stroked around the nipples, rhythmically and gently squeezed. They love having their breasts kissed, and their nipples sucked and playfully licked with the tip of the tongue. The tongue's underside is smooth, like the lips, and its top is rough. By using the smooth and rough sides alternately, a man can give varying sensations to a woman. Only after such exquisitely stimulating preliminaries should he go on to lower areas—buttocks, groin, perineum, vulva, clitoris.

GENITAL CARESSING—AND BEYOND

Love-play progresses naturally to the genital area. Caressing a lover's genitals—with the hand, the mouth, or another part of the body—is the most passionate and intimate form of noncoital erotic communication between lovers. It may end right there, to be repeated some other time; it may result in orgasm; it may lead directly to coitus.

Genital caressing may involve any of a number of techniques: stroking, pressing, rubbing, vibrating, tickling, thrusting, kissing, nibbling, licking, sucking—all carried out with varying pressure, speed, and rhythm. Some people delight in continuous, relentless caresses, while others prefer a teasing, repeated stop-and-go approach.

As all these genital organs are made of tender, sensitive tissue, genital caressing is best begun with slow, light touches; it may then progress to more active, speedier, heavier caresses. Such a gradual buildup prepares the participants not only emotionally but also physically; among other things, it promotes genital lubrication, without which any heavy, passionate caress would be uncomfortable, even painful. Different techniques of caressing suit different zones of the pubic area. Light strokes and soft kisses are most arousing to the insides of the thighs and groin. The cinnabar field and a woman's mons veneris respond favorably to the massaging palm. The fleshy derriere can withstand much heavier caresses, such as kneading, squeezing, and light smacking. Stroking the buttocks with an occasional side excursion to the perineum is quite arousing.

Oral-genital play ranges from lightly kissing a lover's genitals to using the mouth and tongue as sexual organs in simulated copulation. Some people find this thrilling, while others are repelled by it. According to recent polls conducted by *Redbook* and other magazines, a large majority of Americans in higher education and income groups experiment with or regularly practice cunnilingus, fellatio, and such play.

One of the most erotically sensitive zones, and often one of the most neglected, is the perineum, the site of a cluster of sexual nerve endings. It corresponds to the *hui-yin* acupoint, which stimulates male erection as well as female desire. Caressing the perineum lightly with the fingers or the tip of the tongue is very stimulating.

Many think of the anus as solely an excretory organ. Actually, it is connected with sexual nerves, some of which are highly aroused when the anus—washed very clean—is caressed. The

French use the term *postillonage* to describe pressing and poking it with a finger, and *feuille de rose* (rose leaf) to describe licking it and probing into it with the tip of the tongue. Anal caressing is a matter of personal preference.

Genital Secretions

The caressing and the kissing of the genitals inevitably involve genital secretions, nature's ingenious preparation for coitus. By lubricating the sexual organs, these secretions facilitate intercourse. As a pheromone, they also act as a sexual attractant, arousing partners greatly. The ancient Taoists considered ample lubrication of paramount importance for pleasurable sex. So do modern sexologists, who suggest substitutes such as saliva or artificial lubricants in case of emergency. As with food, natural ingredients are always the best.

From a scientific point of view, genital secretions are similar to saliva. The genitals, if carefully cleaned, have a lower bacterial count than the mouth.

Genital secretion from an aroused male comes as a clear, slippery liquid oozing from the mouth of the penis. It originates in two pea-size glands just beneath the prostate, and several smaller ones in the urethra. This secretion is not semen, although if the man becomes highly aroused it may contain a small amount. In the woman, a similar liquid is emitted from four vestibular glands around the vagina opening. Under sexual excitement, the wall of the vagina also "sweats" out a liquid, which at times can be copious.

The semen ejaculated during male orgasm comes from the testicles and the prostate. This sticky, milky fluid becomes more liquid soon after exposure to air. As mentioned earlier, sexologists report that some women ejaculate a fluid when they have a deep uterine orgasm. This transparent liquid serves no biological function and is believed by some sexologists to enhance sexual pleasure.

Warning: Unless a couple has had a strictly monogamous relationship for years, and each partner knows of the other's sexual history, and has tested negative for HIV, it is *not* safe to indulge in any love-play or coitus that involves the exchange of bodily fluids.

CARESSING THE MOON GROTTO

Kissing and caressing by her lover normally are sufficient to arouse a woman so that her moon grotto is lubricated and her clitoris is erect. Her partner can easily ascertain this by occasional quick forays to the vaginal area when he is fondling her thighs and buttocks. The clitoris is very sensitive to touch. Its shaft rather than its sensitive tip should be caressed; in some women the tip can stand only the lightest touch, and a heavy caress could be uncomfortable. Next are the labia minora, or inner lips, of the vulva. By alternately caressing the clitoris and the vulva, first lightly, then moderately, a man may intensify his partner's pleasure rapidly. By stroking along the labia minora and then around the rim of the vagina opening with his middle and index fingers, he can induce more lubrication to flow. If he scoops up these secretions with his fingers, he can rub the shaft of the clitoris with them. If the woman spreads her thighs wide, the classics indicate, she is responding favorably to the manual love-play. When her partner gets this signal, his fingers can probe deeper into her moon grotto. He can intensify her sensations by using one or two fingers to go deep, touch her flower heart, and stroke it lightly.

If the love-play is aimed at the woman's orgasm, the man can bring her to climax by stimulating her clitoris. Some women are capable of multiple orgasms through clitoral stimulation. A few passionate women can go from orgasm to orgasm for a considerable time. The man can bring her to a much more intense uterine orgasm by caressing her G spot; many women, however, appreciate a deep orgasm better during coitus, if the man knows the right positions and dynamics. He can find the G spot by inserting his middle and index fingers about two inches inside the opening of the grotto. With his finger pads facing the front wall of the grotto canal, he massages exploringly. He can tell from the woman's reaction whether he has found the bean-size spot, which may protrude slightly upon stimulation. Once there, he can press the spot lightly and rhythmically. By pushing down on her mons veneris with the palm of the other hand at the same time, the man can increase the pressure on the G spot.

CARESSING THE JADE STALK

Caressing the male genitals can be tricky, depending on whether the man is to ejaculate or not. If he is not, either he should be conversant with the techniques of orgasmic brinkmanship, or there should be prior agreement on what signals he should give the woman to stop as soon as he senses the approach of his crisis. An experienced woman can sense when the man is near the brink even without his signaling, and beat a hasty retreat. But since a man's power to hold back may vary from time to time, it is always safer to prearrange some signals.

Fondling the jade stalk is best done by first lightly stroking the perineum with the fingertips. The woman's fingers then move softly to the back, bottom, and front of the scrotum with half-tickling, half-soothing caresses. As the scrotum is the most vulnerable part of the man's body, the woman should stroke and tickle the testicles delicately. Pinching, squeezing, or nipping them is not love-play; it may cause excruciating pain, injury, or disability. After fondling the man's testicles, the woman's fingers move to his erect stalk. By gripping firmly near the tip with her palms and fingers, and moving her grasp toward the base, she makes its skin more taut. This exposes and tightens the engorged glans, or crown, which she can stimulate with the fingertips of the other hand, with short, light to-and-fro friction. The underside of an erect stalk is more sensitive than the upper side, and the glans and the ridge around its base are even more sensitive. The most sensitive part of the male stalk is the triangular knot-shaped frenulum at the underside of the ridge.

If there has been lubrication of the glans, the woman can smear the secretion with a fingertip in a rotary motion around the glans; she can do the same with her own saliva. The woman can vary the caress by pumping the shaft up and down with her grasping hand, but she must take care not to bring the man to ejaculation, unless this is intended. This stop-and-go technique can help the man delay or avoid ejaculation, while giving him great pleasure and rousing him tremendously.

If she desires, the woman can supplement her caressing with kissing the stalk. While holding the shaft, she can tentatively kiss the glans, then take it from there.

Love-play between partners is an extremely intimate and personal act. It is best tailored by the partners themselves according to their aesthetics and desires. They can create their own play of love—comedy, drama, or fantasy. As the ancient Taoists shrewdly found out, by harmonizing Yin and Yang through love-play, a couple can augment greatly their sexual energy for a fulfilling sexual union.

15

Spring Butterfly and Peacock Tease

Love Games for Grown-ups Only

PLAYING AT LOVE is most delightful when it is spontaneous and whimsical. At times, however, one can enliven it with some choreography. Love games add variety, excite the imagination, and stimulate creativity. Following are suggested love games for modern lovers, adapted from or inspired by ancient Chinese sexologists.

SPRING BUTTERFLY

This titillating game was invented by Chinese painters and calligraphers of yore. It requires a Chinese brush-pen, which has a soft, delicate pointed brush of sable, fox, or rabbit hair set in a thin bamboo tube. These brushes are available in Oriental stationery stores and bookstores; if you cannot find one, buy a Western-style artist's paintbrush. Avoid "flat" or "bright" brushes, which are square-edged. A "round" brush is serviceable, but the best is a "long," or pointed, brush. Avoid also stiff brushes, such as those made of hog bristle; camel or squirrel hair is adequate, but springy, soft sable is the best.

The brush-pen is the butterfly in springtime, and the nude body of the passive partner is the flower-covered landscape of hills and dales. This partner should lie totally relaxed, with eyes closed. Apply the springy tip of the brush to the partner's body like a flirtatious butterfly—here, there, everywhere. The tip of the brush first flits lightly over hands and feet, then moves to arms, legs, and other parts of the body. The "artist" concentrates on such sensitive spots as the fingertips, the palms, the insides of the elbows, the armpits, the soles, between the toes, behind the knees, and especially the insides of the thighs. Various parts of the face, including the lips, are titillated next. Then down the neck to the breasts, the cinnabar field, and the groin. The butterfly touches are delicious to the closed-eyed partner—especially as it is not known where they will land next. The tiny, electric spasms created on the skin are likely to bring forth a plea for firmer caresses. The artist should not give in to such a plea until the moist landing is ready.

For this exquisite stage, dip the tip of the brush in a little aromatic oil. On a woman, caress her areolas and nipples with the oiled brush; go around and around, and flit between the breasts. Next, open her legs and let the butterfly flirt along her perineum and vulva. Then brush her clitoris, first in upward strokes, next in a circular motion. On a man, brush his perineum and scrotum and the exposed glans. You may give your loved one a marvelous, unforgettable hour with this extraordinary game.

A woman with long eyelashes can turn them into spring butterflies by blinking at her partner at extremely close quarters. A man can commandeer his moustache for the same purpose. Such maneuvers may prove exhausting, however, if the whole territory is to be covered.

PEACOCK TEASE

This game was invented centuries ago, when the peacock feather became a decoration of meritorious service to the emperor. Noblemen who were interested in a different type of meritorious service used a peacock feather playfully on their women. Nowadays either partner, male or female, can use the feather on the other. Feathers from ostriches, pheasants, storks, and even chickens also can be used. Be advised that feathers do not have as wide a variation in pressure as an artist's brush.

SPIDER'S LEGS

In this French love-game, *pattes d'araignée,* the fingertips and finger pads play on the partner's body hair, and occasionally skin, with the lightest touches possible. Like the spring butterfly, the spider can go all over the body.

SILK TEASE

For this love game, a scarf or lingerie of genuine silk is preferable; otherwise soft acetate will do. Do not use nylon, as it is too stiff. Crumple the scarf or other item slightly in your hand, and use it to caress various parts of your partner's body. Silk gives a rich, luxurious sensation, quite different from that of brush-pens or feathers.

SNIFF-KISSING

The sniff-kiss is used here to its full extent if your partner's skin is perfumed lightly with crushed jasmine or tuberose, or if your partner's body emits its own sexual aroma. Begin by inhaling and sniffing the breath of your loved one. Nudge your nose on your partner's cheeks, eyelids, and neck, and continue the scented pilgrimage up the peak and down the valley. The natural scent of aroused genitals is a strong aphrodisiac between lovers.

TONGUE SWEEP

This game may—and quite naturally does—start with a roving kiss. The tongue is lavished on a partner with touches ranging from the lightest tickling with the tip to a firm brushing with its rough surface. Zero in on the ear cavity, under the chin, and the palms and soles. Then target the navel, the breasts and nipples, inside the thighs, and the perineum.

A thorough tongue tease will deplete your supply of saliva, no matter how much you may drool. Intersperse the sweep with sniff-kisses.

LOVE POINTS

Among the most fascinating but least known aspects of ancient Chinese erotica is the system of specific acupoints along the body's meridians that when properly stimulated cause immediate sexual arousal, long-term boosting of sexual stamina, and/or tune-up of the autonomic nervous system controlling many sexual sensations and functions. Each of these love points is a carefully mapped acupoint in classical acupuncture. Each has an equivalent international code number used by Western and other non-Chinese researchers in acupuncture. The *hui-yin* point on the perineum, for example, now carries the international label "CV-1" (number 1 point of the conception vessel). In traditional acupuncture, most of these acupoints have general health as well as sexual functions.

The love points are presented here in a very simplified manner, and are selected according to the zones of the body rather than a specific meridian. This is for the practical use of modern lovers who do not have the time or patience to spend months studying such acupoints. The love points can be located on the relevant maps on this page and the following two pages; individual names are given only for selected points.

Love points are scattered all over the human body, but the majority are concentrated on the torso. Acupressure, not acupuncture, may be used on love points; indeed, some love points should *never* be pricked by needles. Some points may be stroked or gently pressed and vibrated with the fingertips, while others may be massaged with the palm. It is at times difficult to locate love points and other acupoints on the body, but in many cases they can be found if finger pressure causes a sensation of tenderness. Partners who want to locate the points, and play the game, should study the maps and explore.

The game of love points may be played as ongoing, long-term therapy for sexual energy, or it may serve as an interlude during love-play. Partners may want to combine love-point acupressure with erotic massage, discussed later.

The major love points are described below, with suggestions on how to stimulate them:

Perineum: The *hui-yin* (sex crossroads), one of the most important love points, is located at the midpoint of the perineum, slightly beneath the skin. In acupuncture, it is important in treating penile pain, vaginitis, irregular menstruation, and prolapse of the uterus. For sexual arousal in love-play, the perineum may be stroked and the point pressed with a fingertip for 4 seconds, then released and pressed again, 40 times or for 5 minutes. This point is one of the two known erection centers for men.

Cinnabar field: From the navel down to the pubic symphysis (at the front of the pubic bone, felt just above the genitals) is a line of seven love points. An approximate way to locate them is to consider the distance between the navel and the pubic symphysis as five segments, each a little over an inch long. The navel itself has a love point. One segment below it is *yin-chiao* (sexual junction). Half a segment below this is *chi-hai* (sea of *chi*), a major love point next to the cinnabar field. Half a segment below it is *shih-men* (stone gate). Below it, at the bottom of each of the next three segments are *kuen-yuan* (pass of primacy), *chung-chi* (ultimate middle), and *chu-ku,* the pubic bone.

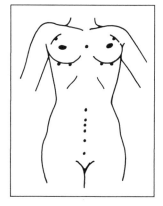

Map of love points

These seven front midline love points are intimately linked with sexual well-being and sexual desire. During love-play all of them should be stroked and pressed with the palm. They should be pressed or rubbed lightly—never heavily—with the fingertip, the finger pad, or the thumb. Press each time for about 3 to 5 seconds; then release and press again. By moving down from the navel to the pubic area, and giving gentle acupressure some 10 times to each point, one progresses to points of increasing arousal. A firmed-up tongue-tip may be used in place of the finger.

Breasts: Love points on the female breasts are both for short-term arousal and long-term enlargement. Each of the nipples contains a love point. On the breastbone, at the same level of the nipples, is another, sometimes called the middle cinnabar field. About an inch up from each nipple toward the corresponding shoulder is another love point. At the base of the breasts are two more pairs. Except for the point on the breastbone, the love points are to be pressed and stroked with the palm and palpated lightly with the finger.

Groin: About two inches down the crease between the abdomen and the thighs are a pair of love points. Touching them, by pressing lightly and stroking along the groin with the fingertips, may alleviate frigidity and impotence.

205

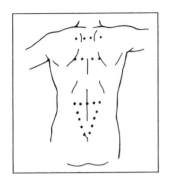

Map of love points

Upper back: There are four pairs of love points on the upper back that may be stimulated for sexual energy. To locate them, imagine, on either side of the spine, two parallel vertical lines, one about 1 ½ inches and the other about 3 inches from the spine. The top points of these lines align with the lower end of the second thoracic vertebra; the bottom ones align with the lower end of the fifth thoracic vertebra. Press each point firmly with the fingertips for a few seconds; then release. Move to the next point. Repeat the acupressure trip a few times.

Lower back: Immediately below the second lumbar vertebra, right on the spine and a little below the back of the waist, is *ming-men* (life gate), an important point for sexual energy and the second erection center for the male. Press this love point firmly with the fingertips for what should be satisfying results. At the same level as this point, on either side of the spine, are two more love points, about 1 ½ and 3 inches from the spine. They should be pressed along with the life gate.

Sacral-coccygeal area: Press firmly with the fingertips on the eight love points lined up in a narrow V on the sacrum. A ninth point is on the tip of the coccyx.

Thighs and legs: On the front of each thigh, about midway between the kneecap and the groin, are two love points. About two inches above the kneecap, at the bulge of muscles slightly toward the inside, is another point. These may be pressed firmly with the thumb.

Lower legs: The most important love point on the lower leg is *san-yin-chiao* (junction of three Yins), which is on the inside of the shin, about three inches above the apex of the medial malleolus, behind the tibia. Pressure on this point may alleviate impotence, frigidity, and premature ejaculation.

EROTIC MASSAGE

One of the most sensual games in love-play is erotic massage. The three-thousand-year-old Chinese massage is aimed not so much at the muscles as at the *chi* meridians and the central nervous system, which controls both body and mind. This venerable classical therapy, when specially adapted for certain areas of the body by a beloved mate, can intensify the alchemy of desire delightfully.

Numerous volumes have been written on this therapeutic art, which requires complicated techniques and much practice to be truly effective. A book of this scope, therefore, will not pretend to cover whole-body erotic massage. Rather, a few simple techniques are presented, and several areas of the body where erotic massage works best are highlighted. Couples who combine these massage techniques with the game of love points on the preceding pages will obtain even greater effects.

Some ground rules: Since massage is a form of nonverbal communication, an unspoken rapport is established between two individuals through the intimate contact of hands and body. In erotic massage, the partners are preferably nude or almost nude, to facilitate the skin-to-skin exchange of life-force and sexual energy. All parts of the body, except the genitals, may be touched. Most areas may be massaged firmly except those vulnerable to injury (e.g., abdomen, female breasts), where gentle stroking is the basic touch. The partner being massaged should lie on a floor mat, a narrow table, a daybed, or a bed with an extrafirm mattress.

Massage can be done without lubricant or, if preferred, with scented water or oil. A good homemade lubricant is a mixture of two-thirds soybean oil, one-third sesame oil, and a sprinkling of aromatic essence such as lavender, chamomile, rose, sandalwood, or ylang-ylang. Sesame oil is very good for the skin; ylang-ylang, from a tropical Asian flower, is considered an aphrodisiac and has a positive effect on blood pressure. Oils are available in Chinese groceries; aromatic essences from natural food stores and pharmacies.

An erotic massage can be a whole-body affair, beginning at fingers and toes and progressing along the limbs to the rest of the body. This easily takes an hour. Partners may prefer an abridged version concentrating on the torso and thighs, which takes 20 minutes or less. The partner being massaged should try to relax, at times with eyes closed, and breathe slowly and deeply with the diaphragm. Manipulative techniques are numerous, and include effleurage (long, rhythmic stroking), tapotement (patting, percussing), petrissage (compressing, kneading), rubbing, pinching, pressing, scraping, grasping, hammering, shaking, and vibrating. The masseur or masseuse performs these with thumb and finger pads, fingers, palms, palm edges, fists, and even soles and elbows. It is fascinating to listen to the rhythm of massage as performed by an expert; it may resemble a work of classical music, from the prelude, through the main section with its changing cadences, to the grand finale.

Head and neck: Stroke with the fingers of both hands, with moderate pressure, from the middle of the forehead to the sides. Press on the temples with the fingertips, moderately and rhythmically. Massage both sides of the chin with the fingers. With the thumb and index finger of one hand, press and pinch the back of the neck, starting from the base of the skull and moving down to the base of the neck. Next stroke the sides of the neck with the fingers of both hands.

Shoulders: With the thumb and index finger of one hand, pinch the tendons between the back and sides of the neck and the shoulders. Start with light pinches; if your partner responds favorably, increase the pressure to firm. Knead the muscles on the outside of both shoulders.

Upper back: With the partner lying prone, the masseur or masseuse kneels astride the waist. The best way to massage the back is with acupressure. Use the thumb pads to press with moderate firmness between the roots of the ribs, about 1 1/2 inches from the spine, and on either side. Press for about 3 or 4 seconds, then release, and move to the next points, and the next, until you reach the waist. An invigorating hammer massage with the fists is great for the fleshy part of the upper back.

Lower back: Stroke the area with fingers and palms, while kneeling astride the partner's knees. Combine the massage with pressure on the love points, especially the important *ming-men.*

Buttocks: After pressing the love points in the sacral-coccygeal area, use the massage techniques best for the fleshy buttocks proper. Kneel astride your partner's thighs. Use the palms to press both cheeks with the force of your body weight for about 10 seconds.

Then soothe the buttocks with fingers stroking upward vertically, left fingers on left buttock, right on right. Start from the valley and stroke to both sides. Next press and palpate the buttocks moderately with both palms, so that vital energy flows from your hands to your partner's body. Grasp a handful of flesh with all your fingers, and knead with firm pressure. Then knead all over the buttocks.

Percussion on the buttocks is particularly stimulating. With the edges of both palms, chop the left and right buttocks alternately, rapidly and with moderate force. You may use your own steady rhythm or follow that of a recorded tune. Progress to another form of percussion by slapping the buttocks with partially cupped hands. Don't mind the resulting noise; the massage is extremely invigorating—and fun too.

Breasts: Let your partner lie supine, with arms slightly extended, and feet about 12 inches apart. The front of the body is to be massaged. With your fingers, sweep your partner's body—from toes to legs, thighs, torso, and finally down the arms. Do this a few times for a tranquilizing effect. To massage a woman's breasts, use only the palms, except when you are pressing love points lightly. Put one palm under a breast, lift it slightly, and stroke it with the palm. Meanwhile, with the spread fingers of the other hand, press very gently, with the same rhythm as for the palm movement. Move to the other breast. Only feather-light stroking should be used on the nipples. Massage of the breasts is best combined with the game of love points for this area and the Breast Circles exercise done by the massaged partner.

Cinnabar field: This soft, unprotected portion of the body is very vulnerable in kung fu—and in love-play. Massage the area with one or both palms, pressing down lightly. This is best done if the active partner kneels astride and on the partner's thighs, or kneels between the partner's spread thighs. Combine the massage with the game of love points for this area and the Cinnabar Field Massage. Since the cinnabar field region is where life-force and sexual *chi* are generated, be sure to recharge it with your deft hands.

Groin: With the pads of three extended fingers, massage along one groin of the partner, then the other. A bit of scented oil will protect the tender skin here from friction. A woman doing the massaging should use her free hand to push the man's genitals slightly to the side.

Thighs: Grasp the front muscles of the thigh with the fingers and thumbs of both hands, and knead. Grasp up and down between the groin and the knee. Then press moderately with the thumb on points about an inch apart, down a line. Move to a line about 1 ½ inches to the side. Finally, stroke lightly on the inside of the thighs with the finger pads. By then the partner being massaged should spread his or her thighs wide apart and bend the knees, to facilitate the next massage.

Perineum: Press the perineum love point, *hui-yin,* rhythmically, and then massage the entire perineum, from the edge of the anus to the edge of the vulva or the bottom of the scrotum. If this is done with finesse, the sexual life-force of the massaged partner will flare up, so that the partners can go directly to coitus, or to more intense love games such as Playing the Flute or Jade Fountain.

THREE FOUNTAINS

The triple game of Three Fountains is based on the Art of the Three Peaks, which enables a man to obtain sexual nutrients from the three peaks of a woman's body: the Red Lotus Peak (tongue), the Twin Lotus Peaks (breasts), and the Purple Agaric Peak (clitoris). On each peak is a fountain: the Heavenly Fountain, the Twin Fountains, and the Jade Fountain, respectively. The triple game may be played separately, or in sequence during love-play. It is described here as three individual games:

Heavenly Fountain: This love game, which can be played between partners during deep kissing, involves stimulating secretion of the partner's saliva, and drinking it as an elixir. While kissing, use your tongue to caress your partner's tongue. Then use the tip of the tongue to sweep over and titillate the roof of your partner's mouth next to the molars on both sides, where ducts leading from saliva glands are located, and to sweep the floor of your partner's mouth along the inside of the teeth and especially next to the tongue's root, where numerous ducts lead from saliva glands in the jaw. The tongue stimulation will produce a rich flow of saliva in the Heavenly Fountain of both partners. Ancient sexologists considered saliva a sexual elixir; modern scientists say it contains a sex hormone and substances called semio-chemicals whose taste is craved by the opposite sex. Drink it from the source.

Twin Fountains: Kissing the female breast is universally done, and a man can give his partner great pleasure by pretending to nurse at her breasts, as if he were a baby. Suck the nipples lightly and rhythmically, occasionally tickling them with the tip of the tongue. Use a hand to "milk" the breast while sucking. Unless your partner is a nursing mother, the milk here is spiritual. And even a dry run is fun.

Jade Fountain: Drinking directly from the jade fountain represented a serious quest for life-nutrients to sexual alchemists. As a modern love game, it is a most delightful experience for women. This is not the run-of-the-mill oral-genital play of kissing the vulva; it involves the more complex eliciting of jade essence from the fountain. The experience of the man in this game has been compared to eating a freshly split pomegranate, or "peach of immortality"; the experience of the woman is indescribable.

The game requires first of all complete cleanliness. The woman lies on her back with her knees bent, her thighs spread wide, her feet on the edge of the bed; she also may slump in an armchair, with her knees bent on the armrests. The man kneels down, facing her. (Alternatively, the partners may both lie in bed on their sides, or one on top of the other, in reverse directions. These two positions are good for this game alone or, when combined with Playing the Flute, in the favorite French game of *soixante-neuf,* or 69—whose very name is a visual representation of mutal oral-genital play.)

The man kisses the woman's mons veneris, then opens the outer lips of her vulva with his fingers, and kisses the inner lips. He should use his tongue to caress the inner lips, which should already be blood-engorged. If you consider the vulva as the sides of a boat, the urethra, the vaginal orifice, and the four vestibular glands are on the bottom of this boat. Sweep the tip of the tongue up and down the boat bottom. Thrust the tongue into the vagina

Soixante-neuf *love-play*

and pull it out, and repeat rhythmically. The tongue caress gradually goes to the clitoral area. Kiss the little button with your lips. Suck it very gently, and tickle its tip with your tongue like a butterfly. Use the rough surface of the tongue to lick upward from the base of the clitoris shaft. Alternate the caresses between the clitoris and the vulva, concentrating on maneuvers that elicit your partner's most enthusiastic responses.

This game will inevitably cause the jade fountain to overflow with jade essence from the vestibular glands and the grotto wall. It may produce some surprising sound effects as well.

PLAYING THE FLUTE

Like Jade Fountain, this game requires scrupulous personal hygiene as well as the utmost delicacy. Some women love it; others dislike it, usually because of the hazards involved: the gag reflex in cases of deep throat, and inadvertent swallowing of the semen if the man is unable or unwilling to practice orgasmic brinkmanship. Some practice and cooperation, however, can get things under control easily. The rest is a matter of personal taste.

The game is best begun with the woman's kissing the man's perineum and scrotum. Then comes the flute-playing. By holding the base of the jade flute firmly with one hand, so that it stands vertically, the woman can control the situation. Give a series of light kisses to the glans, and then hold the glans in your mouth by surrounding the ridge with your lips. Lick the glans, and especially the tiny urethra opening, with the tip of your tongue. Next purse your mouth into a tight O and imagine it as the grotto opening. Move your mouth up and down, or let your partner move the flute in and out, while your fingers play on his perineum and scrotum. Remember that the most sensitive part is the top third of the flute.

Many men, more for psychological than for physical pleasure, like their partners to deep-throat them. When the tip of the flute touches the woman's throat, it will normally—and unpleasantly—activate her gag reflex. By practicing with a gradually deepening approach, a woman can accommodate the intruder easily, if that is what she prefers.

Flute-playing, especially the deep-throat variety, can bring a man to ejaculate in his partner's mouth. Some women avidly swallow the elixir, which scientists say is clean and harmless and which the ancients believed beneficial. Other women, however, do not care for this. If her partner does ejaculate, a woman can keep the fluid in her mouth and then spit it out. Or better yet, she can arrange with him beforehand to signal when he senses the brink is near.

These bedroom games for grown-ups can be played with many variations, according to the desires of the individuals involved. The pace may range from the leisurely to the energetic, the adaptations from the traditional to the bizarre. Whatever the erotic fancy of the lovers, they should avoid any circumstances that might cause mental, physical, or emotional harm to each other.

16

Orgasmic Brinkmanship and Multiple O's

Intensifying and Prolonging Ecstasy

THE BASIC PURPOSE of the ancient Chinese art of lovemaking, as has been suggested, is threefold: to delay the man, accelerate the woman, and prolong and intensify pleasure for both. The various techniques of coitus were developed with these goals in mind.

When we borrow from this art for the modern bedroom, it profits us to experiment, modify, and where possible, refine it. The physiological, psychological, and cultural differences between practitioners today and those in the past, as well as the recognition that there are differences among individuals, demand a flexible rather than a rigid approach.

We can implement the ancient art on at least two levels. First, a trigger-happy man can learn to delay ejaculation until his partner "rejoices." Second, on a higher level, more ambitious couples can reward themselves with some advanced lovemaking. Good lovers can give unbelievable sexual pleasure to their partners. A man can bring a woman to a series of "little deaths" in the form of multiple orgasms, or to an intense, "flower heart," or cervical, orgasm. A woman not only can cooperate with her partner to enhance her own responses, but can energize him to the maximum without pushing him over the brink; she can even seize the initiative. A man and a woman who together have refined the ancient techniques into their own modern art can reap a rich harvest in their sex life. They can intensify and prolong one another's erotic pleasure easily. Any couple can become good lovers, unless they are hindered by physiological or psychological barriers, or unless they do not care.

The ancient "mechanics" of coitus that modern lovers might learn include sexual positions and coital dynamics, which involves movement, speed, angle, and rhythm. But before these possibilities, they must investigate an even more basic aspect of lovemaking—physical compatibility.

COITAL FIT

Some couples are unaware that mere genital incompatibility, especially discrepancy in size, may be the reason for their sexual problems. Anthropologists tell us that human beings have the largest brains and genitals among the primates. The average length of an erect human penis is 6 inches, or 15 centimeters. The average depth of the human vagina is 4 inches, or 10 centimeters. This difference is not a problem in itself, as the vagina is elastic and in intercourse the degree of penetration varies.

Difficulties arise, however, when there is a marked discrepancy of genital size between partners. Unless care is used, for instance, too long a penis or too shallow a vagina could mean pain and injury to a woman in the heat of passion. On the other hand, a small penis may give pleasure to neither partner. In extreme cases, violent penetration by a long penis may lacerate the vaginal vault and induce life-threatening internal bleeding. Unless a woman has a loose vagina, literally speaking, too long a penis is a curse rather than a blessing for her.

Writers of crude pornography the world over extol enormous penises, as if a woman's sexual pleasure were in direct proportion to the length of her partner's organ. If so, a donkey would be a better lover than any human male. In more sophisticated erotic literature, genital size is seldom a matter for concern. And in practice, in fact, there are "remedies" for disproportion. To prevent injury to partners, Frenchmen with undesirably long organs use *bourrelets,* small thick cushions with a hole in the center which are tied with ribbons to the hips. Perhaps partly because of their characteristic slenderness, the Chinese consider a very long penis a disadvantage, and a large clitoris repulsive. The ancient Taoist sexologists valued skill over equipment, and art over skill. As the magician says, it is not the size of the wand, but the magic in it.

Coital fit can be improved to a large extent by choosing an appropriate position for copulation, as shown later in this chapter. Furthermore, size should not be the focus. It is not phallic size but phallic performance, proven through the durability of the erection, and orgasmic brinkmanship that are essential for sexual pleasure.

ORGASMIC BRINKMANSHIP

Talk of sexual pleasure is much ado about nothing, if in coitus a man ejaculates soon after insertion. Here, as we have seen, the ancient Chinese techniques of male delaying or withholding are of immense value.

First a quick look at the physiology of orgasm. During love-play and coitus, if physical and psychological stimulation continue and intensify, the sexual tension in either or both partners mounts until it is suddenly discharged. This sexual release is orgasm, also known as climax or coming. It normally lasts only a few seconds, during which an individual undergoes involuntary muscular contractions, experiences ecstatic pleasure, and becomes oblivious to external surroundings. The French have an apt name for this sexual lightning: *la petite mort* (the little death).

Male and female orgasms are not exactly the same. In a man, orgasm is genitally oriented, explosive, and almost always accompanied by an ejaculation of semen. In a woman, it is a more diffuse, cerebral event, usually without ejaculation. Many women, however, emit a fluid from the urethra when they are deeply stimulated. The man's ejaculation normally demolishes his erection and thus temporarily prevents continued copulation. His erection will return minutes later if he is young and potent, but hours or even days later if he is older or less potent. A woman, with the capacity for multiple orgasms within a short time, usually has no such worry. Herein lies a potential problem for a couple. And it was this very problem that inspired ancient Taoists, who prided themselves in pleasing women sexually, to devise the trick of orgasmic brinkmanship.

The mechanism of male ejaculation is quite complex. When a man reaches orgasm, involuntary muscles of the prostate, seminal ducts, and seminal reservoirs begin a series of contractions, forcing the fluids they contain into the urethra. The man has reached a stage that Masters and Johnson call "ejaculatory inevitability": at this point ejaculation cannot be stopped. Contractions in the urethra and prostate now force the semen out of the penis.

The ancient Taoists considered this process not always inevitable, and because they believed that most if not all bodily processes were affected by the mind, they set out to find a way to stop or delay it. They devised a number of mind-body techniques to arrest the ejaculation of semen, just before the point of "inevitability" was reached. Since orgasm and ejaculation involve mostly the autonomic nervous system and involuntary muscles, a man must deliberately use his mind to train his nervous system to influence his body. When he has mastered the technique, a man can delay ejaculation during sexual intercourse or, if he wants to, avoid ejaculation altogether.

Mentally, the technique of orgasmic brinkmanship involves a relaxed approach, deliberate distraction from sexual sensations, and willpower not to ejaculate. Physically, it requires unhurried, shallow thrustings; deep breathing; a slowdown, pause, or complete withdrawal when sensations mount; and possibly "braking" with pressure on certain acupoints. Knowing exactly when and how to apply these measures is not simple. It is not always clear how close one is to the brink. Practice, self-discipline, and preferably, a cooperative partner are crucial for mastering orgasmic brinkmanship.

The Taoist or Zen attitude is advised for men here. Unwind fully, and enjoy yourself. Do not grit your teeth or tense your muscles; tension is the surest way to premature ejaculation. If you lose control at first, as will happen with beginners, it is no disaster; just try again. Even a master of brinkmanship may fall off the cliff if he is with a new partner. It takes a number of sessions for partners to adjust to one another.

When coitus begins, if you, the male, and your partner have enjoyed sufficient love-play and are in a romantic mood, the moon grotto should be well lubricated and the jade stalk quite rigid. Do not try to penetrate immediately. Instead, use the tip of the jade stalk to tease the shaft of the clitoris and the vestibule of the grotto between the inner lips. This will further arouse your partner and increase lubrication, which reduces friction and makes brinkmanship easier. If your partner wants immediate insertion, resist and withdraw; then tease her again. This will help build your self-confidence.

Advance the jade stalk tentatively and gradually. One Taoist school teaches fifteen deep breaths for the man for each inch he inserts. You need not follow this rigid rule, but you get the idea. For the manipulation of *chi* here, deep diaphragm breathing is of supreme importance. When insertion is complete, remain in without thrusting or letting your partner move. When your sensation quiets down, make shallow, leisurely thrusts. When thrusting, contract your cinnabar field and anus, and breathe deeply the entire time. Avoid deep thrusting during this initial stage.

If any acute sensation develops, slow or stop your movement. If necessary, withdraw completely for about 10 seconds; then reinsert. Your partner may be highly aroused while you try to keep your cool. Strangely, the more she is aroused, the more self-control you may develop in lovemaking. Try to discourage your partner from making any abrupt, impatient movements at this time.

Practice alone can help you sense accurately how close you are to the brink, and when you should slow down or stop before resuming coitus. If you sense yourself too close, apply the emergency brake: Press your middle and index fingers firmly on the *hui-yin* acupoint on your perineum for 4 or 5 seconds, while breathing deeply; repeat if necessary. If done in time, this should prevent any ejaculation; the pressure can be applied while the jade stalk is still inserted or after it is withdrawn. Only a virtuoso in orgasmic brinkmanship can dispense with such measures as pressing the *hui-yin* acupoint or the Tantric-inspired squeezing of the frenulum or base of the stalk (recommended by Masters and Johnson).

When you first begin to practice your self-control during intercourse, inform your partner. Otherwise, your huffing and puffing and other intense efforts might be mistaken as signs of apoplexy or heart attack. Your partner may become frantic or apoplectic herself; she may try to help with mouth-to-mouth resuscitation, which is delightful, or she may call for help, which could be embarrassing. During the early stages of brinkmanship, sympathetic cooperation from your partner is helpful to you both.

Some advice for women is in order here. Your partner's performance during the initial stages of brinkmanship may be frustrating; patience is your best reaction. If you are sexually greedy, unsympathetic, or contemptuous toward your partner's fumbling, you may shatter his self-control. That will lead to premature ejaculation or, worse, temporary impotence. Keep in mind that once he has practiced sufficiently, your partner will have tutored his autonomic nervous system to withstand much of your passionate writhings and wrigglings. Soon he will be bringing you to new orgasmic heights.

As mentioned earlier, even though for most men they take place simultaneously, male orgasm and ejaculation are not the same. The ancient technique of orgasmic brinkmanship enables a man to separate his orgasm from his ejaculation. He can keep himself so near the brink that he experiences a series of smaller, diffuse orgasms—quite similar to those women have—without ejaculation. And multiple orgasms without emission mean that he can have sex much more often than if he ejaculated every time, and that in a single session he can prolong pleasure, in himself and his partner, until either or both reach an explosive orgasm.

More ambitious couples who have discovered what a magic wand the nonemitting phallus is can practice advanced lovemaking. Sophisticated lovemaking depends partly on the choice of positions, and even more so on the coital dynamics.

COITAL POSITIONS

The earliest known systematically listed configurations for sexual intercourse—the Arcane Maid's Nine Positions and the Mystic Master of the Grotto's Thirty—subsequently made their way from China to India and Japan in the East, and then to the West. Today one can count more than a hundred positions, a tally startling to most Westerners. These positions range from the mundane to the exotic, from the sensible to the ridiculous, and they often have been overemphasized. Many "exotic" positions are merely variations of basic ones, with slight changes in the placement of limbs or in the slope of bodies. Quite a few positions are more interesting in concept than in sensation. Others are exclusively for acrobats and contortionists. Because they are titillating and lend themselves to graphic description, sexual positions are a rich source for artists and writers in sexology, pornography, and erotica. Unsophisticated lovers consider attention to coital position the pinnacle of sexual sophistication. In reality, love-play and coital dynamics are far more significant.

Yet finding the right position is important, especially in cases of difference in size or in other circumstances of possible incompatibility. Some positions affect considerably the depth and angle of penetration, ease of movement, and thus the resulting sensations. Most positions may be grouped into the following categories: face to face, side by side, riding, sitting, rear entry, standing, and whimsical. (See chapter 8 for the positions suggested by the Arcane Maid and the Mystic Master; some are referred to below for comparison.)

Face to Face

In the basic face-to-face position, the so-called missionary position, the woman lies on her back with her legs slightly parted, and the man lies on top of her, supporting himself partly with his hands. (The same position is used for the Arcane Maid's Somersaulting Dragons and the Mystic Master's Swifts Sharing a Heart.) The advantages here are that the man and woman can kiss and embrace, converse and make eye contact, and watch one another's expressions. The disadvantages are that penetration is shallow, and genital pressure and stimulation only moderate.

Things can be made more interesting, however, if the woman's pelvic angle and the placement of her legs are modified. A small cushion or pillow under her lumbar region changes the angle of her moon grotto passage, and thereby permits easier and slightly deeper penetration. Similar results obtain if she reclines with her sacrum on the edge of the bed, her thighs spread, and her legs sloping down to the floor. If her partner leans forward between her thighs, his jade stalk can indirectly stimulate her clitoris. At this angle his glans touches the back wall of the grotto, which is not rich in nerves. This position does not permit very deep penetration. The ancient Chinese used it often on wedding nights, as it minimized the pain of virgin brides.

Deeper penetration and greater stimulation result if the woman lies on her back, spreads her thighs wide and bends her knees, as

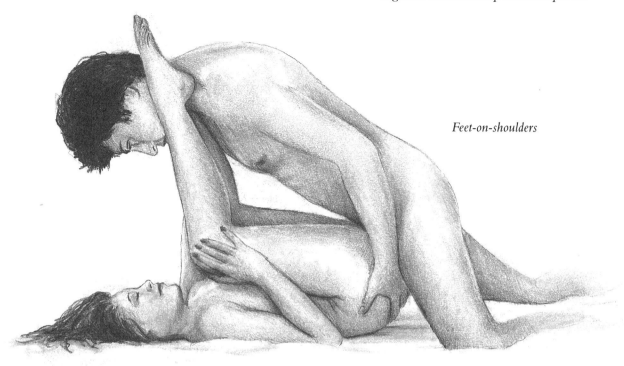

Feet-on-shoulders

she would for a gynecological examination (compare Kingfishers Uniting). A different sensation is achieved if she raises her bent knees to touch her bosom (as in Wrestling Apes or Mounting Tortoises), or touches one knee to her bosom while extending one leg (as in Dragons Twisting).

The woman's wrapping her legs around her partner's waist or hips (compare Silkworms Entangling) permits deeper penetration but limits movement. In this position, novel stimulation can be created if either or both partners contract their pubococcygeus muscles.

The woman can vary her position further: she can raise her legs vertically into the air, hold her feet with her hands, or rest them on her partner's arms (as in Roc Soaring over Dark Sea), or place one leg on his shoulder and stick the other leg high into the air (as in Horse Shaking Its Hoof). The Mystic Master's Wild Horses Leaping, in which the woman puts her feet on the man's shoulders, is an extremely popular variant in China. The position tightens even a roomy grotto. When penetration is shallow and if the angle is right, the sensitive grotto front wall, where the G spot is situated, can be stimulated effectively. When penetration is at its deepest, the glans of the jade stalk can stimulate the flower heart and give extraordinary pleasure to the woman. This position is good for couples aiming at conception. The man must exercise care not to injure his partner in the heat of passion. A man with a long organ should not try it.

Side by Side

The lateral positions are for languid or lazy couples. In one version, the woman lies half on her side and half on her back, and draws up the leg on which she lies; the man faces her (compare Fish Eye-to-Eye). Penetration is shallow, and movement and sensations are limited. In another version, the man faces the woman's back while she bends her legs a little and sticks out her buttocks (as in Mandarin Ducks Joining). This is doing it in the "spoon" fashion, or as the French say, à la paresseuse, the lazy way. Again, penetration is not deep, unless the man has a long stalk. This position is good if the woman is pregnant, or if the couple has children sleeping in the same room, as it is not too noticeable under a blanket.

Riding

The earliest known depiction of sexual positions, which dates back to the Stone Age, shows a woman in a riding position, squatting atop a supine man. Riding positions make the man a captive lover and give the woman all the freedom of movement. Some men like this change, while others, especially those sensitive about their machismo, do not.

The man lies on his back, and the woman kneels or crouches astride him, facing either his head (as in Fish Linking Scales or Butterflies Fluttering) or his feet (as in Bunny Licking Its Fur or Wild Ducks Flying Backward). If the woman faces the man's head, he may place a small cushion under his sacrum to elevate his pelvis, and bend his knees slightly to support her buttocks. If the woman faces his feet, the partners will experience sensations, but without crucial eye contact.

If neither partner has any misgivings, and if the riding position does not become a tired habit, it can be extremely arousing to both partners. The intense sensations created are due to the fact

Woman riding

that the woman's grotto channel is expanded and her cervix lowered by gravity, and as a result the glans of the jade stalk is pressed when penetration is deepest. Any movement, internal or external, will result in the partners' genitals jostling against each other. Deep penetration is possible for even a relatively short stalk.

Riding positions demand agility, coordination, and advanced erotic dynamics from the woman. They are not advised for virgins, pregnant women, or women with a shallow moon grotto, or men with a long jade stalk.

Sitting

Sitting positions are somewhat similar to riding ones. They give both partners some freedom of movement, but because penetration is shallower than in riding positions, sensations are not as sharp as when the man lies on his back. In sitting positions the man sits on a *stiff* armless chair or bench and the woman sits astride him, facing him (as in Cranes Entwining Necks or Humming Ape Embracing the Tree). He spreads her buttocks with his

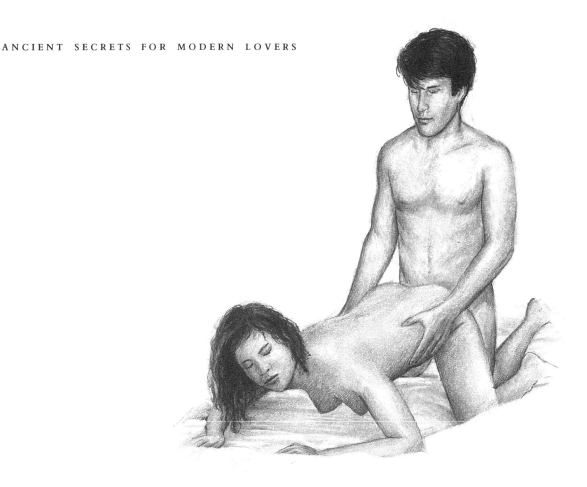

Rear entry knees while she holds on to his neck. By clasping her hips with his hands, he can regulate the thrusts. The woman can control the depth of penetration by leaning backward to increase it and forward to decrease it. In the sitting position the man can fondle the woman's breasts and clitoris, and enjoy her facial expressions.

In the so-called TV position, the woman sits with her back toward the man and her thighs spread (as in Goat Hugging the Tree). This does not allow deep penetration and is easy to disconnect accidentally. Penetration can be deepened if the woman bends forward and the man leans backward. The back-to-face position is useful if the woman is pregnant or the man has an over-long jade stalk.

Rear Entry

Rear-entry positions are another ancient Chinese favorite because they give the woman very keen and unusual sensations. (The

French call such rear-entry positions *en levrette,* "like a grey-hound.") Some people find them unnatural or even debasing because they are characteristic of other mammals. Actually, as quite a few anthropologists and sexologists maintain, rear-entry positions are more natural than face-to-face ones.

Rear-entry positions facilitate deep penetration, except when the woman lies on her stomach below the man (as in Cleaving Cicadas). Here the woman's buttocks get in the way, keeping penetration shallow and causing the man's jade stalk to slip out easily. The man's weight is mostly on the woman, and he cannot stimulate her clitoris. This may be a satisfactory position for thin couples only.

Other versions of rear entry, however, can be very stimulating. The woman may kneel on all fours with the man kneeling behind her (Stepping Tigers). She may lower her head, in the knees-to-chest position, her chest and knees touching the bed. Or she may kneel on the edge of the bed with the man standing behind her (Donkeys of Spring). A rather extreme version, found not in the old Chinese classics but in later erotic paintings, has the woman standing, then bending sharply forward so that her hands touch the floor, while the man stands behind her.

Rear entry is stimulating for a simple geometric reason: The vaginal tube slopes downward while the penis shaft slopes upward. Because of these different angles, once the penis is inserted, its thrusting movements create a stronger friction and give keener sensations. If either or both partners change their postures, even slightly, they can experience any number of different sensations. With the woman on all fours, for example, if the angle is right, the underside of the jade stalk can stimulate the clitoral area. Most rear-entry positions are especially effective for G spot orgasms.

Warning: In cases of rear entry, the female genitals can create a vacuum and suck in air. Then, during the thrusting movement, air sometimes escapes with a disconcerting noise. Rear entry thus may not be suitable for newlyweds or polite lovers. But if familiar partners agree to ignore this occasional sound effect, they can enjoy intense sensations.

Standing

Copulating while standing is awkward and not very rewarding, but it is good for impromptu or quickie lovemaking. The union is easier if the man is shorter, and can be made easier if the woman stands on a low stool or other slight elevation to be higher than the man. Two much more stimulating variations require a muscular man or a light woman. In one, the couple begins in the face-to-face sitting position. The man stands up after insertion, holding the buttocks of the woman, whose legs are wrapped around his back and whose hands cling to his neck. If he is up to it, the man can walk around, making a thrust with each step. The other version is more strenuous for the woman and is possible only if she is lean and supple. Once she and the man are linked, the man stands up. She wraps her legs around him, then disengages her hands from his neck and, using them to support herself, leans back so that her head reaches to the floor.

Whimsy

Then there are more or less playful positions; variations on the standards. Here are a few, requiring certain degrees of athletic ability.

One popular Chinese position is "old man pushing the wheelbarrow." This somewhat strenuous posture usually begins with the woman's kneeling on all fours by the edge of the bed. The man stands upright and enters from the rear. The woman extends her legs, and the man holds her thighs as if gripping the handles of a wheelbarrow. They remain united as he moves slowly backward away from the bed. Using her hands as support and facing the floor, she "walks" on her hands on the floor in a coordinated movement. The man pushes her forward around the room.

Another odd position which might be called "scissors, scissors," has a horizontal and a vertical version. Both feature a novel angle of insertion. The horizontal version is quite restful: The woman lies on her side in bed and raises her upper thigh. The man, lying on his back and spreading his thighs, moves in between her thighs. Their heads point in opposite directions, and their legs interact like two pairs of scissors trying to cut each other. The vertical version is much more athletic: The woman stands on her head, her torso and legs raised vertically with the help of the man, who stands between her spread thighs. The woman supports her upright body with her hands, while the man thrusts by bending his knees and moving up and down.

Coital Dynamics

Inexplicably, most contemporary sexology books ignore or deal cursorily with movement, angle, speed, and rhythm in sexual intercourse. To learn the art of coital dynamics, one has to consult the ancient Taoists. The Mystic Master of the Grotto's Nine Manners of moving the jade stalk and Six Styles of penetration (see chapter 8) are poetic descriptions of the motions of sexual union. In today's bedroom, we can take a few hints from the Mystic Master's flowery advice and work out some pragmatic techniques.

Varied motions in sexual intercourse result in varied forms, degrees, and locations of stimulation. In addition to the stimulation of the usual erogenous zones involved in love-play, partners enjoy having their own genital areas stimulated by their mates' sexual organs. In sexual union, the partners who know where— and how—to stimulate give the greatest pleasure to their mates and themselves.

Nature has endowed men and women differently, so delectable sex depends mostly on the coital dynamics of the male in certain intercourse positions, and mostly on those of the female in others. By experimenting with and controlling the various factors influencing coital motion, a couple can personalize their own pattern of coital dynamics.

Male Dynamics

Men need to understand female anatomy, not just their own, to get the most out of their movement during intercourse. In a woman, the clitoral area is extremely sensitive, the vaginal rim only mildly so. The front vaginal wall in most women is acutely sensitive to friction and deep pressure, while the back wall is much less so. At the depth of the vagina is the cervix, whose stimulation during coitus results in ecstatic sensations in women.

One brilliant bedroom skill from ancient China is variation in male thrusting patterns. Many men believe that the best way to excite a woman is by thrusting deeply, with a regular pumping rhythm. Occasionally this may be so, just before orgasm for example. But regular, deep thrusting may bring on male climax too quickly. Even if the man has enough self-control, the regularity sometimes has a numbing effect on the woman. Deep thrusts are highly stimulating to the woman, especially if the tip of the jade stalk touches the flower heart.

On the other hand, shallower thrusts, with the stalk entering only two or three inches into the moon grotto—to what the ancients called "wheat bud" and "scented mouse"—may excite a woman just as much, though differently. The ridge of the stalk can stimulate the magic spot in the front wall of the grotto. "Nine shallow, one deep" and "eight slow, two fast" are more than just numbers games; in actual coitus such thrusting patterns can excite more than one sensitive zone in the woman.

It is therefore effective to give a series of regular, shallow thrusts first, then follow with a sudden deep thrust, or a series of slow thrusts followed by a quick one. The psychosexual thrill for the woman is all the greater with the element of surprise; a man can give his partner intense pleasure by varying the depth and tempo of his thrusts. Other variations: Advance slowly, while exhaling; then withdraw quickly, while inhaling. Or start by knocking on the sides of the labia; first thrust only a little; continue thrusting, progressively deeper each time.

Whichever technique you choose, alter the depth, speed, and rhythm of your thrusts to fit your own brinkmanship capability and your partner's sensitivity. Verses from a sexology classic give an idea of how coital thrusts can vary:

> Nine shallow, one deep,
> Three right, three left;
> Shake and sway like an eel,
> Advance and crawl like a leech.

A few favorite sexual positions practiced in ancient China show what a good male lover can do for his partner. In some face-to-face positions, for example the aforementioned deflowering position often used on wedding nights, the angle does not permit deep penetration. But if the man dips his stalk downward, he can stimulate the woman's upper grotto entrance and indirectly the clitoral zone.

In Wild Horses Leaping, the celebrated feet-on-shoulders position frequently used in ancient Chinese bedchambers, the initiative lies entirely with the man. The woman is in a helpless position, bent sharply at the hips, with her canal almost vertical; she cannot move or even exercise her sexual muscles, and the man cannot stimulate her clitoral area with his jade stalk. But if it approaches at a different angle, so that its underside presses against the back rim of the grotto, the glans can massage strongly the front wall of her grotto, where it is most sensitive. Also, by changing the angle of his stalk, the man can penetrate deeply enough to reach the woman's flower heart or stimulate her clitoral area with the front of his stalk. The ease in stimulating either the front vaginal wall or the clitoral area with shallow thrusts or the flower heart with deep thrusts—three of the most sensitive genital zones in a woman—by varying the stalk angle only slightly explains the popularity of this position with the ancient eroticists.

Even more popular was Donkeys of Spring and its variations. In most of these rear-entry positions, the man can stimulate the woman's three most sensitive zones (clitoris, front grotto wall, and flower heart) by varying the thrusting angle selectively. The woman can exercise her vaginal muscles, if she has learned the exquisite Butterfly Quiver technique (described below). The free-

Stimulations in feet-on-shoulders positions

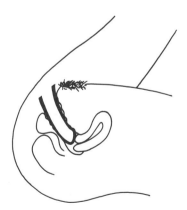 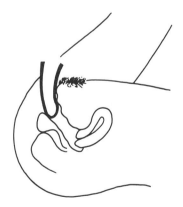 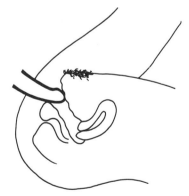

Deepest thrust— stimulating the flower heart

Man on tiptoe— stimulating the clitoral region

Man crouching slightly— stimulating the G spot, on the front wall of the moon grotto

dom of movement for the man is phenomenal with Donkeys of Spring. Here the woman kneels on the edge of a bed or chair, resting on her hands or head, while the man stands behind her; the kneeling surface should be at about the height of the man's knees. The partners' genitals are thus at the same level, and the man can change his angle at each thrust to give the woman various sensations.

If the man makes shallow thrusts from a slightly stooping position, the underside of his jade stalk rubs against the vaginal rim nearest the clitoris and stimulates this area. If he makes shallow thrusts while on tiptoe, his glans can massage the sensitive front wall of the woman's grotto. If he thrusts deeper, he can jostle the flower heart with the tip of his stalk. If he turns his body slightly left or right he can vary the phallic angle, or even make corkscrew movements. This may bring the woman to a deep, shattering orgasm.

Female Dynamics

A woman's role in sexual union is not—or should not be—passive at all. Even in most man-above positions she can make move-

Stimulations in rear-entry positions

Deepest thrust— stimulating the flower heart

Shallow thrust, man on tiptoe— stimulating the G spot

Shallow thrust, man crouching slightly— stimulating the clitoral region

230

ments contrapuntal, reciprocal to her partner's. She can create varying sensations during the union, whether by drumming her heels on the man's back or raising one leg to "shake the hoof."

She can, if she wants to, gain control of the coital dynamics in a number of situations. A woman is virtually in command of the movements when she is atop the man, namely, in riding positions and sitting positions. She has greater freedom of movement in riding positions when she squats rather than kneels astride him. Her legs give her enough leverage for maximum desired stimulation of any area of her moon grotto.

In most riding positions, after insertion the woman moves her torso up and down. Then, to enjoy varying sensations, she can move her pelvis in an oval track. During the downward movement, if she leans slightly forward and pushes her pubis slightly to the back, her clitoral area may be stimulated by her partner's organ. During the upward movement, if she leans slightly backward and pushes her pubis slightly to the front, her sensitive front vaginal wall may be stimulated by the tip of the jade stalk. At the deepest penetration, she may pause for a while, so that his stalk head can massage her flower heart. An adept and creative woman can change her up-and-down, front-and-back movements to varying rice-husking motions—sideways, rotary, or corkscrew. In short, she can stimulate her clitoral area, her front vaginal wall, or her cervix at will.

For centuries many femmes fatales of ancient China—empresses, priestesses, women of literature and art, renowned courtesans—practiced an exquisite erotic technique. This form of internal coital dynamics gives a woman's organ a life of its own, so to speak. Once a woman has learned to control specific sexual nerves and muscles, she is able to bring on vaginal quiverings voluntarily. This ability, unknown to most women, occurs involuntarily to a few women at the height of sexual ecstasy. The ancient Taoists who probably devised the conscious trick and developed it over the centuries did not give it a name; I have dubbed it the Butterfly Quiver.

Today the Butterfly Quiver is not exclusively Chinese. Indians practicing Tantrism know it. The French treasure it as *pompoir.* Even in the United States it is familiar in the form of the Kegel exercise, mentioned earlier. Undoubtedly, there are women all over the world who are gifted with the natural ability, or who have individually discovered and cultivated it, perhaps secretly. In the modern bedroom, a woman who has mastered the Butterfly Quiver can create incredible results for her partner and reap them herself.

The complex muscles in the pelvic area include both voluntary and involuntary muscles. For this erotic technique two specific groups are crucial: the constrictor cunni, which encircles the vaginal rim, and the levator vaginae, which surrounds the vaginal canal farther up (see the illustration on p. 177). Some women can activate all the pelvic muscles together, but very few—either through a natural gift or persistent practice—can activate at will these two groups of muscles, jointly or separately.

If a woman times her internal movements with her partner's thrusting during intercourse, she may experience a many-splendored thrill. She can relax her muscles when the jade stalk is advancing; then, when it is deep inside her, she can activate the constrictor cunni to grip the root of the stalk or use her levator vaginae to massage the middle of the stalk. While her partner is inside her and both are at rest, she can titillate her captive lightly with the Butterfly Quiver, pulsating like butterfly wings, or force

Stimulations in woman-riding positions

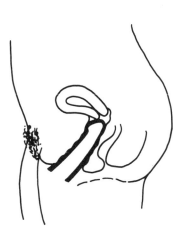 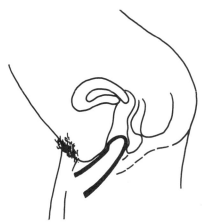 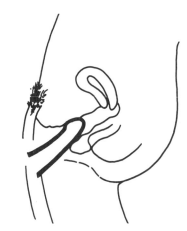

Woman's torso moving down vertically— stimulating the flower heart

Woman leaning forward, moving down partially— stimulating the clitoral region

Woman leaning backward, moving down partially— stimulating the G spot

him to ejaculate with a convulsive milking. After his ejaculation, she can use the constrictor cunni to hold the root of the phallus tightly to prevent the loss of his erection.

To become expert at the Butterfly Quiver, a woman must educate her sexual nerves and muscles. Repeated and persistent practice of erotic exercises centering around the pubic squeeze (see chapter 13) is essential.

MULTIPLE O'S OR THE BIG O?

Individuals who enjoy sophisticated lovemaking control their own orgasm and help control that of their partner. With occasional exceptions, seasoned couples do not zip toward orgasm. Instead, like gourmets at a feast, they sample and savor the delicacies before them, leisurely and repeatedly, until they are satisfied. This is the quintessence of eroticism.

We hear many myths and "authoritative" pronouncements about orgasm. The ancient Taoists ingeniously devised orgasmic brinkmanship, but some of them cherished the dogma of absolute nonejaculation for the man. Some Western sexologists have advocated male ejaculation at every sexual union; others have insisted on simultaneous male and female orgasms. The Victorians believed that women were incapable of orgasms. Freud's distinction between clitoral and vaginal orgasms in women first was accepted, then was discarded, and now may be coming back in a revised version. Fortunately, many of today's sexologists have more liberal views about orgasms than did their predecessors, and many of the old myths and dogmas are behind us.

For today's lovers the choice is wide open. If a man and woman believe that the sole purpose of sex is propagation of the species, they can simply agree to have the man ejaculate as soon as possible. With today's advanced technology, they can even have in vitro fertilization and test-tube babies. Procreation without recreation enables them to bypass any sexual activity. But if partners want to procreate through natural, physical activity, or if they just want to make love without making babies, it pays for them to practice the Art of the Bedchamber. Giving pleasure to each other by mastering erotic techniques and controlling orgasm is a natural and legitimate goal for partners in bed.

All sophisticated lovers know that pleasure delayed is pleasure magnified. Skillful lovers know how to excite and tease their partners to the edge of their precipice, pull them back from the brink, then push them forward again. This stop-and-go strategy, repeatedly and carefully applied, can lift partners from plateau to plateau, each higher than the last, until they explode in ecstasy.

From love-play through coitus, a man who is good in bed can combine brinkmanship and other techniques to lead his partner all the way to her brink. He can try to bring her to a series of orgasms, perhaps superficial and diffuse, or to one Big O, deep and explosive. The former is the likely result of clitoral-oriented love-play and coitus; the latter of techniques aimed especially at the front vaginal wall and the cervix.

Unless she is fettered psychologically or has a physiological defect, any woman can be brought to the height of passion. A woman in ecstasy is one of nature's loveliest sights—not only a boost for her partner's sexual ego, but also one of the most powerful aphrodisiacs available to him. A man who is good in bed is rewarded in more than one respect. In a sexually excited woman, the vulva, clitoris, and vaginal passage are all highly congested; the folds of the vaginal walls swell and bulge, and the cervix dips downward. These alterations, and the ample lubrication of all these parts, mean a soft, warm, elastic embrace for the man.

When a woman is near a much-delayed, intense orgasm, she can please her partner with the Butterfly Quiver. If she has trained herself in the maneuver, she can initiate it herself at the critical moment; if she is untrained, her partner's skill may have brought her to such a state that her grotto muscles go into similar involuntary convulsions. Either way, this can easily send both partners into extraordinary ecstasy.

Recent—and still controversial—findings indicate that in many women the Big O may be accompanied by a gush or spurt. This results especially with such positions as Wild Horses Leaping and Donkeys of Spring, and is often preceded by an acute sensation in the woman similar to an urge to urinate. Unless she starts coitus with a full bladder, this urge is simply an intense orgasmic sensation and is not cause for alarm.

A woman who is good in bed does not stop at practicing her own brand of coital dynamics and the secret Butterfly Quiver. She knows how to arouse her partner with love-play, making him more potent, and can sense how far he is from his brink. This is crucial especially if the man knows no brinkmanship. When a woman feels that her man is near the edge, she can stop him from going over it, then draw him toward it again. A much-teased and much-delayed male orgasm with ejaculation, a Big O, is far more powerful and explosive than an unorchestrated one.

The ancient Art of the Bedchamber, as we can see, has quite a potential in the modern bedroom.

Afterword

During the years of researching and writing *The Yin–Yang Butterfly,* I came to the realization that offering information culled from obscure ancient Chinese sources to contemporary Western readers would require an unorthodox, perhaps even maverick, approach. The subject of the book, sexuality, is universal, but its presentation here has several inherent dichotomies: East versus West, ancient versus modern, mystical versus scientific. My goal, daunting as it may be, has been to minimize these built-in contradictions so that readers can share the universality of an ancient art.

Despite its mystical aspects, dating back to long before the rise of modern science and sexology, the Art of the Bedchamber was a serious study. It was done not in the laboratory of science, but in the ultimate laboratory of human experience. As has been mentioned, some of the aspects of the ancient Taoists' knowledge of sexuality and health, which they considered intimately linked, now seem amazingly "modern." Today's scientists have found validity in various ancient Chinese practices—biofeedback, acupuncture, nutrition and herb therapy, and meditation, for example, all of which are closely associated with sexuality. So while much of ancient mysticism was based on superstition, some of it might be thought of as "new" science.

In this age of instant gratification, when fast food, fleeting fame, and quickie sex are the norm, the leisurely prudence advocated by the ancient bedroom sages may appear quaint. It may, however, be just the style needed to remedy some of our health and sexual malaise.

It was with this conviction, and gleefully, that I wrote the section titled "Ancient Secrets for Modern Lovers." It may merely bring fun and frolic to the bedroom, or result in something more meaningful. You may find something useful among the measures advocated by the ancient Taoists: specific foods and herbs to nurture your sexual vitality; physical exercise and mind–body therapy to train your sexual mechanism; lingering, whimsical love-play to arouse Yin and Yang; varied coital positions for you and your partner to excite each other; orgasmic brinkmanship techniques to prolong union; and ingenious coital dynamics to heighten pleasure.

The Chinese know how to turn humble food ingredients into delicacies. Their main trick is an exchange of flavors among different ingredients, with each ingredient acting as a seasoning for the others. The result is an endless variation of flavors.

Likewise, in their bedchamber art, the ancient Chinese knew how to turn simple physical union into a delicious encounter. Their main trick was mutual stimulation between Yin and Yang, or an exchange of sexual energy, with each partner acting as the aphrodisiac for the other. The result could be an endless variation of pleasure.

This does not mean that ancient Chinese sexologists advocated sexual indulgence and lewdness. They simply believed that with moderation and prudence, sex—like food—could be a celebration of life.

I quote that bedchamber sage the Mystic Master of the Grotto: "Among all the creatures under Heaven, human beings are most precious. What is essential to people is the bedchamber instinct. We imitate Heaven and emulate Earth, measure Yin with the compass and Yang with the square. Those who understand the nature of prudent sex will nurture their vigor and prolong their life. Those who treat its principle with contempt will injure their spirit and shorten their life. . . . If this knowledge benefits all people, why not propagate it for ten thousand generations?"

Glossary

ACUPOINT: acupressure or acupuncture point on the body

ACUPRESSURE: application of pressure on precise points on the body for therapeutic purposes

ACUPUNCTURE: ancient Chinese health treatment in which the body is pierced with needles at specific points

ANIMAL IN THE BOAT: clitoris

APHRODISIAC HEALTH TONICS: nutrients that enhance sexual vitality

CHAN BUDDHISM: *see* Zen Buddhism

CHI: primeval life-energy or life-force

CHI-HAI: "sea of *chi*"; sexual acupoint between the navel and the pubis

CHI-KUNG: "life-energy skill"; meditative breathing exercise to harness life-energy

CHU: chanted verse or ballad

CHU-KU: pubic bone

CHUNG-CHI: "ultimate middle"; sexual acupoint just above the pubis

CINNABAR: red mercuric sulfide, used by ancient Taoist alchemists in search of the elixir of life

CINNABAR FIELD: space inside the abdomen, between the navel and the pubis, regarded by the Taoists as the seat of life-energy and sexual vitality

CINNABAR GROTTO: vagina

CONFUCIANISM: doctrines of the philosopher Confucius (551–479 B.C.) on family, politics, and ethics

CORAL JUICE: human breast milk

COXCOMBS: labia minora

DAO: *see* Tao

DARK GARDEN: prepuce of the clitoris

DIVINE FIELD: prepuce of the clitoris

DRAGON: mythical, auspicious being that symbolized masculinity and the emperor

DRAGON SALIVA: ambergris, a substance from the intestines of the sperm whale, used in perfumes and aphrodisiacs

DRINKING AT THE JADE FOUNTAIN: oral stimulation of the moon grotto, or cunnilingus

DUAL TRAINING: erotic techniques for health and pleasure for both partners

DUSTER HANDLE: penis

EXAMINATION HALL: vulva

FANG-CHUNG: "inside the bedchamber"; ancient Chinese sexology, considered a branch of medicine

FANG-NEI: *see Fang-chung*

FLOWER HEART: cervix

FLOWER PISTIL: cervix

FROG MOUTH: orifice of the penis

FU: poetic essay

GOLDEN GULCH: upper vulva where the labia minora meet

GRAIN SEED: five inches inside the vagina

HEAVENLY COURT: vaginal vestibule; also the name of a high peak which may indicate the male organ

HEAVENLY ROOT: penis

HIDDEN VALLEY: *see* Heavenly court

HSIEN: Taoist immortal who has acquired godlike powers but retains the appearance of a human being

HUI-CHUN: "recapture the spring"; exercises for enhancing sexual vitality

HUI-YIN: "sex crossroads"; sexual acupoint in the perineum

I CHING: *The Book of Changes,* an ancient Chinese classic of philosophy and oracles

JADE CHAMBER: boudoir

JADE FOUNTAIN: lubricated vagina

JADE GATE: vagina

JADE ROOT: penis

JADE SPOON: penis

JADE STALK: penis

JADE VEIN: lower vulva where the labia minora meet

JEWEL TERRACE: clitoris

KUEN-YUAN: "pass of primacy"; sexual acupoint between the navel and the pubis

LIFE-NURTURE: use of food, herbs, and mind-body therapy to maintain or enhance life-energy

LING-CHIH: "divine mushrooms"; fungus with reputed magical powers

LOVE POINT: sexual acupoint

LUTE STRINGS: one inch inside the vagina

MANDARIN: scholar appointed as a high-level government official

MERIDIAN: channel through which *chi*, or life-energy, flows through the body

MING-MEN: "life gate"; sexual acupoint in the small of the back

MIXED ROCK: four inches inside the vagina

MOON GROTTO: vagina

NEO-CONFUCIANISM: form of Confucianism developed during the last eight centuries, which has borrowed the theory of Yin and Yang, and other metaphysical beliefs from Taoism, while at the same time exaggerating loyalty to the emperor and the importance of sexual propriety, especially for women

NURTURE: taking food and herbs to nourish health as well as sexual vitality

PEACH: symbol of longevity; literary metaphor for female genitals

PLAYING THE FLUTE: oral stimulation of the jade stalk, or fellatio

PLUCK-AND-NURTURE: sexual practice at which one partner tries to bring the other to orgasmic ejaculation and absorb the resulting secretions as nourishment

PURPLE AGARIC PEAK: clitoris

QI-GONG: *see Chi-kung*

SAN-YIN-CHIAO: "junction of three Yins"; sexual acupoint on the lower leg

SAND MOUND: mons veneris or mons pubis

SCARLET CHAMBER: uterus

SCARLET PEARLS: labia minora

SCENTED MOUSE: three inches inside the vagina

SHIH CHING: *The Book of Odes* (ancient Chinese poetry classic)

SHIH-MEN: "stone gate"; sexual acupoint between the navel and the pubis

SHUANG-HSIU: *see* Dual training

TAI CHI: "Grand Ultimate" or "Great Ultimate"; primeval energy of the universe

TAI CHI CHUAN: "great ultimate fist"; health and self-defense exercise involving shadow-boxing, deep breathing, and meditation

TAN-TIEN: *see* Cinnabar field

TAO: the Way, born of the mating of Yin and Yang, the Way that cannot be charted, the Name that cannot be described, the Truth that is unknowable

TAOISM: philosophy based on Tao, founded by Lao Tzu (c. sixth century B.C.)

TASSELED SPEAR: penis

TSAI-PU: *see* Pluck-and-nurture

TWIN LOTUS PEAKS: female breasts

TZU: form of poetry combining the classical and the vernacular

VAST FOUNTAIN: female urethral orifice

WATER FROM THE HEAVENLY POOL: saliva

WHEAT BUD: two inches inside the vagina

YANG: masculine sexual energy

YANG IMPLEMENT: penis

YANG PEAK: penis

YANG STEM: penis

YEN-SHIH: voluptuous poetry

YIN: female sexual energy

YIN-CHIAO: "sexual junction"; sexual acupoint below the navel

YIN GATE: vagina

YUN-YU: "clouds and rain"; literary metaphor for sexual intercourse

ZEN BUDDHISM: Chinese form of Buddhism based on India's Mahayana Buddhism and influenced by Taoism

Major Chinese Dynasties

Age of the Five Rulers (legendary period)	c. 2852–2205 B.C.
Hsia	c. 2205–1765 B.C.
Shang-Yin	1766–1122 B.C.
Chou	1122–722 B.C.
Era of Spring and Autumn	722–480 B.C.
Era of Warring States	480–221 B.C.
Chin	221–206 B.C.
Han	206 B.C.–A.D. 220
Era of Three Kingdoms	221–277
Western Tsin	265–317
Eastern Tsin	317–420
Era of South-North Dynasties	420–589
Sui	589–618
Tang	618–907
Era of Five Dynasties	907–960
Sung	960–1126
Southern Sung	1127–1280
Yuan (Mongol)	1280–1368
Ming	1368–1644
Ching (Manchu)	1644–1911

Bibliography

Ananga Ranga—Hindu Art of Love, trans. Sir Richard Burton. Cleveland: Classics Library, n.d.

Beurdelay, Michel. *Chinese Erotic Art.* Secaucus, NJ: Chartwell, 1969.

Douglas, Nik, and Penny Slinger. *Sexual Secrets.* New York: Destiny, 1979.

Franzblau, Abraham N. *Erotic Art of China.* New York: Crown, 1977.

Ishihara, Akira, and Howard S. Levy. *The Tao of Sex: An Annotated Translation of the 28th Section of "The Essence of Medical Prescriptions."* New York: Harper & Row, 1968.

Jou Pu Tuan: A 17th Century Erotic Novel, trans. Richard Martin, from a German trans. by Franz Kuhn. New York: Grove, 1963.

The Kama Sutra of Vatsyayana, trans. Sir Richard Burton and F. F. Arbuthnot. New York: G. P. Putnam's Sons, 1984.

Kinsey, Alfred Charles, Wardell Pomeroy, and Clyde E. Martin. *Sexual Behavior in the Human Female.* Philadelphia: W. B. Saunders, 1953.

————, and Paul H. Gebhard. *Sexual Behavior in the Human Male.* Philadelphia: W. B. Saunders, 1948.

Kline-Graber, Georgia, and Benjamin Graber. *Women's Orgasm.* New York: Bobbs-Merrill, 1975.

Ladas, Alice K., Beverly Whipple, and John D. Perry. *The G Spot—and Other Recent Discoveries About Human Sexuality.* New York: Dell, 1983.

McIlvenna, Raymond L. *The Pleasure Quest.* San Francisco: Specific Press, 1988.

Masters, William H., and Virginia E. Johnson. *Human Sexual Inadequacy.* Boston: Little, Brown, 1970.

————. *Human Sexual Response.* Boston: Little, Brown, 1966.

————. *The Pleasure Bond.* Boston: Little, Brown, 1975.

————, and Robert C. Kolodny. *Masters and Johnson on Sex and Human Loving.* Boston: Little, Brown, 1986.

Mookerjee, Ajit, and Madhu Khanna. *The Tantric Way.* Boston: New York Graphic Society, 1977.

Needham, Joseph. *Science and Civilisation in China.* Cambridge, England: Cambridge University Press, 1956-.

Ovid. *The Art of Love.* New York: Grosset & Dunlap, 1959.

The Perfumed Garden of the Shaykh Nefzawi, trans. Sir Richard Burton. New York: G. P. Putnam's Sons, 1964.

Rawson, Philip. *The Art of Tantra.* Greenwich, CT: New York Graphic Society, 1973.

———. *Erotic Art of the East.* New York: G. P. Putnam's Sons, 1968.

The Secret of the Golden Flower—A Chinese Book of Life, trans. Cary F. Baynes, from a German trans. by Richard Wilhelm; commentary by Carl G. Jung. New York: Causeway, 1975.

Sevely, Josephine Lowndes. *Eve's Secrets: A New Theory of Female Sexuality.* New York: Random House, 1987.

Tavris, Carol, and Susan Sadd. *The Redbook Report on Female Sexuality.* New York: Delacorte, 1977.

Temple, Robert. *The Genius of China.* New York: Simon & Schuster, 1986.

Van de Velde, Theodore H. *Ideal Marriage.* London: William Heinemann Medical, 1953 (originally pub. 1928).

Van Gulik, R. H. *Sexual Life in Ancient China.* Leiden, Netherlands: E. J. Brill, 1961.

CHINESE SOURCES

This book is based for the most part directly on ancient Chinese sources; for practical reasons, only the best-known sexology classics and a few erotic novels are listed here. The authors of many of these ancient texts are not known; since the texts are not protected by copyright, they have been copied and reprinted by various publishers. Dates are the nearest estimates given by scholars.

The Classic of the Arcane Maid (Hsuan Nu Ching), c. fifth century

The Classic of the Elemental Maid (Su Nu Ching), c. first century A.D.

The Classic of the Iridescent Maid (Tsai Nu Ching), c. fifth century

Collected Works of the Dark Image of Double Plum Trees (Shuang Mei Ching An Tsung Shu), by Yeh Teh-hui, 1914

The Dream of the Red Chamber (Hung Lou Meng), by Tsao Hsueh-chin, mid–eighteenth century

The Essence of Medical Prescriptions (I Shim Po, or I Shing Fang), ed. and comp. Tamba Yasuyori, 984

Essentials of the Jade Chamber (Yu Fang Chih Yao), c. 6th century

Gold Vase Plum (Chin Ping Mei), later sixteenth century

The Master Who Embraces Simplicity (Pao Pu Tzu), by Ko Hung, c. 300

Materia Medica, by Li Shih-chen, 1578

The Mystic Master of the Grotto (Tung Hsuan Tzu), c. 5th–7th centuries

The Poetical Essay on the Supreme Joy of the Pleasurable Union of Heaven and Earth, and Yin and Yang (Ta Lo Fu), by Po Hsing-chien, ninth century

The Prayer Cushion of Flesh (Jou Pu Tuan), also known as *The Zen of Latter-Day Enlightenment (Chuen Hou Chan),* by Ching Yin, 1634

The Secret Art of the Jade Chamber (Yu Fang Pi Chueh), c. sixth century

Shen Nung's Medical Herb Classic, c. 550

Index

About the Author

VALENTIN CHU was born and educated in Shanghai. As a winner of an international writing award, he was invited to be a guest observer at United Nations headquarters in New York. He worked as a correspondent for *Time* magazine in Hong Kong, then as an editor at Time-Life Books in New York and, later, at Reader's Digest General Books. His byline articles have appeared in *Time, Life, U.S. News & World Report, The New Leader,* and the *U.S. Congressional Record,* and in periodicals in Britain, France, Italy, and the Far East. For the past decade, Chu has been a student of ancient Chinese sexology. He has always been fascinated by the interplay between East and West, in sexology and other fields. He now lives in the San Francisco Bay area.